CANDIDE
or Optimism

A FRESH TRANSLATION
BACKGROUNDS
CRITICISM

Second Edition

A NORTON CRITICAL EDITION

Voltaire
CANDIDE
OR OPTIMISM

A FRESH TRANSLATION
BACKGROUNDS
CRITICISM

Second Edition

Translated and Edited by

ROBERT M. ADAMS
PROFESSOR EMERITUS OF ENGLISH
UNIVERSITY OF CALIFORNIA AT LOS ANGELES

W · W · NORTON & COMPANY · *New York* · *London*

Printed in the United States of America.

The text of this book is composed in Electra, with the display set in
Bernhard Modern. Composition by PennSet, Inc.
Manufacturing by Courier.
Book design by Antonina Krass.

Library of Congress Cataloging-in-Publication Data
Voltaire, 1694–1778
[Candide. English]
Candide, or, Optimism : a fresh translation, backgrounds, criticism / Voltaire ;
translated and edited by Robert M. Adams. — 2nd ed.
p.   cm. — (A Norton critical edition)
Includes bibliographical references.
ISBN 0-393-96058-7
1. Voltaire, 1694–1778, Candide. I. Adams, Robert Martin, 1915–
II. Title. III. Title: Candide. IV. Title: Optimism.
PQ2082.C3E5   1990

843'.5—dc20   90-36677

ISBN 0-393-96058-7
W. W. Norton & Company, Inc., 500 Fifth Avenue, New York, N.Y. 10110
W. W. Norton & Company, Ltd., 10 Coptic Street, London WC1A 1PU
2 3 4 5 6 7 8 9 0

Contents

The Climate of Controversy

Preface to the Second Edition

When Candide first set forth into the world, in January 1759, he did not do so under the aegis of M. de Voltaire, the well-known poet, tragedian, historian, philosopher, and friend of Frederick the Great. As illegitimate as its hero, the book *Candide* proposed itself as the work of "Dr. Ralph"; and if it had not been signed extravagantly between the lines with another and better-known autograph, would doubtless figure today only in Barbier and Billard's labyrinthine listing of anonymous literature.

The little book made its way, in other words, on its own—was read because it was amusing, and for that reason alone, and has only lately started to appear on assigned-reading lists and enumerations of "the world's great books." Now that it is a classic, I suppose the first thing the startled student must be told is that it is still funny.

The other things about the story, and there are a good many of them, come a long way after this first article.

Candide is a cruel and destructive book as well as a funny one. Funny and cruel: the qualities go together more easily perhaps than we like to think. But they would not suffice for the peculiar vitality of *Candide*, unless something else were added. If all it did was demolish a long-outdated system of German philosophy, its fun might feel as antiquated and its cruelty as gratuitous as Shakespeare's puns or Pope's malignant hounding after dunces. But *Candide*'s cruelty is not sour, and its fun remains modern and relevant. Dozens of heroes in modern fiction are Candides under one disguise or another,* as our standard heroine is a reworked Madame Bovary—who herself has more than a touch of Candide in her complexion. Why Voltaire's little book feels so modern clearly has something to do with the things it destroys and the way in which it carries out that work of destruction. But it is neither necessary nor possible to be peremptory in defining its targets, for satire generally works more widely than even its creator realizes. There's something in it for everyone. So the book's exact import is evidently up to the decision of the duly informed and sensitive reader—for whose individual re-

---

* For example, all the Evelyn Waugh and Aldous Huxley heroes, as well as Augie March, Holden Caulfield, Huckleberry Finn and all his multitu- dinous descendants, not to mention the "étranger" of Camus, good soldier Schweik, and an infinity of other battered innocents.

sponses to the actual work of art there neither is nor can be any substitute.

Though its action scampers dizzily around the perimeter of the civilized world, *Candide* is an essentially European book in its passionate addiction to, and scepticism of, the reasonable life. It could easily have a number of subtitles other than "Optimism"; one good one would be "Civilization and Its Discontents."

The present translation has aimed to be neither literal nor loose, but to preserve a decent respect for English idiom while rendering a French intent. It was made from the old standard Morize edition, still a classic despite its age, and especially useful for the dry, neat erudition of its notes. But in its late stages, the English text was read against, and modified to conform with, M. René Pomeau's 1959 edition, which introduces a few recent textual modifications. The text of *Candide* contains little that is problematic; it is clean and clear with only a couple of unimportant and relatively unsuccessful afterthoughts. When and where exactly the first printing of the first edition appeared is still doubtful; Voltaire was both a master of publicity and a past master at covering his tracks. But these fine points are for the difficult determinations of textual scholars.

As for Voltaire's prose, it is late in the day to pronounce in its favor; a translator, however, may speak with special feeling of its lucidity, lightness, and swiftness of tonal variation. It is a joy to experience.

ROBERT M. ADAMS

The Text of
CANDIDE
or Optimism

translated from the German of Doctor Ralph
with the additions which were found in the Doctor's pocket
when he died at Minden in the Year of Our Lord 1759

Translated by Robert M. Adams

"Candide" and Mademoiselle "Cunégonde": A Note on Their Names

The name of the character Candide comes unchanged from a standard French adjective, direct counterpart of the English adjective "candid." Both words derive from the Latin "candidus," the primary meaning of which was *white*. Snow, swans, and stones were some of the objects to which the Romans applied the adjective in its primary sense. An extended meaning came when men standing for public office were expected to wear clean white togas, hence our modern word *candidate*. But the word expanded in other directions too. When applied to people, it took on the extra import of *beautiful*; Virgil refers to both Queen Dido and the goddess Maia as *candida* (*Aeneid* 5.70 and 8.138). Another set of Roman meanings grew out of the concept *unspotted*, hence *honest* and *fair-minded*. Horace refers to Albus as an unbiased judge of his poems, *nostrorum sermonum candide iudex* (*Epistles* 1.4.1).

Though an English writer as late as Dryden used "candid" in the old sense of *white*, it was in a translation from the Latin of Ovid (*Metamorphoses* 15.60), and the more common usage, both in England and in France, carried the import of *uncorrupted* and *fair-minded*. Pope and Swift use the word repeatedly in the sense of *unbiased*; and in disputes over the American Revolution appeals to "the candid reader" will frequently be found. Quite a few of these secondary implications of the word cling to Voltaire's hero; he is untouched by the smut of the world; he is pure of soul, completely trusting, and always ready to give the philosophy of Pangloss another trial. He is such a white innocent that, like Dagwood Bumstead, he never learns anything and so never grows old.

Mademoiselle Cunégonde—she is always "Mademoiselle" for Voltaire, being single, as the song has it, "just in the legal sense"—gets her name from either or both of two high-born Germanic ladies of the eleventh century. Kunigunde was the daughter of Siegfried count of Luxembourg; in 1001 she married Henry duke of Bavaria, who the year after was elected Holy Roman Emperor. With their wedding vows the happy couple seem to have taken vows of permanent chastity. (Voltaire would have been amused by the contrast with his much-traveled and vigorously used heroine.) Another source for the name might have been Kunegonde, sister of Welf or Guelph III, duke of Carinthia; sometime in the first half of the eleventh century, she married Alberto Azzo II, founder of the Italian house of Este. But in any event all Voltaire was really interested in was the archaic-sounding Germanic name.

Candide

CHAPTER 1

How Candide Was Brought up in a Fine Castle and How He Was Driven Out of It

There lived in Westphalia,[1] in the castle of the Baron of Thunder-Ten-Tronckh, a young man on whom nature had bestowed the perfection of gentle manners. His features admirably expressed his soul, he combined an honest mind with great simplicity of heart; and I think it was for this reason that they called him Candide. The old servants of the house suspected that he was the son of the Baron's sister by a respectable, honest gentleman of the neighborhood, whom she had refused to marry because he could prove only seventy-one quarterings,[2] the rest of his family tree having been lost in the passage of time.

The Baron was one of the most mighty lords of Westphalia, for his castle had a door and windows. His great hall was even hung with a tapestry. The dogs of his courtyard made up a hunting pack on occasion, with the stableboys as huntsmen; the village priest was his grand almoner. They all called him "My Lord," and laughed at his stories.

The Baroness, who weighed in the neighborhood of three hundred and fifty pounds, was greatly respected for that reason, and did the honors of the house with a dignity which rendered her even more imposing. Her daughter Cunégonde,[3] aged seventeen, was a ruddy-cheeked girl, fresh, plump, and desirable. The Baron's son seemed in every way worthy of his father. The tutor Pangloss was the oracle of the household, and little Candide listened to his lectures with all the good faith of his age and character.

Pangloss gave instruction in metaphysico-theologico-cosmoloonigology.[4] He proved admirably that there cannot possibly be an effect without

1. Westphalia is a province of western Germany, near Holland and the lower Rhineland. Flat, boggy, and drab, it is noted chiefly for its excellent ham. In a letter to his niece, written during his German expedition of 1750, Voltaire described the "vast, sad, sterile, detestable countryside of Westphalia."

2. Quarterings are genealogical divisions of one's family tree. Seventy-one of them is a grotesque number to have, representing something over two thousand years of uninterrupted aristocracy. Cunégonde, who is of flawless nobility, has seventy-two quarterings.

3. On the names Candide and Cunégonde, see page xi. Pangloss gets his name from Greek words meaning *all-tongue.*

4. The "looney" I have buried in this burlesque word corresponds to a buried *nigaud*—"booby" in the French. Christian Wolff, disciple of Leibniz, invented and popularized the word "cosmology."

a cause and that in this best of all possible worlds[5] the Baron's castle was the most beautiful of all castles and his wife the best of all possible Baronesses.

—It is clear, said he, that things cannot be otherwise than they are, for since everything is made to serve an end, everything necessarily serves the best end. Observe: noses were made to support spectacles, hence we have spectacles. Legs, as anyone can plainly see, were made to be breeched, and so we have breeches. Stones were made to be shaped and to build castles with; thus My Lord has a fine castle, for the greatest Baron in the province should have the finest house; and since pigs were made to be eaten, we eat pork all year round.[6] Consequently, those who say everything is well are uttering mere stupidities; they should say everything is for the best.

Candide listened attentively and believed implicitly; for he found Miss Cunégonde exceedingly pretty, though he never had the courage to tell her so. He decided that after the happiness of being born Baron of Thunder-Ten-Tronckh, the second order of happiness was to be Miss Cunégonde; the third was seeing her every day, and the fourth was listening to Master Pangloss, the greatest philosopher in the province and consequently in the entire world.

One day, while Cunégonde was walking near the castle in the little woods that they called a park, she saw Dr. Pangloss in the underbrush; he was giving a lesson in experimental physics to her mother's maid, a very attractive and obedient brunette. As Miss Cunégonde had a natural bent for the sciences, she watched breathlessly the repeated experiments which were going on; she saw clearly the doctor's sufficient reason, observed both cause and effect, and returned to the house in a distracted and pensive frame of mind, yearning for knowledge and dreaming that she might be the sufficient reason of young Candide—who might also be hers.

As she was returning to the castle, she met Candide, and blushed; Candide blushed too. She greeted him in a faltering tone of voice; and Candide talked to her without knowing what he was saying. Next day, as everyone was rising from the dinner table, Cunégonde and Candide found themselves behind a screen; Cunégonde dropped her handkerchief, Candide picked it up; she held his hand quite innocently, he kissed her hand quite innocently with remarkable vivacity, grace, and emotion; their lips met, their eyes lit up, their knees trembled, their hands wandered. The Baron of Thunder-Ten-Tronckh passed by the

5. These catch phrases, echoed by popularizers of Leibniz, make reference to the determinism of his system, its linking of cause with effect, and its optimism. As his correspondence indicates, Voltaire habitually thought of Leibniz's philosophy (which, having been published in definitive form as early as 1710, had been in the air for a long time) in terms of these catch phrases.

6. The argument from design supposes that everything in this world exists for a specific reason; Voltaire objects not to the argument as a whole, but to the abuse of it. Noses, he would say, were not designed to support spectacles, but spectacles were adapted to the pre-existing fact of noses. His full view finds expression in the article on "causes finales" in the *Philosophical Dictionary*

screen and, taking note of this cause and this effect, drove Candide out of the castle by kicking him vigorously on the backside. Cunégonde fainted; as soon as she recovered, the Baroness slapped her face; and everything was confusion in the most beautiful and agreeable of all possible castles.

CHAPTER 2

What Happened to Candide Among the Bulgars[7]

Candide, ejected from the earthly paradise, wandered for a long time without knowing where he was going, weeping, raising his eyes to heaven, and gazing back frequently on the most beautiful of castles which contained the most beautiful of Baron's daughters. He slept without eating, in a furrow of a plowed field, while the snow drifted over him; next morning, numb with cold, he dragged himself into the neighboring village, which was called Waldberghofftrarbk-dikdorff; he was penniless, famished, and exhausted. At the door of a tavern he paused forlornly. Two men dressed in blue[8] took note of him:

—Look, chum, said one of them, there's a likely young fellow of just about the right size.

They approached Candide and invited him very politely to dine with them.

—Gentlemen, Candide replied with charming modesty, I'm honored by your invitation, but I really don't have enough money to pay my share.

—My dear sir, said one of the blues, people of your appearance and your merit don't have to pay; aren't you five feet five inches tall?

—Yes, gentlemen, that is indeed my stature, said he, making a bow.

—Then, sir, you must be seated at once; not only will we pay your bill this time, we will never allow a man like you to be short of money; for men were made only to render one another mutual aid.

—You are quite right, said Candide; it is just as Dr. Pangloss always told me, and I see clearly that everything is for the best.

They beg him to accept a couple of crowns, he takes them, and offers an I.O.U.; they won't hear of it, and all sit down at table together.

—Don't you love dearly . . . ?

—I do indeed, says he, I dearly love Miss Cunégonde.

—No, no, says one of the gentlemen, we are asking if you don't love dearly the King of the Bulgars.

---

7. Voltaire chose this name to represent the Prussian troops of Frederick the Great because he wanted to make an insinuation of pederasty against both the soldiers and their master. Cf. French *bougre*, English "bugger."

8. The recruiting officers of Frederick the Great, much feared in eighteenth-century Europe, wore blue uniforms. Frederick had a passion for sorting out his soldiers by size; several of his regiments would accept only six-footers.

—Not in the least, says he, I never laid eyes on him.

—What's that you say? He's the most charming of kings, and we must drink his health.

—Oh, gladly, gentlemen; and he drinks.

—That will do, they tell him; you are now the bulwark, the support, the defender, the hero of the Bulgars; your fortune is made and your future assured.

Promptly they slip irons on his legs and lead him to the regiment. There they cause him to right face, left face, present arms, order arms, aim, fire, doubletime, and they give him thirty strokes of the rod. Next day he does the drill a little less awkwardly and gets only twenty strokes; the third day, they give him only ten, and he is regarded by his comrades as a prodigy.

Candide, quite thunderstruck, did not yet understand very clearly how he was a hero. One fine spring morning he took it into his head to go for a walk, stepping straight out as if it were a privilege of the human race, as of animals in general, to use his legs as he chose.[9] He had scarcely covered two leagues when four other heroes, each six feet tall, overtook him, bound him, and threw him into a dungeon. At the court-martial they asked which he preferred, to be flogged thirty-six times by the entire regiment or to receive summarily a dozen bullets in the brain. In vain did he argue that the human will is free and insist that he preferred neither alternative; he had to choose; by virtue of the divine gift called "liberty" he decided to run the gauntlet thirty-six times, and actually endured two floggings. The regiment was composed of two thousand men. That made four thousand strokes, which laid open every muscle and nerve from his nape to his butt. As they were preparing for the third beating, Candide, who could endure no more, begged as a special favor that they would have the goodness to smash his head. His plea was granted; they bandaged his eyes and made him kneel down. The King of the Bulgars, passing by at this moment, was told of the culprit's crime; and as this king had a rare genius, he understood, from everything they told him of Candide, that this was a young metaphysician, extremely ignorant of the ways of the world, so he granted his royal pardon, with a generosity which will be praised in every newspaper in every age. A worthy surgeon cured Candide in three weeks with the ointments described by Dioscorides.[1] He already had a bit of skin back

---

9. This episode was suggested by the experience of a Frenchman named Courtilz, who had deserted from the Prussian army and been bastinadoed for it. Voltaire intervened with Frederick to gain his release. But it also reflects the story that Wolff, Leibniz's disciple, got into trouble with Frederick's father when someone reported that his doctrine denying free will had encouraged several soldiers to desert. "The argument of the grenadier," who was said to have pleaded pre-established harmony to justify his desertion, so infuriated the king that he had Wolff expelled from the country.

1. Dioscorides' treatise on *materia medica*, dating from the first century A.D., was not the most up to date.

and was able to walk when the King of the Bulgars went to war with the King of the Abares.[2]

CHAPTER 3

How Candide Escaped from the Bulgars, and What Became of Him

Nothing could have been so fine, so brisk, so brilliant, so well-drilled as the two armies. The trumpets, the fifes, the oboes, the drums, and the cannon produced such a harmony as was never heard in hell. First the cannons battered down about six thousand men on each side; then volleys of musket fire removed from the best of worlds about nine or ten thousand rascals who were cluttering up its surface. The bayonet was a sufficient reason for the demise of several thousand others. Total casualties might well amount to thirty thousand men or so. Candide, who was trembling like a philosopher, hid himself as best he could while this heroic butchery was going on.

Finally, while the two kings in their respective camps celebrated the victory by having *Te Deums* sung,[3] Candide undertook to do his reasoning of cause and effect somewhere else. Passing by mounds of the dead and dying, he came to a nearby village which had been burnt to the ground. It was an Abare village, which the Bulgars had burned, in strict accordance with the laws of war. Here old men, stunned from beatings, watched the last agonies of their butchered wives, who still clutched their infants to their bleeding breasts; there, disemboweled girls, who had first satisfied the natural needs of various heroes, breathed their last; others, half-scorched in the flames, begged for their death stroke. Scattered brains and severed limbs littered the ground.

Candide fled as fast as he could to another village; this one belonged to the Bulgars, and the heroes of the Abare cause had given it the same treatment. Climbing over ruins and stumbling over twitching torsos, Candide finally made his way out of the war area, carrying a little food in his knapsack and never ceasing to dream of Miss Cunégonde. His supplies gave out when he reached Holland; but having heard that everyone in that country was rich and a Christian, he felt confident of being treated as well as he had been in the castle of the Baron before he was kicked out for the love of Miss Cunégonde.

He asked alms of several grave personages, who all told him that if

---

2. The name "Abares" actually designates a tribe of semicivilized Scythians, who might be supposed at war with the Bulgars; allegorically, the Abares are the French, who opposed the Prussians in the conflict known to hindsight history as the Seven Years' War (1756–63). For Voltaire, at the moment of writing *Candide*, it was simply the current war. One notes that according to the title page of 1761, "Doctor Ralph," the dummy author of *Candide*, himself perished at the battle of Minden (Westphalia) in 1759.

3. *Te Deums* are hymns sung to give thanks for a victory; having both sides sing at the same time is obviously ridiculous. After hideous casualties, the war actually ended in stalemate, so neither side was entitled to a triumph.

he continued to beg, he would be shut up in a house of correction and set to hard labor.

Finally he approached a man who had just been talking to a large crowd for an hour on end; the topic was charity. Looking doubtfully at him, the orator demanded:

—What are you doing here? Are you here to serve the good cause?

—There is no effect without a cause, said Candide modestly; all events are linked by the chain of necessity and arranged for the best. I had to be driven away from Miss Cunégonde, I had to run the gauntlet, I have to beg my bread until I can earn it; none of this could have happened otherwise.

—Look here, friend, said the orator, do you think the Pope is Antichrist?[4]

—I haven't considered the matter, said Candide; but whether he is or not, I'm in need of bread.

—You don't deserve any, said the other; away with you, you rascal, you rogue, never come near me as long as you live.

Meanwhile, the orator's wife had put her head out of the window, and, seeing a man who was not sure the Pope was Antichrist, emptied over his head a pot full of —— Scandalous! The excesses into which women are led by religious zeal!

A man who had never been baptized, a good Anabaptist named Jacques, saw this cruel and heartless treatment being inflicted on one of his fellow creatures, a featherless biped possessing a soul[5]; he took Candide home with him, washed him off, gave him bread and beer, presented him with two florins, and even undertook to give him a job in his Persian-rug factory—for these items are widely manufactured in Holland. Candide, in an ecstasy of gratitude, cried out:

—Master Pangloss was right indeed when he told me everything is for the best in this world; for I am touched by your kindness far more than by the harshness of that black-coated gentleman and his wife.

Next day, while taking a stroll about town, he met a beggar who was covered with pustules, his eyes were sunken, the end of his nose rotted off, his mouth twisted, his teeth black, he had a croaking voice and a hacking cough, and spat a tooth every time he tried to speak.

4. Voltaire is satirizing extreme Protestant sects that have sometimes seemed to make hatred of Rome the sum and substance of their creed. Holland, as the home of religious liberty, had offered asylum to the Anabaptists, whose radical views on property and religious discipline had made them unpopular during the sixteenth century. Granted tolerance, they settled down into respectable burghers. Since this behavior confirmed some of Voltaire's major prejudices, he had a high opinion of contemporary Anabaptists.

5. Plato's famous minimal definition of a man, which he corrected by the addition of a soul to distinguish man from a plucked chicken. The point is that the Anabaptist sympathizes with men simply because they are human.

CHAPTER 4

How Candide Met His Old Philosophy Tutor, Doctor Pangloss, and What Came of It

Candide, more touched by compassion even than by horror, gave this ghastly beggar the two florins that he himself had received from his honest Anabaptist friend Jacques. The phantom stared at him, burst into tears, and fell on his neck. Candide drew back in terror.

—Alas, said one wretch to the other, don't you recognize your dear Pangloss any more?

—What are you saying? You, my dear master! you, in this horrible condition? What misfortune has befallen you? Why are you no longer in the most beautiful of castles? What has happened to Miss Cunégonde, that pearl among young ladies, that masterpiece of Nature?

—I am perishing, said Pangloss.

—Candide promptly led him into the Anabaptist's stable, where he gave him a crust of bread, and when he had recovered: —Well, said he, Cunégonde?

—Dead, said the other.

Candide fainted. His friend brought him around with a bit of sour vinegar which happened to be in the stable. Candide opened his eyes.

—Cunégonde, dead! Ah, best of worlds, what's become of you now? But how did she die? It wasn't of grief at seeing me kicked out of her noble father's elegant castle?

—Not at all, said Pangloss; she was disemboweled by the Bulgar soldiers, after having been raped to the absolute limit of human endurance; they smashed the Baron's head when he tried to defend her, cut the Baroness to bits, and treated my poor pupil exactly like his sister.[6] As for the castle, not one stone was left on another, not a shed, not a sheep, not a duck, not a tree; but we had the satisfaction of revenge, for the Abares did exactly the same thing to a nearby barony belonging to a Bulgar nobleman.

At this tale Candide fainted again; but having returned to his senses and said everything appropriate to the occasion, he asked about the cause and effect, the sufficient reason, which had reduced Pangloss to his present pitiful state.

—Alas, said he, it was love; love, the consolation of the human race, the preservative of the universe, the soul of all sensitive beings, love, gentle love.

—Unhappy man, said Candide, I too have had some experience of this love, the sovereign of hearts, the soul of our souls; and it never got

---

6. The theme of homosexuality that attaches to Cunégonde's brother seems to have no general satiric point, but its presence is unmistakable. See chapters 14, 15, and 28. Note also that the sides in this lunatic war are scrambled; though Candide is fighting for the Bulgars, they loot his home; but he gets "revenge" when the Abares also loot a Bulgar castle.

me anything but a single kiss and twenty kicks in the rear. How could this lovely cause produce in you such a disgusting effect?

Pangloss replied as follows: —My dear Candide! you knew Paquette, that pretty maidservant to our august Baroness. In her arms I tasted the delights of paradise, which directly caused these torments of hell, from which I am now suffering. She was infected with the disease, and has perhaps died of it. Paquette received this present from an erudite Franciscan, who took the pains to trace it back to its source; for he had it from an elderly countess, who picked it up from a captain of cavalry, who acquired it from a marquise, who caught it from a page, who had received it from a Jesuit, who during his novitiate got it directly from one of the companions of Christopher Columbus.[7] As for me, I shall not give it to anyone, for I am a dying man.

—Oh, Pangloss, cried Candide, that's a very strange genealogy. Isn't the devil at the root of the whole thing?

—Not at all, replied that great man; it's an indispensable part of the best of worlds, a necessary ingredient; if Columbus had not caught, on an American island, this sickness which attacks the source of generation and sometimes prevents generation entirely—which thus strikes at and defeats the greatest end of Nature herself—we should have neither chocolate nor cochineal.[8] It must also be noted that until the present time this malady, like religious controversy, has been wholly confined to the continent of Europe. Turks, Indians, Persians, Chinese, Siamese, and Japanese know nothing of it as yet; but there is a sufficient reason for which they in turn will make its acquaintance in a couple of centuries. Meanwhile, it has made splendid progress among us, especially among those big armies of honest, well-trained mercenaries who decide the destinies of nations. You can be sure that when thirty thousand men fight a pitched battle against the same number of the enemy, there will be about twenty thousand with the pox on either side.

—Remarkable indeed, said Candide, but we must see about curing you.

—And how can I do that, said Pangloss, seeing I don't have a cent to my name? There's not a doctor in the whole world who will let your blood or give you an enema without demanding a fee. If you can't pay yourself, you must find someone to pay for you.

These last words decided Candide; he hastened to implore the help of his charitable Anabaptist, Jacques, and painted such a moving picture of his friend's wretched state that the good man did not hesitate to take in Pangloss and have him cured at his own expense. In the course of the cure, Pangloss lost only an eye and an ear. Since he wrote a fine

7. Syphilis was the first contribution of the New World to the happiness of the Old. Voltaire's information comes from Astruc, *Traité des maladies vénériennes* (1734).

8. Cochineal was a scarlet dye prepared from insects living exclusively in Mexico and Peru. Chocolate, prepared from the cacao bean, was perhaps a greater gift from the Americas to the world.

hand and knew arithmetic, the Anabaptist made him his bookkeeper. At the end of two months, being obliged to go to Lisbon on business, he took his two philosophers on the boat with him. Pangloss still maintained that everything was for the best, but Jacques didn't agree with him.

—It must be, said he, that men have somehow corrupted Nature, for they are not born wolves, yet that is what they become. God gave them neither twenty-four-pound cannon nor bayonets, yet they have manufactured both in order to destroy themselves. Bankruptcies have the same effect, and so does the justice which seizes the goods of bankrupts in order to prevent the creditors from getting them.[9]

—It was all indispensable, replied the one-eyed doctor, since private misfortunes make for public welfare, and therefore the more private misfortunes there are, the better everything is.

While he was reasoning, the air grew dark, the winds blew from all directions, and the vessel was attacked by a horrible tempest within sight of Lisbon harbor.

CHAPTER 5

Tempest, Shipwreck, Earthquake, and What Happened to Doctor Pangloss, Candide, and the Anabaptist, Jacques

Half of the passengers, weakened by the frightful anguish of seasickness and the distress of tossing about on stormy waters, were incapable of noticing their danger. The other half shrieked aloud and fell to their prayers, the sails were ripped to shreds, the masts snapped, the vessel opened at the seams. Everyone worked who could stir, nobody listened for orders or issued them. The Anabaptist was lending a hand in the after part of the ship when a frantic sailor struck him and knocked him to the deck; but just at that moment, the sailor lurched so violently that he fell head first over the side, where he hung, clutching a fragment of the broken mast. The good Jacques ran to his aid, and helped him to climb back on board, but in the process was himself thrown into the sea under the very eyes of the sailor, who allowed him to drown without even glancing at him. Candide rushed to the rail, and saw his benefactor rise for a moment to the surface, then sink forever. He wanted to dive to his rescue; but the philosopher Pangloss prevented him by proving that the bay of Lisbon had been formed expressly for this Anabaptist to drown in. While he was proving the point *a priori*,[1] the vessel opened up and everyone perished except for Pangloss, Candide, and the brutal sailor who had caused the virtuous Anabaptist to drown; this rascal swam

---

9. Voltaire had suffered losses from various bankruptcy proceedings, which lend a personal edge to his satire here, besides diverting its point a bit.

1. By deduction from general principles.

easily to shore, while Pangloss and Candide drifted there on a plank.

When they had recovered a bit of energy, they set out for Lisbon; they still had a little money with which they hoped to stave off hunger after escaping the storm.

Scarcely had they set foot in the town, still bewailing the loss of their benefactor, when they felt the earth quake underfoot; the sea was lashed to a froth, burst into the port, and smashed all the vessels lying at anchor there. Whirlwinds of fire and ash swirled through the streets and public squares; houses crumbled, roofs came crashing down on foundations, foundations split; thirty thousand inhabitants of every age and either sex were crushed in the ruins.[2] The sailor whistled through his teeth, and said with an oath:—There'll be something to pick up here.

—What can be the sufficient reason of this phenomenon? asked Pangloss.

—The Last Judgment is here, cried Candide.

But the sailor ran directly into the middle of the ruins, heedless of danger in his eagerness for gain; he found some money, laid violent hands on it, got drunk, and, having slept off his wine, bought the favors of the first streetwalker he could find amid the ruins of smashed houses, amid corpses and suffering victims on every hand. Pangloss however tugged at his sleeve.

—My friend, said he, this is not good form at all; your behavior falls short of that required by the universal reason; it's untimely, to say the least.

—Bloody hell, said the other, I'm a sailor, born in Batavia; I've been four times to Japan and stamped four times on the crucifix;[3] get out of here with your universal reason.

Some falling stonework had struck Candide; he lay prostrate in the street, covered with rubble, and calling to Pangloss:—For pity's sake bring me a little wine and oil; I'm dying.

—This earthquake is nothing novel, Pangloss replied; the city of Lima, in South America, underwent much the same sort of tremor, last year; same causes, same effects; there is surely a vein of sulphur under the earth's surface reaching from Lima to Lisbon.

—Nothing is more probable, said Candide; but, for God's sake, a little oil and wine.

—What do you mean, probable? replied the philosopher; I regard the case as proved.

---

2. The great Lisbon earthquake and fire occurred on November 1, 1755; between thirty and forty thousand deaths resulted.
3. The Japanese, originally receptive to foreign visitors, grew fearful that priests and proselytizers were merely advance agents of empire, and expelled both the Portuguese and the Spanish early in the seventeenth century. Only the Dutch were allowed to retain a small foothold, under humiliating conditions, of which the notion of stamping on the crucifix is symbolic. It was never what Voltaire suggests here, an actual requirement for entering the country.

Candide fainted and Pangloss brought him some water from a nearby fountain.

Next day, as they wandered amid the ruins, they found a little food which restored some of their strength. Then they fell to work like the others, bringing relief to those of the inhabitants who had escaped death. Some of the citizens whom they rescued gave them a dinner as good as was possible under the circumstances; it is true that the meal was a melancholy one, and the guests watered their bread with tears; but Pangloss consoled them by proving that things could not possibly be otherwise.

—For, said he, all this is for the best, since if there is a volcano at Lisbon, it cannot be somewhere else, since it is unthinkable that things should not be where they are, since everything is well.

A little man in black, an officer of the Inquisition,[4] who was sitting beside him, politely took up the question, and said:—It would seem that the gentleman does not believe in original sin, since if everything is for the best, man has not fallen and is not liable to eternal punishment.

—I most humbly beg pardon of your excellency, Pangloss answered, even more politely, but the fall of man and the curse of original sin entered necessarily into the best of all possible worlds.

—Then you do not believe in free will? said the officer.

—Your excellency must excuse me, said Pangloss; free will agrees very well with absolute necessity, for it was necessary that we should be free, since a will which is determined . . .

Pangloss was in the middle of his sentence, when the officer nodded significantly to the attendant who was pouring him a glass of port, or Oporto, wine.

CHAPTER 6

How They Made a Fine Auto-da-Fé to Prevent Earthquakes, and How Candide Was Whipped

After the earthquake had wiped out three quarters of Lisbon, the learned men of the land could find no more effective way of averting total destruction than to give the people a fine auto-da-fé;[5] the University of Coimbra had established that the spectacle of several persons being roasted over a slow fire with full ceremonial rites is an infallible specific against earthquakes.

In consequence, the authorities had rounded up a Biscayan convicted of marrying a woman who had stood godmother to his child, and two

4. Specifically, a *familier* or *poursuivant*, an undercover agent with powers of arrest.
5. Literally, "act of faith," a public ceremony of repentance and humiliation. Such an auto-da-fé was actually held in Lisbon, June 20, 1756.

Portuguese who while eating a chicken had set aside a bit of bacon used for seasoning.[6] After dinner, men came with ropes to tie up Doctor Pangloss and his disciple Candide, one for talking and the other for listening with an air of approval; both were taken separately to a set of remarkably cool apartments, where the glare of the sun is never bothersome; eight days later they were both dressed in *san-benitos* and crowned with paper mitres;[7] Candide's mitre and *san-benito* were decorated with inverted flames and with devils who had neither tails nor claws; but Pangloss's devils had both tails and claws, and his flames stood upright. Wearing these costumes, they marched in a procession, and listened to a very touching sermon, followed by a beautiful concert of plainsong. Candide was flogged in cadence to the music; the Biscayan and the two men who had avoided bacon were burned, and Pangloss was hanged, though hanging is not customary. On the same day there was another earthquake, causing frightful damage.[8]

Candide, stunned, stupefied, despairing, bleeding, trembling, said to himself:—If this is the best of all possible worlds, what are the others like? The flogging is not so bad, I was flogged by the Bulgars. But oh my dear Pangloss, greatest of philosophers, was it necessary for me to watch you being hanged, for no reason that I can see? Oh my dear Anabaptist, best of men, was it necessary that you should be drowned in the port? Oh Miss Cunégonde, pearl of young ladies, was it necessary that you should have your belly slit open?

He was being led away, barely able to stand, lectured, lashed, absolved, and blessed, when an old woman approached and said,—My son, be of good cheer and follow me.

CHAPTER 7

How an Old Woman Took Care of Candide, and How He Regained What He Loved

Candide was of very bad cheer, but he followed the old woman to a shanty; she gave him a jar of ointment to rub himself, left him food and drink; she showed him a tidy little bed; next to it was a suit of clothing.

—Eat, drink, sleep, she said; and may Our Lady of Atocha, Our Lord St. Anthony of Padua, and Our Lord St. James of Compostela watch over you. I will be back tomorrow.

Candide, still completely astonished by everything he had seen and suffered, and even more by the old woman's kindness, offered to kiss her hand.

---

6. The Biscayan's fault lay in marrying someone within the forbidden bounds of relationship, an act of spiritual incest. The men who declined pork or bacon were understood to be crypto-Jews.
7. The cone-shaped paper cap (intended to resem-

ble a bishop's mitre) and flowing yellow cape were customary garb for those pleading before the Inquisition.
8. In fact, the second quake occurred December 21, 1755.

—It's not *my* hand you should be kissing, said she. I'll be back to-morrow; rub yourself with the ointment, eat and sleep.

In spite of his many sufferings, Candide ate and slept. Next day the old woman returned bringing breakfast; she looked at his back and rubbed it herself with another ointment; she came back with lunch; and then she returned in the evening, bringing supper. Next day she repeated the same routine.

—Who are you? Candide asked continually. Who told you to be so kind to me? How can I ever repay you?

The good woman answered not a word; she returned in the evening, and without food.

—Come with me, says she, and don't speak a word.

Taking him by the hand, she walks out into the countryside with him for about a quarter of a mile; they reach an isolated house, quite surrounded by gardens and ditches. The old woman knocks at a little gate, it opens. She takes Candide up a secret stairway to a gilded room furnished with a fine brocaded sofa; there she leaves him, closes the door, disappears. Candide stood as if entranced; his life, which had seemed like a nightmare so far, was now starting to look like a delightful dream.

Soon the old woman returned; on her feeble shoulder leaned a trembling woman, of a splendid figure, glittering in diamonds, and veiled.

—Remove the veil, said the old woman to Candide.

The young man stepped timidly forward, and lifted the veil. What an event! What a surprise! Could it be Miss Cunégonde? Yes, it really was! She herself! His knees give way, speech fails him, he falls at her feet, Cunégonde collapses on the sofa. The old woman plies them with brandy, they return to their senses, they exchange words. At first they could utter only broken phrases, questions and answers at cross purposes, sighs, tears, exclamations. The old woman warned them not to make too much noise, and left them alone.

—Then it's really you, said Candide, you're alive, I've found you again in Portugal. Then you never were raped? You never had your belly ripped open, as the philosopher Pangloss assured me?

—Oh yes, said the lovely Cunégonde, but one doesn't always die of these two accidents.

—But your father and mother were murdered then?

—All too true, said Cunégonde, in tears.

—And your brother?

—Killed too.

—And why are you in Portugal? and how did you know I was here? and by what device did you have me brought to this house?

—I shall tell you everything, the lady replied; but first you must tell me what has happened to you since that first innocent kiss we exchanged and the kicking you got because of it.

Candide obeyed her with profound respect; and though he was overcome, though his voice was weak and hesitant, though he still had twinges of pain from his beating, he described as simply as possible everything that had happened to him since the time of their separation. Cunégonde lifted her eyes to heaven; she wept at the death of the good Anabaptist and at that of Pangloss; after which she told the following story to Candide, who listened to every word while he gazed on her with hungry eyes.

CHAPTER 8

Cunégonde's Story

—I was in my bed and fast asleep when heaven chose to send the Bulgars into our castle of Thunder-Ten-Tronckh. They butchered my father and brother, and hacked my mother to bits. An enormous Bulgar, six feet tall, seeing that I had swooned from horror at the scene, set about raping me; at that I recovered my senses, I screamed and scratched, bit and fought, I tried to tear the eyes out of that big Bulgar—not realizing that everything which had happened in my father's castle was a mere matter of routine. The brute then stabbed me with a knife on my left thigh, where I still bear the scar.

—What a pity! I should very much like to see it, said the simple Candide.

—You shall, said Cunégonde; but shall I go on?

—Please do, said Candide.

So she took up the thread of her tale:—A Bulgar captain appeared, he saw me covered with blood and the soldier too intent to get up. Shocked by the monster's failure to come to attention, the captain killed him on my body. He then had my wound dressed, and took me off to his quarters, as a prisoner of war. I laundered his few shirts and did his cooking; he found me attractive, I confess it, and I won't deny that he was a handsome fellow, with a smooth, white skin; apart from that, however, little wit, little philosophical training; it was evident that he had not been brought up by Doctor Pangloss. After three months, he had lost all his money and grown sick of me; so he sold me to a jew named Don Issachar, who traded in Holland and Portugal, and who was mad after women. This jew developed a mighty passion for my person, but he got nowhere with it; I held him off better than I had done with the Bulgar soldier; for though a person of honor may be raped once, her virtue is only strengthened by the experience. In order to keep me hidden, the jew brought me to his country house, which you see here. Till then I had thought there was nothing on earth so beautiful as the castle of Thunder-Ten-Tronckh; I was now undeceived.

—One day the Grand Inquisitor took notice of me at mass; he ogled me a good deal, and made known that he must talk to me on a matter of secret business. I was taken to his palace; I told him of my rank; he pointed out that it was beneath my dignity to belong to an Israelite. A suggestion was then conveyed to Don Issachar that he should turn me over to My Lord the Inquisitor. Don Issachar, who is court banker and a man of standing, refused out of hand. The inquisitor threatened him with an auto-da-fé. Finally my jew, fearing for his life, struck a bargain by which the house and I would belong to both of them as joint tenants; the jew would get Mondays, Wednesdays, and the Sabbath, the inquisitor would get the other days of the week. That has been the arrangement for six months now. There have been quarrels; sometimes it has not been clear whether the night from Saturday to Sunday belonged to the old or the new dispensation. For my part, I have so far been able to hold both of them off; and that, I think, is why they are both still in love with me.

—Finally, in order to avert further divine punishment by earthquake, and to terrify Don Issachar, My Lord the Inquisitor chose to celebrate an auto-da-fé. He did me the honor of inviting me to attend. I had an excellent seat; the ladies were served with refreshments between the mass and the execution. To tell you the truth, I was horrified to see them burn alive those two jews and that decent Biscayan who had married his child's godmother; but what was my surprise, my terror, my grief, when I saw, huddled in a *san-benito* and wearing a mitre, someone who looked like Pangloss! I rubbed my eyes, I watched his every move, I saw him hanged; and I fell back in a swoon. Scarcely had I come to my senses again, when I saw you stripped for the lash; that was the peak of my horror, consternation, grief, and despair. I may tell you, by the way, that your skin is even whiter and more delicate than that of my Bulgar captain. Seeing you, then, redoubled the torments which were already overwhelming me. I shrieked aloud, I wanted to call out, 'Let him go, you brutes!' but my voice died within me, and my cries would have been useless. When you had been thoroughly thrashed: 'How can it be,' I asked myself, 'that agreeable Candide and wise Pangloss have come to Lisbon, one to receive a hundred whiplashes, the other to be hanged by order of My Lord the Inquisitor, whose mistress I am? Pangloss must have deceived me cruelly when he told me that all is for the best in this world.'

—Frantic, exhausted, half out of my senses, and ready to die of weakness, I felt as if my mind were choked with the massacre of my father, my mother, my brother, with the arrogance of that ugly Bulgar soldier, with the knife slash he inflicted on me, my slavery, my kitchen-drudgery, my Bulgar captain, my nasty Don Issachar, my abominable inquisitor, with the hanging of Doctor Pangloss, with that great plainsong *miserere*[9] which they sang while they flogged you—and above all, my mind was full of the kiss which I gave you behind the screen, on the day I saw you for the last time. I praised God, who had brought you back to me after so many trials. I asked my old woman to look out for you, and to bring you here as soon as she could. She did just as I asked; I have had the indescribable joy of seeing you again, hearing you and talking with you once more. But you must be frightfully hungry; I am, myself; let us begin with a dinner.

So then and there they sat down to table; and after dinner, they adjourned to that fine brocaded sofa, which has already been mentioned; and there they were when the eminent Don Issachar, one of the masters of the house, appeared. It was the day of the Sabbath; he was arriving to assert his rights and express his tender passion.

CHAPTER 9

What Happened to Cunégonde, Candide, the Grand Inquisitor, and a Jew

This Issachar was the most choleric Hebrew seen in Israel since the Babylonian captivity.

—What's this, says he, you bitch of a Christian, you're not satisfied with the Grand Inquisitor? Do I have to share you with this rascal, too?

So saying, he drew a long dagger, with which he always went armed, and, supposing his opponent defenseless, flung himself on Candide. But our good Westphalian had received from the old woman, along with his suit of clothes, a fine sword. Out it came, and though his manners were of the gentlest, in short order he laid the Israelite stiff and cold on the floor, at the feet of the lovely Cunégonde.

—Holy Virgin! she cried. What will become of me now? A man killed in my house! If the police find out, we're done for.

—If Pangloss had not been hanged, said Candide, he would give us good advice in this hour of need, for he was a great philosopher. Lacking him, let's ask the old woman.

She was a sensible body, and was just starting to give her opinion of the situation, when another little door opened. It was just one o'clock in the morning, Sunday morning. This day belonged to the inquisitor. In he came, and found the whipped Candide with a sword in his hand, a corpse at his feet, Cunégonde in terror, and an old woman giving them both good advice.

Here now is what passed through Candide's mind in this instant of time; this is how he reasoned:—If this holy man calls for help, he will

9. The fiftieth Psalm in the Vulgate (Latin) Bible begins with the word *Miserere* (have mercy); it is fittingly included among the penitential psalms.   Plainsong is a particularly unadorned form of medieval music.

certainly have me burned, and perhaps Cunégonde as well; he has already had me whipped without mercy; he is my rival; I have already killed once; why hesitate?

It was a quick, clear chain of reasoning; without giving the inquisitor time to recover from his surprise, he ran him through, and laid him beside the jew.

—Here you've done it again, said Cunégonde; there's no hope for us now. We'll be excommunicated, our last hour has come. How is it that you, who were born so gentle, could kill in two minutes a jew and a prelate?

—My dear girl, replied Candide, when a man is in love, jealous, and just whipped by the Inquisition, he is no longer himself.

The old woman now spoke up and said:—There are three Andalusian steeds[1] in the stable, with their saddles and bridles; our brave Candide must get them ready: my lady has some gold coin and diamonds; let's take to horse at once, though I can only ride on one buttock; we will go to Cadiz. The weather is as fine as can be, and it is pleasant to travel in the cool of the evening.

Promptly, Candide saddled the three horses. Cunégonde, the old woman, and he covered thirty miles without a stop. While they were fleeing, the Holy Brotherhood[2] came to investigate the house; they buried the inquisitor in a fine church, and threw Issachar on the dunghill.

Candide, Cunégonde, and the old woman were already in the little town of Avacena, in the middle of the Sierra Morena; and there, as they sat in a country inn, they had this conversation.

CHAPTER 10

In Deep Distress, Candide, Cunégonde, and the Old Woman Reach Cadiz; They Put to Sea

—Who then could have robbed me of my gold and diamonds? said Cunégonde, in tears. How shall we live? what shall we do? where shall I find other inquisitors and jews to give me some more?

—Ah, said the old woman, I strongly suspect that reverend Franciscan friar who shared the inn with us yesterday at Badajoz. God save me from judging him unfairly! But he came into our room twice, and he left long before us.

—Alas, said Candide, the good Pangloss often proved to me that the fruits of the earth are a common heritage of all, to which each man has equal right. On these principles, the Franciscan should at least have left us enough to finish our journey. You have nothing at all, my dear Cunégonde?

1. Spanish horses, proverbially swift and strong.   active in eighteenth-century Spain.
2. A semireligious order with police powers, very

—Not a maravedi, said she.

—What to do? said Candide.

—We'll sell one of the horses, said the old woman; I'll ride on the croup behind my mistress, though only on one buttock, and so we will get to Cadiz.

There was in the same inn a Benedictine prior; he bought the horse cheap. Candide, Cunégonde, and the old woman passed through Lucena, Chillas, and Lebrixa, and finally reached Cadiz. There a fleet was being fitted out and an army assembled, to reason with the Jesuit fathers in Paraguay, who were accused of fomenting among their flock a revolt against the kings of Spain and Portugal near the town of St. Sacrement.[3] Candide, having served in the Bulgar army, performed the Bulgar manual of arms before the general of the little army with such grace, swiftness, dexterity, fire, and agility, that they gave him a company of infantry to command. So here he is, a captain; and off he sails with Miss Cunégonde, the old woman, two valets, and the two Andalusian steeds which had belonged to My Lord the Grand Inquisitor of Portugal.

Throughout the crossing, they spent a great deal of time reasoning about the philosophy of poor Pangloss.

—We are destined, in the end, for another universe, said Candide; no doubt that is the one where everything is well. For in this one, it must be admitted, there is some reason to grieve over our physical and moral state.

—I love you with all my heart, said Cunégonde; but my soul is still harrowed by thoughts of what I have seen and suffered.

—All will be well, replied Candide; the sea of this new world is already better than those of Europe, calmer and with steadier winds. Surely it is the New World which is the best of all possible worlds.

—God grant it, said Cunégonde; but I have been so horribly unhappy in the world so far, that my heart is almost dead to hope.

—You pity yourselves, the old woman told them; but you have had no such misfortunes as mine.

Cunégonde nearly broke out laughing; she found the old woman comic in pretending to be more unhappy than she.

—Ah, you poor old thing, said she, unless you've been raped by two Bulgars, been stabbed twice in the belly, seen two of your castles destroyed, witnessed the murder of two of your mothers and two of your fathers, and watched two of your lovers being whipped in an auto-da-fé, I do not see how you can have had it worse than me. Besides, I was born a baroness, with seventy-two quarterings, and I have worked in a scullery.

---

3. Actually, Colonia del Sacramento. Voltaire took great interest in the Jesuit role in Paraguay, which he has much oversimplified and largely misrepresented here in the interests of his satire. In 1750 they did, however, offer armed resistance to an agreement made between Spain and Portugal. They were subdued and expelled in 1769.

—My lady, replied the old woman, you do not know my birth and rank; and if I showed you my rear end, you would not talk as you do, you might even speak with less assurance.

These words inspired great curiosity in Candide and Cunégonde, which the old woman satisfied with this story.

CHAPTER 11

The Old Woman's Story

—My eyes were not always bloodshot and red-rimmed, my nose did not always touch my chin, and I was not born a servant. I am in fact the daughter of Pope Urban the Tenth and the Princess of Palestrina.[4] Till the age of fourteen, I lived in a palace so splendid that all the castles of all your German barons would not have served it as a stable; a single one of my dresses was worth more than all the assembled magnificence of Westphalia. I grew in beauty, in charm, in talent, surrounded by pleasures, dignities, and glowing visions of the future. Already I was inspiring the young men to love; my breast was formed—and what a breast! white, firm, with the shape of the Venus de Medici; and what eyes! what lashes, what black brows! What fire flashed from my glances and outshone the glitter of the stars, as the local poets used to tell me! The women who helped me dress and undress fell into ecstasies, whether they looked at me from in front or behind; and all the men wanted to be in their place.

—I was engaged to the ruling prince of Massa-Carrara; and what a prince he was! as handsome as I, softness and charm compounded, brilliantly witty, and madly in love with me. I loved him in return as one loves for the first time, with a devotion approaching idolatry. The wedding preparations had been made, with a splendor and magnificence never heard of before; nothing but celebrations, masks, and comic operas, uninterruptedly; and all Italy composed in my honor sonnets of which not one was even passable. I had almost attained the very peak of bliss, when an old marquise who had been the mistress of my prince invited him to her house for a cup of chocolate. He died in less than two hours, amid horrifying convulsions. But that was only a trifle. My mother, in complete despair (though less afflicted than I), wished to escape for a while the oppressive atmosphere of grief. She owned a handsome property near Gaeta.[5] We embarked on a papal galley gilded like the altar of St. Peter's in Rome. Suddenly a pirate ship from Salé swept down and boarded us. Our soldiers defended themselves as papal

4. Voltaire left behind a comment on this passage, a note first published in 1829: "Note the extreme discretion of the author; hitherto there has never been a pope named Urban X; he avoided attrib-uting a bastard to a known pope. What circumspection! what an exquisite conscience!"
5. About halfway between Rome and Naples. Salé: a seaport town in Morocco.

troops usually do; falling on their knees and throwing down their arms, they begged of the corsair absolution *in articulo mortis.*[6]

—They were promptly stripped as naked as monkeys, and so was my mother, and so were our maids of honor, and so was I too. It's a very remarkable thing, the energy these gentlemen put into stripping people. But what surprised me even more was that they stuck their fingers in a place where we women usually admit only a syringe. This ceremony seemed a bit odd to me, as foreign usages always do when one hasn't traveled. They only wanted to see if we didn't have some diamonds hidden there; and I soon learned that it's a custom of long standing among the genteel folk who swarm the seas. I learned that my lords the very religious knights of Malta never overlook this ceremony when they capture Turks, whether male or female; it's one of those international laws which have never been questioned.

—I won't try to explain how painful it is for a young princess to be carried off into slavery in Morocco with her mother. You can imagine everything we had to suffer on the pirate ship. My mother was still very beautiful; our maids of honor, our mere chambermaids, were more charming than anything one could find in all Africa. As for myself, I was ravishing, I was loveliness and grace supreme, and I was a virgin. I did not remain so for long; the flower which had been kept for the handsome prince of Massa-Carrara was plucked by the corsair captain; he was an abominable negro, who thought he was doing me a great favor. My Lady the Princess of Palestrina and I must have been strong indeed to bear what we did during our journey to Morocco. But on with my story; these are such common matters that they are not worth describing.

—Morocco was knee deep in blood when we arrived. Of the fifty sons of the emperor Muley-Ismael,[7] each had his faction, which produced in effect fifty civil wars, of blacks against blacks, of blacks against browns, halfbreeds against halfbreeds; throughout the length and breadth of the empire, nothing but one continual carnage.

—Scarcely had we stepped ashore, when some negroes of a faction hostile to my captor arrived to take charge of his plunder. After the diamonds and gold, we women were the most prized possessions. I was now witness of a struggle such as you never see in the temperate climate of Europe. Northern people don't have hot blood; they don't feel the absolute fury for women which is common in Africa. Europeans seem to have milk in their veins; it is vitriol or liquid fire that pulses through these people around Mount Atlas. The fight for possession of us raged with the fury of the lions, tigers, and poisonous vipers of that land. A

6. Literally, when at the point of death. Absolution from a corsair in the act of murdering one is of very dubious validity.
7. Having reigned for more than fifty years, a po-

tent and ruthless sultan of Morocco, he died in 1727 and left his kingdom in much the condition described.

Moor snatched my mother by the right arm, the first mate held her by the left; a Moorish soldier grabbed one leg, one of our pirates the other. In a moment's time almost all our girls were being dragged four different ways. My captain held me behind him while with his scimitar he killed everyone who braved his fury. At last I saw all our Italian women, including my mother, torn to pieces, cut to bits, murdered by the monsters who were fighting over them. My captive companions, their captors, soldiers, sailors, blacks, browns, whites, mulattoes, and at last my captain, all were killed, and I remained half dead on a mountain of corpses. Similar scenes were occurring, as is well known, for more than three hundred leagues around, without anyone skimping on the five prayers a day decreed by Mohammed.

—With great pain, I untangled myself from this vast heap of bleeding bodies, and dragged myself under a great orange tree by a neighboring brook, where I collapsed, from terror, exhaustion, horror, despair, and hunger. Shortly, my weary mind surrendered to a sleep which was more of a swoon than a rest. I was in this state of weakness and languor, between life and death, when I felt myself touched by something which moved over my body. Opening my eyes, I saw a white man, rather attractive, who was groaning and saying under his breath: '*O che sciagura d'essere senza coglioni!*'[8]

CHAPTER 12

The Old Woman's Story Continued

—Amazed and delighted to hear my native tongue, and no less surprised by what this man was saying, I told him that there were worse evils than those he was complaining of. In a few words, I described to him the horrors I had undergone, and then fainted again. He carried me to a nearby house, put me to bed, gave me something to eat, served me, flattered me, comforted me, told me he had never seen anyone so lovely, and added that he had never before regretted so much the loss of what nobody could give him back.

'I was born at Naples, he told me, where they caponize two or three thousand children every year; some die of it, others acquire a voice more beautiful than any woman's, still others go on to become governors of kingdoms.[9] The operation was a great success with me, and I became court musician to the Princess of Palestrina . . .

'Of my mother,' I exclaimed.

'Of your mother,' cried he, bursting into tears; 'then you must be the princess whom I raised till she was six, and who already gave promise of becoming as beautiful as you are now!'

8. "Oh what a misfortune to have no testicles!"
9. The castrate Farinelli (1705–82), originally a singer, came to exercise considerable political influence on the kings of Spain, Philip V and Ferdinand VI.

'I am that very princess; my mother lies dead, not a hundred yards from here, cut into quarters and buried under a pile of corpses.'

—I told him my adventures, he told me his: that he had been sent by a Christian power to the King of Morocco, to conclude a treaty granting him gunpowder, cannon, and ships with which to liquidate the traders of the other Christian powers.

'My mission is concluded,' said this honest eunuch; 'I shall take ship at Ceuta and bring you back to Italy. *Ma che sciagura d'essere senza coglioni!*'

—I thanked him with tears of gratitude, and instead of returning me to Italy, he took me to Algiers and sold me to the dey of that country. Hardly had the sale taken place, when that plague which has made the rounds of Africa, Asia, and Europe broke out in full fury at Algiers. You have seen earthquakes; but tell me, young lady, have you ever had the plague?

—Never, replied the baroness.

—If you had had it, said the old woman, you would agree that it is far worse than an earthquake. It is very frequent in Africa, and I had it. Imagine, if you will, the situation of a pope's daughter, fifteen years old, who in three months' time had experienced poverty, slavery, had been raped almost every day, had seen her mother quartered, had suffered from famine and war, and who now was dying of pestilence in Algiers. As a matter of fact, I did not die; but the eunuch and the dey and nearly the entire seraglio of Algiers perished.

—When the first horrors of this ghastly plague had passed, the slaves of the dey were sold. A merchant bought me and took me to Tunis; there he sold me to another merchant, who resold me at Tripoli; from Tripoli I was sold to Alexandria, from Alexandria resold to Smyrna, from Smyrna to Constantinople. I ended by belonging to an aga of janizaries, who was shortly ordered to defend Azov against the besieging Russians.[1]

—The aga, who was a gallant soldier, took his whole seraglio with him, and established us in a little fort amid the Maeotian marshes,[2] guarded by two black eunuchs and twenty soldiers. Our side killed a prodigious number of Russians, but they paid us back nicely. Azov was put to fire and sword without respect for age or sex; only our little fort continued to resist, and the enemy determined to starve us out. The twenty janizaries had sworn never to surrender. Reduced to the last extremities of hunger, they were forced to eat our two eunuchs, lest they violate their oaths. After several more days, they decided to eat the women too.

1. Azov, near the mouth of the Don, was besieged by the Russians under Peter the Great in 1695–96. An aga or agha is, in Mohammedan countries, a military commander about equivalent to a major; janizaries were slaves, prisoners, or captured Christians who served the sultan as an elite group of mercenary soldiers.
2. The Roman name of the so-called Sea of Azov, a shallow swampy lake near the town.

—We had an imam,[3] very pious and sympathetic, who delivered an excellent sermon, persuading them not to kill us altogether.

'Just cut off a single rumpsteak from each of these ladies,' he said, 'and you'll have a fine meal. Then if you should need another, you can come back in a few days and have as much again; heaven will bless your charitable action, and you will be saved.'

—His eloquence was splendid, and he persuaded them. We underwent this horrible operation. The imam treated us all with the ointment that they use on newly circumcised children. We were at the point of death.

—Scarcely had the janizaries finished the meal for which we furnished the materials, when the Russians appeared in flat-bottomed boats; not a janizary escaped. The Russians paid no attention to the state we were in; but there are French physicians everywhere, and one of them, who knew his trade, took care of us. He cured us, and I shall remember all my life that when my wounds were healed, he made me a proposition. For the rest, he counselled us simply to have patience, assuring us that the same thing had happened in several other sieges, and that it was according to the laws of war.

—As soon as my companions could walk, we were herded off to Moscow. In the division of booty, I fell to a boyar who made me work in his garden, and gave me twenty whiplashes a day; but when he was broken on the wheel after about two years, with thirty other boyars, over some little court intrigue,[4] I seized the occasion; I ran away; I crossed all Russia; I was for a long time a chambermaid in Riga, then at Rostock, Wismar, Leipzig, Cassel, Utrecht, Leyden, The Hague, Rotterdam; I grew old in misery and shame, having only half a backside and remembering always that I was the daughter of a Pope. A hundred times I wanted to kill myself, but always I loved life more. This ridiculous weakness is perhaps one of our worst instincts; is anything more stupid than choosing to carry a burden that really one wants to cast on the ground? to hold existence in horror, and yet to cling to it? to fondle the serpent which devours us till it has eaten out our heart?

—In the countries through which I have been forced to wander, in the taverns where I have had to work, I have seen a vast number of people who hated their existence; but I never saw more than a dozen who deliberately put an end to their own misery: three negroes, four Englishmen, four Genevans, and a German professor named Robeck.[5]

---

3. In effect, a chaplain.

4. Boyars were a class of petty Russian nobility; the "little court intrigue" that Voltaire has in mind here was an ineffectual conspiracy against Peter the Great known as the "revolt of the strelitz" or musketeers, which took place in 1698. Though easily put down, it provoked from the emperor a massive and atrocious program of reprisals.

5. Johann Robeck (1672–1739) published a treatise advocating suicide and showed his conviction by drowning himself. But he waited till he was 67 before putting his theory to the test. For a larger view of the issue, see L. G. Crocker, "The Discussion of Suicide in the 18th Century," *Journal of the History of Ideas* 13(1952): 47–72.

My last post was as servant to the jew Don Issachar; he attached me to your service, my lovely one; and I attached myself to your destiny, till I have become more concerned with your fate than with my own. I would not even have mentioned my own misfortunes, if you had not irked me a bit, and if it weren't the custom, on shipboard, to pass the time with stories. In a word, my lady, I have had some experience of the world, I know it; why not try this diversion? Ask every passenger on this ship to tell you his story, and if you find a single one who has not often cursed the day of his birth, who has not often told himself that he is the most miserable of men, then you may throw me overboard head first.

CHAPTER 13

How Candide Was Forced to Leave the Lovely Cunégonde and the Old Woman

Having heard out the old woman's story, the lovely Cunégonde paid her the respects which were appropriate to a person of her rank and merit. She took up the wager as well, and got all the passengers, one after another, to tell her their adventures. She and Candide had to agree that the old woman had been right.

—It's certainly too bad, said Candide, that the wise Pangloss was hanged, contrary to the custom of autos-da-fé; he would have admirable things to say of the physical evil and moral evil which cover land and sea, and I might feel within me the impulse to dare to raise several polite objections.

As the passengers recited their stories, the boat made steady progress, and presently landed at Buenos Aires. Cunégonde, Captain Candide, and the old woman went to call on the governor, Don Fernando d'Ibaraa y Figueroa y Mascarenes y Lampourdos y Souza. This nobleman had the pride appropriate to a man with so many names. He addressed everyone with the most aristocratic disdain, pointing his nose so loftily, raising his voice so mercilessly, lording it so splendidly, and assuming so arrogant a pose, that everyone who met him wanted to kick him. He loved women to the point of fury; and Cunégonde seemed to him the most beautiful creature he had ever seen. The first thing he did was to ask directly if she were the captain's wife. His manner of asking this question disturbed Candide; he did not dare say she was his wife, because in fact she was not; he did not dare say she was his sister, because she wasn't that either; and though this polite lie was once common enough among the ancients,[6] and sometimes serves moderns very well, he was too pure of heart to tell a lie.

6. Voltaire has in mind Abraham's adventures with Sarah (Genesis 12) and Isaac's with Rebecca (Genesis 26).

—Miss Cunégonde, said he, is betrothed to me, and we humbly beg your excellency to perform the ceremony for us.

Don Fernando d'Ibaraa y Figueroa y Mascarenes y Lampourdos y Souza twirled his moustache, smiled sardonically, and ordered Captain Candide to go drill his company. Candide obeyed. Left alone with my lady Cunégonde, the governor declared his passion, and protested that he would marry her tomorrow, in church or in any other manner, as it pleased her charming self. Cunégonde asked for a quarter-hour to collect herself, consult the old woman, and make up her mind.

The old woman said to Cunégonde:—My lady, you have seventy-two quarterings and not one penny; if you wish, you may be the wife of the greatest lord in South America, who has a really handsome moustache; are you going to insist on your absolute fidelity? You have already been raped by the Bulgars; a jew and an inquisitor have enjoyed your favors; miseries entitle one to privileges. I assure you that in your position I would make no scruple of marrying my lord the Governor, and making the fortune of Captain Candide.

While the old woman was talking with all the prudence of age and experience, there came into the harbor a small ship bearing an alcalde and some alguazils.[7] This is what had happened.

As the old woman had very shrewdly guessed, it was a long-sleeved Franciscan who stole Cunégonde's gold and jewels in the town of Badajoz, when she and Candide were in flight. The monk tried to sell some of the gems to a jeweler, who recognized them as belonging to the Grand Inquisitor. Before he was hanged, the Franciscan confessed that he had stolen them, indicating who his victims were and where they were going. The flight of Cunégonde and Candide was already known. They were traced to Cadiz, and a vessel was hastily dispatched in pursuit of them. This vessel was now in the port of Buenos Aires. The rumor spread that an alcalde was aboard, in pursuit of the murderers of my lord the Grand Inquisitor. The shrewd old woman saw at once what was to be done.

—You cannot escape, she told Cunégonde, and you have nothing to fear. You are not the one who killed my lord, and, besides, the governor, who is in love with you, won't let you be mistreated. Sit tight.

And then she ran straight to Candide:—Get out of town, she said, or you'll be burned within the hour.

There was not a moment to lose; but how to leave Cunégonde, and where to go?

---

7. Police officers accompanying a mayor, or royal official.

CHAPTER 14

How Candide and Cacambo Were Received
by the Jesuits of Paraguay

Candide had brought from Cadiz a valet of the type one often finds in the provinces of Spain and in the colonies. He was one quarter Spanish, son of a halfbreed in the Tucuman;[8] he had been choirboy, sacristan, sailor, monk, merchant, soldier, and lackey. His name was Cacambo, and he was very fond of his master because his master was a very good man. In hot haste he saddled the two Andalusian steeds.

—Hurry, master, do as the old woman says; let's get going and leave this town without a backward look.

Candide wept:—O my beloved Cunégonde! must I leave you now, just when the governor is about to marry us! Cunégonde, brought from so far, what will ever become of you?

—She'll become what she can, said Cacambo; women can always find something to do with themselves; God sees to it; let's get going.

—Where are you taking me? where are we going? what will we do without Cunégonde? said Candide.

—By Saint James of Compostela, said Cacambo, you were going to make war against the Jesuits, now we'll go make war for them. I know the roads pretty well, I'll bring you to their country, they will be delighted to have a captain who knows the Bulgar drill; you'll make a prodigious fortune. If you don't get your rights in one world, you will find them in another. And isn't it pleasant to see new things and do new things?

—Then you've already been in Paraguay? said Candide.

—Indeed I have, replied Cacambo; I was cook in the College of the Assumption, and I know the government of Los Padres[9] as I know the streets of Cadiz. It's an admirable thing, this government. The kingdom is more than three hundred leagues across; it is divided into thirty provinces. Los Padres own everything in it, and the people nothing; it's a masterpiece of reason and justice. I myself know nothing so divine as Los Padres, who in this hemisphere make war on the kings of Spain and Portugal, but in Europe hear their confessions; who kill Spaniards here, and in Madrid send them to heaven; that really tickles me; let's get moving, you're going to be the happiest of men. Won't Los Padres be delighted when they learn they have a captain who knows the Bulgar drill!

As soon as they reached the first barricade, Cacambo told the frontier guard that a captain wished to speak with my lord the Commander. A Paraguayan officer ran to inform headquarters by laying the news at the

8. A city and province of Argentina, to the northwest of Buenos Aires, just at the juncture of the Andes and the Grand Chaco.
9. The Jesuit fathers. R. B. Cunningham-Grahame has written an account of the Jesuits in Paraguay 1607–1767, under the title *A Vanished Arcadia*.

feet of the commander. Candide and Cacambo were first disarmed and deprived of their Andalusian horses. They were then placed between two files of soldiers; the commander was at the end, his three-cornered hat on his head, his cassock drawn up, a sword at his side, and a pike in his hand. He nods, and twenty-four soldiers surround the newcomers. A sergeant then informs them that they must wait, that the commander cannot talk to them, since the reverend father provincial has forbidden all Spaniards from speaking, except in his presence, and from remaining more than three hours in the country.[1]

—And where is the reverend father provincial? says Cacambo.

—He is reviewing his troops after having said mass, the sergeant replies, and you'll only be able to kiss his spurs in three hours.

—But, says Cacambo, my master the captain, who, like me, is dying from hunger, is not Spanish at all, he is German; can't we have some breakfast while waiting for his reverence?

The sergeant promptly went off to report this speech to the commander.

—God be praised, said this worthy; since he is German, I can talk to him; bring him into my bower.

Candide was immediately led into a leafy nook surrounded by a handsome colonnade of green and gold marble and trellises amid which sported parrots, birds of paradise,[2] humming birds, guinea fowl, and all the rarest species of birds. An excellent breakfast was prepared in golden vessels; and while the Paraguayans ate corn out of wooden bowls in the open fields under the glare of the sun, the reverend father commander entered into his bower.

He was a very handsome young man, with an open face, rather blonde in coloring, with ruddy complexion, arched eyebrows, liquid eyes, pink ears, bright red lips, and an air of pride, but a pride somehow different from that of a Spaniard or a Jesuit. Their confiscated weapons were restored to Candide and Cacambo, as well as their Andalusian horses; Cacambo fed them oats alongside the bower, always keeping an eye on them for fear of an ambush.

First Candide kissed the hem of the commander's cassock, then they sat down at the table.

—So you are German? said the Jesuit, speaking in that language.

—Yes, your reverence, said Candide.

As they spoke these words, both men looked at one another with great surprise, and another emotion which they could not control.

1. In fact, the Jesuits, who had organized their Indian parishes into villages under a system of tribal communism, did their best to discourage contact with the outside world.

2. In this passage and several later ones, Voltaire uses in conjunction two words, both of which mean humming bird. The French system of classifying humming birds, based on the work of the celebrated Buffon, distinguishes *oiseaux-mouches* with straight bills from *colibris* with curved bills. This distinction is wholly fallacious. Humming birds have all manner of shaped bills, and the division of species must be made on other grounds entirely. At the expense of ornithological accuracy, I have therefore introduced birds of paradise to get the requisite sense of glitter and sheen.

—From what part of Germany do you come? said the Jesuit.

—From the nasty province of Westphalia, said Candide; I was born in the castle of Thunder-Ten-Tronckh.

—Merciful heavens! cries the commander. Is it possible?

—What a miracle! exclaims Candide.

—Can it be you? asks the commander.

—It's impossible, says Candide.

They both fall back in their chairs, they embrace, they shed streams of tears.

—What, can it be you, reverend father! you, the brother of the lovely Cunégonde! you, who were killed by the Bulgars! you, the son of my lord the Baron! you, a Jesuit in Paraguay! It's a mad world, indeed it is. Oh, Pangloss! Pangloss! how happy you would be, if you hadn't been hanged.

The commander dismissed his negro slaves and the Paraguayans who served his drink in crystal goblets. He thanked God and Saint Ignatius a thousand times, he clasped Candide in his arms, their faces were bathed in tears.

—You would be even more astonished, even more delighted, even more beside yourself, said Candide, if I told you that my lady Cunégonde, your sister, who you thought was disemboweled, is enjoying good health.

—Where?

—Not far from here, in the house of the governor of Buenos Aires; and to think that I came to make war on you!

Each word they spoke in this long conversation added another miracle. Their souls danced on their tongues, hung eagerly at their ears, glittered in their eyes. As they were Germans, they sat a long time at table, waiting for the reverend father provincial; and the commander spoke in these terms to his dear Candide.

CHAPTER 15

How Candide Killed the Brother of His Dear Cunégonde

—All my life long I shall remember the horrible day when I saw my father and mother murdered and my sister raped. When the Bulgars left, that adorable sister of mine was nowhere to be found; so they loaded a cart with my mother, my father, myself, two serving girls, and three little butchered boys, to carry us all off for burial in a Jesuit chapel some two leagues from our ancestral castle. A Jesuit sprinkled us with holy water; it was horribly salty, and a few drops got into my eyes; the father noticed that my lid made a little tremor; putting his hand on my heart, he felt it beat; I was rescued, and at the end of three weeks was as good as new. You know, my dear Candide, that I was a very pretty boy; I became even more so; the reverend father Croust,[3] superior of the abbey, conceived a most tender friendship for me; he accepted me as a novice, and shortly after, I was sent to Rome. The Father General had need of a resupply of young German Jesuits. The rulers of Paraguay accept as few Spanish Jesuits as they can; they prefer foreigners, whom they think they can control better. I was judged fit, by the Father General, to labor in this vineyard. So we set off, a Pole, a Tyrolean, and myself. Upon our arrival, I was honored with the posts of subdeacon and lieutenant; today I am a colonel and a priest. We will be giving a vigorous reception to the King of Spain's men; I assure you they will be excommunicated as well as trounced on the battlefield. Providence has sent you to help us. But is it really true that my dear sister, Cunégonde, is in the neighborhood, with the governor of Buenos Aires?

Candide reassured him with a solemn oath that nothing could be more true. Their tears began to flow again.

The baron could not weary of embracing Candide; he called him his brother, his savior.

—Ah, my dear Candide, said he, maybe together we will be able to enter the town as conquerors, and be united with my sister Cunégonde.

—That is all I desire, said Candide; I was expecting to marry her, and I still hope to.

—You insolent dog, replied the baron, you would have the effrontery to marry my sister, who has seventy-two quarterings! It's a piece of presumption for you even to mention such a crazy project in my presence.

Candide, terrified by this speech, answered:—Most reverend father, all the quarterings in the world don't affect this case; I have rescued your sister out of the arms of a jew and an inquisitor; she has many obligations to me, she wants to marry me. Master Pangloss always taught me that men are equal; and I shall certainly marry her.

—We'll see about that, you scoundrel, said the Jesuit baron of Thunder-Ten-Tronckh; and so saying, he gave him a blow across the face with the flat of his sword. Candide immediately drew his own sword and thrust it up to the hilt in the baron's belly; but as he drew it forth all dripping, he began to weep.

—Alas, dear God! said he, I have killed my old master, my friend, my brother-in-law; I am the best man in the world, and here are three men I've killed already, and two of the three were priests.

Cacambo, who was standing guard at the entry of the bower, came running.

—We can do nothing but sell our lives dearly, said his master; someone will certainly come; we must die fighting.

Cacambo, who had been in similar scrapes before, did not lose his head; he took the Jesuit's cassock, which the commander had been

3. It is the name of a Jesuit rector at Colmar with whom Voltaire had quarreled in 1754.

wearing, and put it on Candide; he stuck the dead man's square hat on Candide's head, and forced him onto horseback. Everything was done in the wink of an eye.

—Let's ride, master; everyone will take you for a Jesuit on his way to deliver orders; and we will have passed the frontier before anyone can come after us.

Even as he was pronouncing these words, he charged off, crying in Spanish:—Way, make way for the reverend father colonel!

CHAPTER 16

What Happened to the Two Travelers with Two Girls, Two Monkeys, and the Savages Named Biglugs

Candide and his valet were over the frontier before anyone in the camp knew of the death of the German Jesuit. Foresighted Cacambo had taken care to fill his satchel with bread, chocolate, ham, fruit, and several bottles of wine. They pushed their Andalusian horses forward into unknown country, where there were no roads. Finally a broad prairie divided by several streams opened before them. Our two travelers turned their horses loose to graze; Cacambo suggested that they eat too, and promptly set the example. But Candide said:—How can you expect me to eat ham when I have killed the son of my lord the Baron, and am now condemned never to see the lovely Cunégonde for the rest of my life? Why should I drag out my miserable days, since I must exist far from her in in the depths of despair and remorse? And what will the *Journal de Trévoux* say of all this?[4]

Though he talked this way, he did not neglect the food. Night fell. The two wanderers heard a few weak cries which seemed to be voiced by women. They could not tell whether the cries expressed grief or joy; but they leaped at once to their feet, with that uneasy suspicion which one always feels in an unknown country. The outcry arose from two girls, completely naked, who were running swiftly along the edge of the meadow, pursued by two monkeys who snapped at their buttocks. Candide was moved to pity; he had learned marksmanship with the Bulgars, and could have knocked a nut off a bush without touching the leaves. He raised his Spanish rifle, fired twice, and killed the two monkeys.

—God be praised, my dear Cacambo! I've saved these two poor creatures from great danger. Though I committed a sin in killing an inquisitor and a Jesuit, I've redeemed myself by saving the lives of two girls. Perhaps they are two ladies of rank, and this good deed may gain us special advantages in the country.

He had more to say, but his mouth shut suddenly when he saw the

4. A journal published by the Jesuit order, founded in 1701 and consistently hostile to Voltaire.

girls embracing the monkeys tenderly, weeping over their bodies, and filling the air with lamentations.

—I wasn't looking for quite so much generosity of spirit, said he to Cacambo; the latter replied:—You've really fixed things this time, master; you've killed the two lovers of these young ladies.

—Their lovers! Impossible! You must be joking, Cacambo; how can I believe you?

—My dear master, Cacambo replied, you're always astonished by everything. Why do you think it so strange that in some countries monkeys succeed in obtaining the good graces of women? They are one quarter human, just as I am one quarter Spanish.

—Alas, Candide replied, I do remember now hearing Master Pangloss say that such things used to happen, and that from these mixtures there arose pans, fauns, and satyrs,[5] and that these creatures had appeared to various grand figures of antiquity; but I took all that for fables.

—You should be convinced now, said Cacambo; it's true, and you see how people make mistakes who haven't received a measure of education. But what I fear is that these girls may get us into real trouble.

These sensible reflections led Candide to leave the field and to hide in a wood. There he dined with Cacambo; and there both of them, having duly cursed the inquisitor of Portugal, the governor of Buenos Aires, and the baron, went to sleep on a bed of moss. When they woke up, they found themselves unable to move; the reason was that during the night the Biglugs,[6] natives of the country, to whom the girls had complained of them, had tied them down with cords of bark. They were surrounded by fifty naked Biglugs, armed with arrows, clubs, and stone axes. Some were boiling a caldron of water, others were preparing spits, and all cried out:—It's a Jesuit, a Jesuit! We'll be revenged and have a good meal; let's eat some Jesuit, eat some Jesuit!

—I told you, my dear master, said Cacambo sadly, I said those two girls would play us a dirty trick.

Candide, noting the caldron and spits, cried out:—We are surely going to be roasted or boiled. Ah, what would Master Pangloss say if he could see these men in a state of nature? All is for the best, I agree; but I must say it seems hard to have lost Miss Cunégonde and to be stuck on a spit by the Biglugs.

Cacambo did not lose his head.

—Don't give up hope, said he to the disconsolate Candide; I understand a little of the jargon these people speak, and I'm going to talk to them.

5. Hybrid creatures of mythology, half-animal, half-human.
6. Voltaire's name is "Oreillons" from Spanish "Orejones," a name mentioned in Garcilaso de Vega's *Historia General del Perú* (1609), on which Voltaire drew for many of the details in his picture of South America. See Richard A. Brooks, "Voltaire and Garcilaso de Vega" *Studies in Voltaire and the 18th Century* 30:189–204.

—Don't forget to remind them, said Candide, of the frightful inhumanity of eating their fellow men, and that Christian ethics forbid it.

—Gentlemen, said Cacambo, you have a mind to eat a Jesuit today? An excellent idea; nothing is more proper than to treat one's enemies so. Indeed, the law of nature teaches us to kill our neighbor, and that's how men behave the whole world over. Though we Europeans don't exercise our right to eat our neighbors, the reason is simply that we find it easy to get a good meal elsewhere; but you don't have our resources, and we certainly agree that it's better to eat your enemies than to let the crows and vultures have the fruit of your victory. But, gentlemen, you wouldn't want to eat your friends. You think you will be spitting a Jesuit, and it's your defender, the enemy of your enemies, whom you will be roasting. For my part, I was born in your country; the gentleman whom you see is my master, and far from being a Jesuit, he has just killed a Jesuit, the robe he is wearing was stripped from him; that's why you have taken a dislike to him. To prove that I am telling the truth, take his robe and bring it to the nearest frontier of the kingdom of Los Padres; find out for yourselves if my master didn't kill a Jesuit officer. It won't take long; if you find that I have lied, you can still eat us. But if I've told the truth, you know too well the principles of public justice, customs, and laws, not to spare our lives.

The Biglugs found this discourse perfectly reasonable; they appointed chiefs to go posthaste and find out the truth; the two messengers performed their task like men of sense, and quickly returned bringing good news. The Biglugs untied their two prisoners, treated them with great politeness, offered them girls, gave them refreshments, and led back to the border of their state, crying joyously:—He isn't a Jesuit, he isn't a Jesuit!

Candide could not weary of exclaiming over his preservation.

—What a people! he said. What men! what customs! If I had not had the good luck to run a sword through the body of Miss Cunégonde's brother, I would have been eaten on the spot! But, after all, it seems that uncorrupted nature is good, since these folk, instead of eating me, showed me a thousand kindnesses as soon as they knew I was not a Jesuit.

CHAPTER 17

Arrival of Candide and His Servant at the Country of Eldorado,[7] *and What They Saw There*

When they were out of the land of the Biglugs, Cacambo said to Candide:—You see that this hemisphere is no better than the other; take my advice, and let's get back to Europe as soon as possible.

7. The myth of this land of gold somewhere in Central or South America had been widespread since the sixteenth century.

—How to get back, asked Candide, and where to go? If I go to my own land, the Bulgars and Abares are murdering everyone in sight; if I go to Portugal, they'll burn me alive; if we stay here, we risk being skewered any day. But how can I ever leave this part of the world where Miss Cunégonde lives?

—Let's go toward Cayenne, said Cacambo, we shall find some Frenchmen there, for they go all over the world; they can help us; perhaps God will take pity on us.

To get to Cayenne was not easy; they knew more or less which way to go, but mountains, rivers, cliffs, robbers, and savages obstructed the way everywhere. Their horses died of weariness; their food was eaten; they subsisted for one whole month on wild fruits, and at last they found themselves by a little river fringed with coconut trees, which gave them both life and hope.

Cacambo, who was as full of good advice as the old woman, said to Candide:—We can go no further, we've walked ourselves out; I see an abandoned canoe on the bank, let's fill it with coconuts, get into the boat, and float with the current; a river always leads to some inhabited spot or other. If we don't find anything pleasant, at least we may find something new.

—Let's go, said Candide, and let Providence be our guide.

They floated some leagues between banks sometimes flowery, sometimes sandy, now steep, now level. The river widened steadily; finally it disappeared into a chasm of frightful rocks that rose high into the heavens. The two travelers had the audacity to float with the current into this chasm. The river, narrowly confined, drove them onward with horrible speed and a fearful roar. After twenty-four hours, they saw daylight once more; but their canoe was smashed on the snags. They had to drag themselves from rock to rock for an entire league; at last they emerged to an immense horizon, ringed with remote mountains. The countryside was tended for pleasure as well as profit; everywhere the useful was joined to the agreeable.[8] The roads were covered, or rather decorated, with elegantly shaped carriages made of a glittering material, carrying men and women of singular beauty, and drawn by great red sheep which were faster than the finest horses of Andalusia, Tetuan, and Mequinez.[9]

—Here now, said Candide, is a country that's better than Westphalia.

Along with Cacambo, he climbed out of the river at the first village he could see. Some children of the town, dressed in rags of gold brocade,

---

8. This journey down an underground river is probably adapted from a similar episode in the story of Sinbad the Sailor. The phrase below about the useful being everywhere joined to the agreeable echoes a famous tag from Horace's *Art of Poetry* 343, "miscere utile dulci." The Eldoradan land-scape is like a well-composed humanist poem.

9. Mequinez or Meknes is in North Africa; its horses are Berber steeds, swift as or even swifter than Spanish stallions. The sheep of Eldorado come from Voltaire's reading of travelers' tales; we know them now as llamas and alpacas.

were playing quoits at the village gate; our two men from the other world paused to watch them; their quoits were rather large, yellow, red, and green, and they glittered with a singular luster. On a whim, the travelers picked up several; they were of gold, emeralds, and rubies, and the least of them would have been the greatest ornament of the Grand Mogul's throne.

—Surely, said Cacambo, these quoit players are the children of the king of the country.

The village schoolmaster appeared at that moment, to call them back to school.

—And there, said Candide, is the tutor of the royal household.

The little rascals quickly gave up their game, leaving on the ground their quoits and playthings. Candide picked them up, ran to the schoolmaster, and presented them to him humbly, giving him to understand by sign language that their royal highnesses had forgotten their gold and jewels. With a smile, the schoolmaster tossed them to the ground, glanced quickly but with great surprise at Candide's face, and went his way.

The travelers did not fail to pick up the gold, rubies, and emeralds.

—Where in the world are we? cried Candide. The children of this land must be well trained, since they are taught contempt for gold and jewels.[1]

Cacambo was as much surprised as Candide. At last they came to the finest house of the village; it was built like a European palace. A crowd of people surrounded the door, and even more were in the entry; delightful music was heard, and a delicious aroma of cooking filled the air. Cacambo went up to the door, listened, and reported that they were talking Peruvian; that was his native language, for every reader must know that Cacambo was born in Tucuman, in a village where they talk that language exclusively.[2]

—I'll act as interpreter, he told Candide; it's an hotel, let's go in.

Promptly two boys and two girls of the staff, dressed in cloth of gold, and wearing ribbons in their hair, invited them to sit at the host's table. The meal consisted of four soups, each one garnished with a brace of parakeets, a boiled condor which weighed two hundred pounds, two roast monkeys of an excellent flavor, three hundred birds of paradise in one dish and six hundred humming birds in another, exquisite stews, delicious pastries, the whole thing served up in plates of what looked like rock crystal. The boys and girls of the staff poured them various beverages made from sugar cane.

The diners were for the most part merchants and travelers, all ex-

---

1. Training in contempt for precious metals and gemstones was a conspicuous feature of the Utopian society imagined by Sir Thomas More (1516).
2. Cacambo's linguistic skills are an obvious joke; even in Peru there is no Peruvian language, and in Tucuman, which is a province of Argentina, they speak Spanish predominantly.

tremely polite, who questioned Cacambo with the most discreet circumspection, and answered his questions very directly.

When the meal was over, Cacambo as well as Candide supposed he could settle his bill handsomely by tossing onto the table two of those big pieces of gold which they had picked up; but the host and hostess burst out laughing, and for a long time nearly split their sides. Finally they subsided.

—Gentlemen, said the host, we see clearly that you're foreigners; we don't meet many of you here. Please excuse our laughing when you offered us in payment a couple of pebbles from the roadside. No doubt you don't have any of our local currency, but you don't need it to eat here. All the hotels established for the promotion of commerce are maintained by the state. You have had meager entertainment here, for we are only a poor town; but everywhere else you will be given the sort of welcome you deserve.[3]

Cacambo translated for Candide all the host's explanations, and Candide listened to them with the same admiration and astonishment that his friend Cacambo showed in reporting them.

—What is this country, then, said they to one another, unknown to the rest of the world, and where nature itself is so different from our own? This probably is the country where everything is for the best; for it's absolutely necessary that such a country should exist somewhere. And whatever Master Pangloss said of the matter, I often had occasion to notice that things went pretty badly in Westphalia.

CHAPTER 18

What They Saw in the Land of Eldorado

Cacambo revealed his curiosity to the host, and the host told him:—I am an ignorant man and content to remain so; but we have here an old man, retired from the court, who is the most knowing person in the kingdom, and the most talkative.

Thereupon he brought Cacambo to the old man's house. Candide now played second fiddle, and acted as servant to his own valet. They entered an austere little house, for the door was merely of silver and the paneling of the rooms was only gold, though so tastefully wrought that the finest paneling would not surpass it. If the truth must be told, the lobby was only decorated with rubies and emeralds; but the patterns in which they were arranged atoned for the extreme simplicity.

The old man received the two strangers on a sofa stuffed with bird-of-paradise feathers, and offered them several drinks in diamond carafes; then he satisfied their curiosity in these terms.

3. Voltaire's imaginary South America owes this special feature partly to his anticlericalism, partly to his readings about Quaker customs in (!) Pennsylvania. Without a Catholic hierarchy, he supposed, people would be more natural in their feelings, hence more generous toward visitors.

—I am a hundred and seventy-two years old, and I heard from my late father, who was liveryman to the king, about the astonishing revolutions in Peru which he had seen. Our land here was formerly the native land of the Incas, who rashly left it in order to conquer another part of the world, and who were ultimately destroyed by the Spaniards. The wisest princes of their house were those who never left their native valley; they decreed, with the consent of the nation, that henceforth no inhabitant of our little kingdom should ever leave it; and this rule is what has preserved our innocence and our happiness. The Spaniards heard vague rumors about this land, they called it El Dorado; and an English knight named Raleigh[4] even came somewhere close to it about a hundred years ago; but as we are surrounded by unscalable mountains and precipices, we have managed so far to remain hidden from the rapacity of the European nations, who have an inconceivable rage for the pebbles and mud of our land, and who, in order to get some, would butcher us all to the last man.

The conversation was a long one; it turned on the form of the government, the national customs, on women, public shows, the arts. At last Candide, whose taste always ran to metaphysics, told Cacambo to ask if the country had any religion.

The old man grew a bit red.

—How's that? he said. Can you have any doubt of it? Do you suppose we are altogether thankless scoundrels?

Cacambo asked meekly what was the religion of Eldorado. The old man flushed again.

—Can there be two religions? he asked. I suppose our religion is the same as everyone's, we worship God from morning to evening.

—Then you worship a single deity? said Cacambo, who acted throughout as interpreter of the questions of Candide.

—It's obvious, said the old man, that there aren't two or three or four of them. I must say the people of your world ask very remarkable questions.

Candide could not weary of putting questions to this good old man; he wanted to know how the people of Eldorado prayed to God.

—We don't pray to him at all, said the good and respectable sage; we have nothing to ask him for, since everything we need has already been granted; we thank God continually.

Candide was interested in seeing the priests; he had Cacambo ask where they were. The old gentleman smiled.

—My friends, said he, we are all priests; the king and all the heads of household sing formal psalms of thanksgiving every morning, and five or six thousand voices accompany them.

4. *The Discovery of Guiana*, published in 1595, described Sir Walter Raleigh's infatuation with the myth of Eldorado and served to spread the story across Europe.

—What! you have no monks to teach, argue, govern, intrigue, and burn at the stake everyone who disagrees with them?

—We should have to be mad, said the old man; here we are all of the same mind, and we don't understand what you're up to with your monks.

Candide was overjoyed at all these speeches, and said to himself:— This is very different from Westphalia and the castle of My Lord the Baron; if our friend Pangloss had seen Eldorado, he wouldn't have called the castle of Thunder-Ten-Tronckh the finest thing on earth; to know the world one must travel.

After this long conversation, the old gentleman ordered a carriage with six sheep made ready, and gave the two travelers twelve of his servants for their journey to the court.

—Excuse me, said he, if old age deprives me of the honor of accompanying you. The king will receive you after a style which will not altogether displease you, and you will doubtless make allowance for the customs of the country if there are any you do not like.

Candide and Cacambo climbed into the coach; the six sheep trotted off like the wind, and in less than four hours they reached the king's palace at the edge of the capital. The entryway was two hundred and twenty feet high and a hundred wide; it is impossible to describe all the materials of which it was made. But you can imagine how much finer it was than those pebbles and sand which we call gold and jewels.

Twenty beautiful girls of the guard detail welcomed Candide and Cacambo as they stepped from the carriage, took them to the baths, and dressed them in robes woven of humming-bird feathers; then the high officials of the crown, both male and female, led them to the royal chamber between two long lines, each of a thousand musicians, as is customary. As they approached the throne room, Cacambo asked an officer what was the proper method of greeting his majesty: if one fell to one's knees or on one's belly; if one put one's hands on one's head or on one's rear; if one licked up the dust of the earth—in a word, what was the proper form?[5]

—The ceremony, said the officer, is to embrace the king and kiss him on both cheeks.

Candide and Cacambo warmly embraced his majesty, who received them with all the dignity imaginable, and asked them politely to dine.

In the interim, they were taken about to see the city, the public buildings rising to the clouds, the public markets and arcades, the fountains of pure water and of rose water, those of sugar cane liquors which flowed perpetually in the great plazas paved with a sort of stone which gave off odors of gillyflower and rose petals. Candide asked to see the

5. Candide's questions may be related to those of Gulliver on a somewhat similar occasion; see *Gulliver's Travels*, book 4.

supreme court and the hall of parliament; they told him there was no such thing, that lawsuits were unknown. He asked if there were prisons, and was told there were not. What surprised him more, and gave him most pleasure, was the palace of sciences, in which he saw a gallery two thousand paces long, entirely filled with mathematical and physical instruments.

Having passed the whole afternoon seeing only a thousandth part of the city, they returned to the king's palace. Candide sat down to dinner with his majesty, his own valet Cacambo, and several ladies. Never was better food served, and never did a host preside more jovially than his majesty. Cacambo explained the king's witty sayings to Candide, and even when translated they still seemed witty. Of all the things which astonished Candide, this was not, in his eyes, the least astonishing.

They passed a month in this refuge. Candide never tired of saying to Cacambo:—It's true, my friend, I'll say it again, the castle where I was born does not compare with the land where we now are; but Miss Cunégonde is not here, and you doubtless have a mistress somewhere in Europe. If we stay here, we shall be just like everybody else, whereas if we go back to our own world, taking with us just a dozen sheep loaded with Eldorado pebbles, we shall be richer than all the kings put together, we shall have no more inquisitors to fear, and we shall easily be able to retake Miss Cunégonde.

This harangue pleased Cacambo; wandering is such pleasure, it gives a man such prestige at home to be able to talk of what he has seen abroad, that the two happy men resolved to be so no longer, but to take their leave of his majesty.

—You are making a foolish mistake, the king told them; I know very well that my kingdom is nothing much; but when you are pretty comfortable somewhere, you had better stay there. Of course I have no right to keep strangers against their will, that sort of tyranny is not in keeping with our laws or our customs; all men are free; depart when you will, but the way out is very difficult. You cannot possibly go up the river by which you miraculously came; it runs too swiftly through its underground caves. The mountains which surround my land are ten thousand feet high, and steep as walls; each one is more than ten leagues across; the only way down is over precipices. But since you really must go, I shall order my engineers to make a machine which can carry you conveniently. When we take you over the mountains, nobody will be able to go with you, for my subjects have sworn never to leave their refuge, and they are too sensible to break their vows. Other than that, ask of me what you please.

—We only request of your majesty, Cacambo said, a few sheep loaded with provisions, some pebbles, and some of the mud of your country.

The king laughed.

—I simply can't understand, said he, the passion you Europeans have for our yellow mud; but take all you want, and much good may it do you.

He promptly gave orders to his technicians to make a machine for lifting these two extraordinary men out of his kingdom. Three thousand good physicists worked at the problem; the machine was ready in two weeks' time, and cost no more than twenty million pounds sterling, in the money of the country. Cacambo and Candide were placed in the machine; there were two great sheep, saddled and bridled to serve them as steeds when they had cleared the mountains, twenty pack sheep with provisions, thirty which carried presents consisting of the rarities of the country, and fifty loaded with gold, jewels, and diamonds. The king bade tender farewell to the two vagabonds.

It made a fine spectacle, their departure, and the ingenious way in which they were hoisted with their sheep up to the top of the mountains. The technicians bade them good-bye after bringing them to safety, and Candide had now no other desire and no other object than to go and present his sheep to Miss Cunégonde.

—We have, said he, enough to pay off the governor of Buenos Aires—if, indeed, a price can be placed on Miss Cunégonde. Let us go to Cayenne, take ship there, and then see what kingdom we can find to buy up.

CHAPTER 19

What Happened to Them at Surinam, and How Candide
Got to Know Martin

The first day was pleasant enough for our travelers. They were encouraged by the idea of possessing more treasures than Asia, Europe, and Africa could bring together. Candide, in transports, carved the name of Cunégonde on the trees. On the second day two of their sheep bogged down in a swamp and were lost with their loads; two other sheep died of fatigue a few days later; seven or eight others starved to death in a desert; still others fell, a little after, from precipices. Finally, after a hundred days' march, they had only two sheep left. Candide told Cacambo:—My friend, you see how the riches of this world are fleeting; the only solid things are virtue and the joy of seeing Miss Cunégonde again.

—I agree, said Cacambo, but we still have two sheep, laden with more treasure than the king of Spain will ever have; and I see in the distance a town which I suspect is Surinam; it belongs to the Dutch. We are at the end of our trials and on the threshold of our happiness.

As they drew near the town, they discovered a negro stretched on the ground with only half his clothes left, that is, a pair of blue drawers; the poor fellow was also missing his left leg and his right hand.

—Good Lord, said Candide in Dutch, what are you doing in that horrible condition, my friend?

—I am waiting for my master, Mr. Vanderdendur,[6] the famous merchant, answered the negro.

—Is Mr. Vanderdendur, Candide asked, the man who treated you this way?

—Yes, sir, said the negro, that's how things are around here. Twice a year we get a pair of linen drawers to wear. If we catch a finger in the sugar mill where we work, they cut off our hand; if we try to run away, they cut off our leg: I have undergone both these experiences. This is the price of the sugar you eat in Europe. And yet, when my mother sold me for ten Patagonian crowns on the coast of Guinea, she said to me: 'My dear child, bless our witch doctors, reverence them always, they will make your life happy; you have the honor of being a slave to our white masters, and in this way you are making the fortune of your father and mother.' Alas! I don't know if I made their fortunes, but they certainly did not make mine. The dogs, monkeys, and parrots are a thousand times less unhappy than we are. The Dutch witch doctors who converted me tell me every Sunday that we are all sons of Adam, black and white alike. I am no genealogist; but if these preachers are right, we must all be remote cousins; and you must admit no one could treat his own flesh and blood in a more horrible fashion.

—Oh Pangloss! cried Candide, you had no notion of these abominations! I'm through, I must give up your optimism after all.

—What's optimism? said Cacambo.

—Alas, said Candide, it is a mania for saying things are well when one is in hell.[7]

And he shed bitter tears as he looked at his negro, and he was still weeping as he entered Surinam.

The first thing they asked was if there was not some vessel in port which could be sent to Buenos Aires. The man they asked was a Spanish merchant who undertook to make an honest bargain with them. They arranged to meet in a cafe; Candide and the faithful Cacambo, with their two sheep, went there to meet with him.

Candide, who always said exactly what was in his heart, told the Spaniard of his adventures, and confessed that he wanted to recapture Miss Cunégonde.

—I shall take good care *not* to send you to Buenos Aires, said the merchant; I should be hanged, and so would you. The lovely Cunégonde is his lordship's favorite mistress.

This was a thunderstroke for Candide; he wept for a long time; finally he drew Cacambo aside.

6. A name intended to suggest VanDuren, a Dutch bookseller with whom Voltaire had quarreled.
7. The story of European mistreatment of slaves on the sugar plantations—apart from being basically true—reached Voltaire through the treatise *De L'Esprit* by Helvetius (1758).

—Here, my friend, said he, is what you must do. Each one of us has in his pockets five or six millions' worth of diamonds; you are cleverer than I; go get Miss Cunégonde in Buenos Aires. If the governor makes a fuss, give him a million; if that doesn't convince him, give him two millions; you never killed an inquisitor, nobody will suspect you. I'll fit out another boat and go wait for you in Venice. That is a free country, where one need have no fear either of Bulgars or Abares or jews or inquisitors.

Cacambo approved of this wise decision. He was in despair at leaving a good master who had become a bosom friend: but the pleasure of serving him overcame the grief of leaving him. They embraced, and shed a few tears; Candide urged him not to forget the good old woman. Cacambo departed that very same day; he was a very good fellow, that Cacambo.

Candide remained for some time in Surinam, waiting for another merchant to take him to Italy, along with the two sheep which were left him. He hired servants and bought everything necessary for the long voyage; finally Mr. Vanderdendur, master of a big ship, came calling.

—How much will you charge, Candide asked this man, to take me to Venice—myself, my servants, my luggage, and those two sheep over there?

The merchant set a price of ten thousand piastres; Candide did not blink an eye.

—Oh ho, said the prudent Vanderdendur to himself, this stranger pays out ten thousand piastres at once, he must be pretty well fixed.

Then, returning a moment later, he made known that he could not set sail under twenty thousand.

—All right, you shall have them, said Candide.

—Whew, said the merchant softly to himself, this man gives twenty thousand piastres as easily as ten.

He came back again to say he could not go to Venice for less than thirty thousand piastres.

—All right, thirty then, said Candide.[8]

—Ah ha, said the Dutch merchant, again speaking to himself; so thirty thousand piastres mean nothing to this man; no doubt the two sheep are loaded with immense treasures; let's say no more; we'll pick up the thirty thousand piastres first, and then we'll see.

Candide sold two little diamonds, the least of which was worth more than all the money demanded by the merchant. He paid him in advance. The two sheep were taken aboard. Candide followed in a little boat, to board the vessel at its anchorage. The merchant bides his time, sets sail,

8. The business of jacking up one's price in the middle of a bargain points directly at the bookseller Van Duren, to whom Voltaire had successively offered 1,000, 1,500, 2,000, and 3,000 florins for the return of the manuscript of Frederick the Great's *Anti-Machiavel*.

and makes his escape with a favoring wind. Candide, aghast and stupefied, soon loses him from view.

—Alas, he cries, now there is a trick worthy of the old world!

He returns to shore sunk in misery; for he had lost riches enough to make the fortunes of twenty monarchs.

Now he rushes to the house of the Dutch magistrate, and, being a bit disturbed, he knocks loudly at the door; goes in, tells the story of what happened, and shouts a bit louder than is customary. The judge begins by fining him ten thousand piastres for making such a racket; then he listens patiently to the story, promises to look into the matter as soon as the merchant comes back, and charges another ten thousand piastres as the costs of the hearing.

This legal proceeding completed the despair of Candide. In fact he had experienced miseries a thousand times more painful, but the coldness of the judge, and that of the merchant who had robbed him, roused his bile and plunged him into a black melancholy. The malice of men rose up before his spirit in all its ugliness, and his mind dwelt only on gloomy thoughts. Finally, when a French vessel was ready to leave for Bordeaux, since he had no more diamond-laden sheep to transport, he took a cabin at a fair price, and made it known in the town that he would pay passage and keep, plus two thousand piastres, to any honest man who wanted to make the journey with him, on condition that this man must be the most disgusted with his own condition and the most unhappy man in the province.

This drew such a crowd of applicants as a fleet could not have held. Candide wanted to choose among the leading candidates, so he picked out about twenty who seemed companionable enough, and of whom each pretended to be more miserable than all the others. He brought them together at his inn and gave them a dinner, on condition that each would swear to tell truthfully his entire history. He would select as his companion the most truly miserable and rightly discontented man, and among the others he would distribute various gifts.

The meeting lasted till four in the morning. Candide, as he listened to all the stories, remembered what the old woman had told him on the trip to Buenos Aires, and of the wager she had made, that there was nobody on the boat who had not undergone great misfortunes. At every story that was told him, he thought of Pangloss.

—That Pangloss, he said, would be hard put to prove his system. I wish he was here. Certainly if everything goes well, it is in Eldorado and not in the rest of the world.

At last he decided in favor of a poor scholar who had worked ten years for the booksellers of Amsterdam. He decided that there was no trade in the world with which one should be more disgusted.

This scholar, who was in fact a good man, had been robbed by his wife, beaten by his son, and deserted by his daughter, who had got

herself abducted by a Portuguese. He had just been fired from the little
job on which he existed; and the preachers of Surinam were persecuting
him because they took him for a Socinian.[9] The others, it is true, were
at least as unhappy as he, but Candide hoped the scholar would prove
more amusing on the voyage. All his rivals declared that Candide was
doing them a great injustice, but he pacified them with a hundred piastres
apiece.

CHAPTER 20

What Happened to Candide and Martin at Sea

The old scholar, whose name was Martin, now set sail with Candide
for Bordeaux. Both men had seen and suffered much; and even if the
vessel had been sailing from Surinam to Japan via the Cape of Good
Hope, they would have been able to keep themselves amused during
the entire trip with instances of moral and physical evil.

However, Candide had one great advantage over Martin, that he still
hoped to see Miss Cunégonde again, while Martin had nothing to hope
for; besides, he had gold and diamonds, and though he had lost a hundred
big red sheep loaded with the greatest treasures of the earth, though he
had always at his heart a memory of the Dutch merchant's villainy, yet,
when he thought of the wealth that remained in his hands, and when
he talked of Cunégonde, especially just after a good dinner, he still
inclined to the system of Pangloss.

—But what about you, Monsieur Martin, he asked the scholar, what
do you think of all that? What is your idea of moral evil and physical
evil?

—Sir, answered Martin, those priests accused me of being a Socinian,
but the truth is that I am a Manichee.[1]

—You're joking, said Candide; there aren't any more Manichees in
the world.

—There's me, said Martin; I don't know what to do about it, but I
can't think otherwise.

—You must be possessed of the devil, said Candide.

—He's mixed up with so many things of this world, said Martin, that
he may be in me as well as elsewhere; but I assure you, as I survey this
globe, or globule rather, I think that God has abandoned it to some evil

---

9. A follower of Faustus and Laelius Socinus, sixteenth-century Polish theologians, who proposed
a form of "rational" Christianity that exalted the
rational conscience and minimized such mysteries
as the trinity. The Socinians, by a special irony,
were vigorous optimists. But in Voltaire's day, "Socinian" was used mostly as a loose term of theological abuse.
1. Mani, a Persian mage and philosopher of the
third century A.D., taught (probably under the in-

fluence of traditions stemming from Zoroaster and
the worshippers of the sun god Mithra) that the
earth is a field of dispute between two almost equal
powers, one of light and one of darkness, both of
which must be propitiated. Saint Augustine was
much exercised by the heresy, to which he was at
one time himself addicted, and Voltaire came to
some knowledge of it through the encyclopedic
learning of the seventeenth-century scholar Pierre
Bayle.

spirit—all of it except Eldorado. I have scarcely seen one town that did not wish to destroy its neighboring town, no family that did not wish to exterminate some other family. Everywhere the weak loathe the powerful, before whom they cringe, and the powerful treat them like brute cattle, to be sold for their meat and fleece. A million regimented assassins roam Europe from one end to the other, plying the trades of murder and robbery in an organized way for a living, because there is no more honest form of work for them; and in the cities which seem to enjoy peace and where the arts are flourishing, men are devoured by more envy, cares, and anxieties than a whole town experiences when it's under siege. Private griefs are worse even than public trials. In a word, I have seen so much and suffered so much, that I am a Manichee.

—Still there is some good, said Candide.

—That may be, said Martin, but I don't know it.

In the middle of this discussion, the rumble of cannon was heard. From minute to minute the noise grew louder. Everyone reached for his spyglass. At a distance of some three miles they saw two vessels fighting; the wind brought both of them so close to the French vessel that they had a pleasantly comfortable seat to watch the fight. Presently one of the vessels caught the other with a broadside so low and so square as to send it to the bottom. Candide and Martin saw clearly a hundred men on the deck of the sinking ship; they all raised their hands to heaven, uttering fearful shrieks; and in a moment everything was swallowed up.

—Well, said Martin, that is how men treat one another.

—It is true, said Candide, there's something devilish in this business.

As they chatted, he noticed something of a striking red color floating near the sunken vessel. They sent out a boat to investigate; it was one of his sheep. Candide was more joyful to recover this one sheep than he had been afflicted to lose a hundred of them, all loaded with big Eldorado diamonds.

The French captain soon learned that the captain of the victorious vessel was Spanish and that of the sunken vessel was a Dutch pirate. It was the same man who had robbed Candide. The enormous riches which this rascal had stolen were sunk beside him in the sea, and nothing was saved but a single sheep.

—You see, said Candide to Martin, crime is punished sometimes; this scoundrel of a Dutch merchant has met the fate he deserved.

—Yes, said Martin; but did the passengers aboard his ship have to perish too? God punished the scoundrel, the devil drowned the others.[2]

Meanwhile the French and Spanish vessels continued on their journey, and Candide continued his talks with Martin. They disputed for fifteen days in a row, and at the end of that time were just as much in agreement as at the beginning. But at least they were talking, they

2. Martin claims to be a Manichee, but this snappy formula closely parallels a dictum of Cicero's, *De Natura Deorum* 3.37.

exchanged ideas, they consoled one another. Candide caressed his sheep.

—Since I have found you again, said he, I may well rediscover Miss Cunégonde.

CHAPTER 21

Candide and Martin Approach the Coast of France: They Reason Together

At last the coast of France came in view.

—Have you ever been in France, Monsieur Martin? asked Candide.

—Yes, said Martin, I have visited several provinces. There are some where half the inhabitants are crazy, others where they are too sly, still others where they are quite gentle and stupid, some where they venture on wit; in all of them the principal occupation is lovemaking, the second is slander, and the third stupid talk.

—But, Monsieur Martin, were you ever in Paris?

—Yes, I've been in Paris; it contains specimens of all these types; it is a chaos, a mob, in which everyone is seeking pleasure and where hardly anyone finds it, at least from what I have seen. I did not live there for long; as I arrived, I was robbed of everything I possessed by thieves at the fair of St. Germain; I myself was taken for a thief, and spent eight days in jail, after which I took a proofreader's job to earn enough money to return on foot to Holland. I knew the writing gang, the intriguing gang, the gang with fits and convulsions.[3] They say there are some very civilized people in that town; I'd like to think so.

—I myself have no desire to visit France, said Candide; you no doubt realize that when one has spent a month in Eldorado, there is nothing else on earth one wants to see, except Miss Cunégonde. I am going to wait for her at Venice; we will cross France simply to get to Italy; wouldn't you like to come with me?

—Gladly, said Martin; they say Venice is good only for the Venetian nobles, but that on the other hand they treat foreigners very well when they have plenty of money. I don't have any; you do, so I'll follow you anywhere.

—By the way, said Candide, do you believe the earth was originally all ocean, as they assure us in that big book belonging to the ship's captain?[4]

—I don't believe any of that stuff, said Martin, nor any of the dreams which people have been peddling for some time now.

—But why, then, was this world formed at all? asked Candide.

3. The Jansenists, a sect of strict Catholics, became notorious for spiritual ecstasies. Their public displays reached a height during the 1720s, and Voltaire described them in *Le Siècle de Louis XIV* (chap. 37), as well as in the article on "Convul-sions" in the *Philosophical Dictionary*. Voltaire's older brother, Armand Arouet, was for a while an associate of the convulsionaries.

4. The Bible. Voltaire is straining at a dark passage in Genesis 1.

—To drive us mad, answered Martin.

—Aren't you astonished, Candide went on, at the love which those two girls showed for the monkeys in the land of the Biglugs that I told you about?

—Not at all, said Martin, I see nothing strange in these sentiments; I have seen so many extraordinary things that nothing seems extraordinary any more.

—Do you believe, asked Candide, that men have always massacred one another as they do today? That they have always been liars, traitors, ingrates, thieves, weaklings, sneaks, cowards, backbiters, gluttons, drunkards, misers, climbers, killers, calumniators, sensualists, fanatics, hypocrites, and fools?

—Do you believe, said Martin, that hawks have always eaten pigeons when they could get them?

—Of course, said Candide.

—Well, said Martin, if hawks have always had the same character, why do you suppose that men have changed?

—Oh, said Candide, there's a great deal of difference, because freedom of the will . . .

As they were disputing in this manner, they reached Bordeaux.

CHAPTER 22

What Happened in France to Candide and Martin

Candide paused in Bordeaux only long enough to sell a couple of Dorado pebbles and to fit himself out with a fine two-seater carriage, for he could no longer do without his philosopher Martin; only he was very unhappy to part with his sheep, which he left to the academy of science in Bordeaux. They proposed, as the theme of that year's prize contest, the discovery of why the wool of the sheep was red; and the prize was awarded to a northern scholar who demonstrated by A plus B minus C divided by Z that the sheep ought to be red and die of sheep rot.[5]

But all the travelers with whom Candide talked in the roadside inns told him: —We are going to Paris.

This general consensus finally inspired in him too a desire to see the capital; it was not much out of his road to Venice.

He entered through the Faubourg Saint-Marceau,[6] and thought he was in the meanest village of Westphalia.

5. The satire is pointed at Maupertuis Le Lapon, philosopher and mathematician, whom Voltaire had accused of trying to adduce mathematical proofs of the existence of God and whose algebraic formulae were easily ridiculed.

6. A district on the left bank, notably grubby in the eighteenth century. " 'As I entered [Paris] through the Faubourg Saint-Marceau, I saw nothing but dirty stinking little streets, ugly black houses, a general air of squalor and poverty, beggars, carters, menders of clothes, sellers of herb-drinks and old hats,' J.-J. Rousseau, Confessions, Book IV."

Scarcely was Candide in his hotel, when he came down with a mild illness caused by exhaustion. As he was wearing an enormous diamond ring, and people had noticed among his luggage a tremendously heavy safe, he soon found at his bedside two doctors whom he had not called, several intimate friends who never left him alone, and two pious ladies who helped to warm his broth. Martin said: —I remember that I too was ill on my first trip to Paris; I was very poor; and as I had neither friends, pious ladies, nor doctors, I got well.

However, as a result of medicines and bleedings, Candide's illness became serious. A resident of the neighborhood came to ask him politely to fill out a ticket, to be delivered to the porter of the other world.[7] Candide wanted nothing to do with it. The pious ladies assured him it was a new fashion; Candide replied that he wasn't a man of fashion. Martin wanted to throw the resident out the window. The cleric swore that without the ticket they wouldn't bury Candide. Martin swore that he would bury the cleric if he continued to be a nuisance. The quarrel grew heated; Martin took him by the shoulders and threw him bodily out the door; all of which caused a great scandal, from which developed a legal case.

Candide got better; and during his convalescence he had very good company in to dine. They played cards for money; and Candide was quite surprised that none of the aces were ever dealt to him, and Martin was not surprised at all.

Among those who did the honors of the town for Candide there was a little abbé from Perigord, one of those busy fellows, always bright, always useful, assured, obsequious, and obliging, who waylay passing strangers, tell them the scandal of the town, and offer them pleasures at any price they want to pay. This fellow first took Candide and Martin to the theatre. A new tragedy was being played. Candide found himself seated next to a group of wits. That did not keep him from shedding a few tears in the course of some perfectly played scenes. One of the commentators beside him remarked during the intermission: —You are quite mistaken to weep, this actress is very bad indeed; the actor who plays with her is even worse; and the play is even worse than the actors in it. The author knows not a word of Arabic, though the action takes place in Arabia; and besides, he is a man who doesn't believe in innate ideas.[8] Tomorrow I will show you twenty pamphlets written against him.[9]

—Tell me, sir, said Candide to the abbé, how many plays are there for performance in France?

---

7. In the middle of the eighteenth century, it became customary to require persons who were grievously ill to sign *billets de confession*, without which they could not be given absolution, admitted to the last sacraments, or buried in consecrated ground.

8. Descartes proposed certain ideas as innate; Voltaire followed Locke in categorically denying innate ideas. The point is simply that in faction fights all the issues get muddled together.

9. Here begins a long passage interpolated by Voltaire in 1761; it ends on p. 52.

—Five or six thousand, replied the other.

—That's a lot, said Candide; how many of them are any good?

—Fifteen or sixteen, was the answer.

—That's a lot, said Martin.

Candide was very pleased with an actress who took the part of Queen Elizabeth in a rather dull tragedy[1] that still gets played from time to time.

—I like this actress very much, he said to Martin, she bears a slight resemblance to Miss Cunégonde; I should like to meet her.

The abbé from Perigord offered to introduce him. Candide, raised in Germany, asked what was the protocol, how one behaved in France with queens of England.

—You must distinguish, said the abbé; in the provinces, you take them to an inn; at Paris they are respected while still attractive, and thrown on the dunghill when they are dead.[2]

—Queens on the dunghill! said Candide.

—Yes indeed, said Martin, the abbé is right; I was in Paris when Miss Monime herself passed, as they say, from this life to the other; she was refused what these folk call 'the honors of burial,' that is, the right to rot with all the beggars of the district in a dirty cemetery; she was buried all alone by her troupe at the corner of the Rue de Bourgogne; this must have been very disagreeable to her, for she had a noble character.[3]

—That was extremely rude, said Candide.

—What do you expect? said Martin; that is how these folk are. Imagine all the contradictions, all the incompatibilities you can, and you will see them in the government, the courts, the churches, and the plays of this crazy nation.

—Is it true that they are always laughing in Paris? asked Candide.

—Yes, said the abbé, but with a kind of rage too; when people complain of things, they do so amid explosions of laughter; they even laugh as they perform the most detestable actions.

—Who was that fat swine, said Candide, who spoke so nastily about the play over which I was weeping, and the actors who gave me so much pleasure?

—He is a living illness, answered the abbé, who makes a business of slandering all the plays and books; he hates the successful ones, as eunuchs hate successful lovers; he's one of those literary snakes who live on filth and venom; he's a folliculator . . .

—What's this word *folliculator?* asked Candide.

1. *Le Comte d'Essex* by Thomas Corneille.

2. Voltaire engaged in a long and vigorous campaign against the rule that actors and actresses could not be buried in consecrated ground. The superstition probably arose from a feeling that by assuming false identities they denied their own souls.

3. Adrienne Lecouvreur (1690–1730), so called because she made her debut as Monime in Racine's *Mithridate*. Voltaire had assisted at her secret midnight funeral and wrote an indignant poem about it.

—It's a folio filler, said the abbé, a Fréron.[4]

It was after this fashion that Candide, Martin, and the abbé from Perigord chatted on the stairway as they watched the crowd leaving the theatre.

—Although I'm in a great hurry to see Miss Cunégonde again, said Candide, I would very much like to dine with Miss Clairon,[5] for she seemed to me admirable.

The abbé was not the man to approach Miss Clairon, who saw only good company.

—She has an engagement tonight, he said; but I shall have the honor of introducing you to a lady of quality, and there you will get to know Paris as if you had lived here four years.

Candide, who was curious by nature, allowed himself to be brought to the lady's house, in the depths of the Faubourg St.-Honoré; they were playing faro[6]; twelve melancholy punters held in their hands a little sheaf of cards, blank summaries of their bad luck. Silence reigned supreme, the punters were pallid, the banker uneasy; and the lady of the house, seated beside the pitiless banker, watched with the eyes of a lynx for the various illegal redoublings and bets at long odds which the players tried to signal by folding the corners of their cards; she had them unfolded with a determination which was severe but polite, and concealed her anger lest she lose her customers. The lady caused herself to be known as the Marquise of Parolignac.[7] Her daughter, fifteen years old, sat among the punters and tipped off her mother with a wink to the sharp practices of these unhappy players when they tried to recoup their losses. The abbé from Perigord, Candide, and Martin came in; nobody arose or greeted them or looked at them; all were lost in the study of their cards.

—My Lady the Baroness of Thunder-Ten-Tronckh was more civil, thought Candide.

However, the abbé whispered in the ear of the marquise, who, half rising, honored Candide with a gracious smile and Martin with a truly noble nod; she gave a seat and dealt a hand of cards to Candide, who lost fifty thousand francs in two turns; after which they had a very merry supper. Everyone was amazed that Candide was not upset over his losses;

4. A successful and popular journalist, who had attacked several of Voltaire's plays, including *Tancrède*. Voltaire had a fine story that the devil attended the first night of *Tancrède* disguised as Fréron: when a lady in the balcony wept at the play's pathos, her tear dropped on the devil's nose; he thought it was holy water and shook it off—psha! psha! G. Desnoiresterres, *Voltaire et Jean-Jacques Rousseau*, pp. 3–4.

5. Actually Claire Leris (1723–1803). She had played the lead role in *Tancrède* and was for many years a leading figure on the Paris stage.

6. A game of cards, about which it is necessary to know only that a number of punters (bettors) play against a banker or dealer. The pack is dealt out two cards at a time, and each player may bet on any card as much as he pleases. The sharp practices of the punters consist essentially of tricks for increasing their winnings without corresponding risks.

7. A *paroli* is an illegal redoubling of one's bet; her name therefore implies a title grounded in cardsharping.

the lackeys, talking together in their usual lackey language, said: —He must be some English milord.

The supper was like most Parisian suppers: first silence, then an indistinguishable rush of words; then jokes, mostly insipid, false news, bad logic, a little politics, a great deal of malice. They even talked of new books.

—Have you seen the new novel by Dr. Gauchat, the theologian?[8] asked the abbé from Perigord.

—Oh yes, answered one of the guests; but I couldn't finish it. We have a horde of impudent scribblers nowadays, but all of them put together don't match the impudence of this Gauchat, this doctor of theology. I have been so struck by the enormous number of detestable books which are swamping us that I have taken up punting at faro.

—And the *Collected Essays* of Archdeacon T—[9] asked the abbé, what do you think of them?

—Ah, said Madame de Parolignac, what a frightful bore he is! He takes such pains to tell you what everyone knows; he discourses so learnedly on matters which aren't worth a casual remark! He plunders, and not even wittily, the wit of other people! He spoils what he plunders, he's disgusting! But he'll never disgust me again; a couple of pages of the archdeacon have been enough for me.

There was at table a man of learning and taste, who supported the marquise on this point. They talked next of tragedies; the lady asked why there were tragedies which played well enough but which were wholly unreadable. The man of taste explained very clearly how a play could have a certain interest and yet little merit otherwise; he showed succinctly that it was not enough to conduct a couple of intrigues, such as one can find in any novel, and which never fail to excite the spectator's interest; but that one must be new without being grotesque, frequently touch the sublime but never depart from the natural; that one must know the human heart and give it words; that one must be a great poet without allowing any character in the play to sound like a poet; and that one must know the language perfectly, speak it purely, and maintain a continual harmony without ever sacrificing sense to mere sound.

—Whoever, he added, does not observe all these rules may write one or two tragedies which succeed in the theatre, but he will never be ranked among the good writers; there are very few good tragedies; some are idylls in well-written, well-rhymed dialogue, others are political arguments which put the audience to sleep, or revolting pomposities; still others are the fantasies of enthusiasts, barbarous in style, incoherent in logic, full of long speeches to the gods because the author does not

8. He had written against Voltaire, and Voltaire suspected him (wrongly) of having committed a novel, *L'Oracle des nouveaux philosophes*.
9. His name was Trublet, and he had said, among other disagreeable things, that Voltaire's epic poem, the *Henriade*, made him yawn and that Voltaire's genius was "the perfection of mediocrity."

know how to address men, full of false maxims and emphatic commonplaces.

Candide listened attentively to this speech and conceived a high opinion of the speaker; and as the marquise had placed him by her side, he turned to ask her who was this man who spoke so well.

—He is a scholar, said the lady, who never plays cards and whom the abbé sometimes brings to my house for supper; he knows all about tragedies and books, and has himself written a tragedy that was hissed from the stage and a book, the only copy of which ever seen outside his publisher's office was dedicated to me.

—What a great man, said Candide, he's Pangloss all over.

Then, turning to him, he said: —Sir, you doubtless think everything is for the best in the physical as well as the moral universe, and that nothing could be otherwise than as it is?

—Not at all, sir, replied the scholar, I believe nothing of the sort. I find that everything goes wrong in our world; that nobody knows his place in society or his duty, what he's doing or what he ought to be doing, and that outside of mealtimes, which are cheerful and congenial enough, all the rest of the day is spent in useless quarrels, as of Jansenists against Molinists,[1] parliament-men against churchmen, literary men against literary men, courtiers against courtiers, financiers against the plebs, wives against husbands, relatives against relatives—it's one unending warfare.

Candide answered: —I have seen worse; but a wise man, who has since had the misfortune to be hanged, taught me that everything was marvelously well arranged. Troubles are just the shadows in a beautiful picture.

—Your hanged philosopher was joking, said Martin; the shadows are horrible ugly blots.

—It is human beings who make the blots, said Candide, and they can't do otherwise.

—Then it isn't their fault, said Martin.

Most of the faro players, who understood this sort of talk not at all, kept on drinking; Martin disputed with the scholar, and Candide told part of his story to the lady of the house.

After supper, the marquise brought Candide into her room and sat him down on a divan.

—Well, she said to him, are you still madly in love with Miss Cunégonde of Thunder-Ten-Tronckh?

—Yes, ma'am, replied Candide. The marquise turned upon him a tender smile.

—You answer like a young man of Westphalia, said she; a Frenchman

---

1. The Jansenists (from Corneille Jansen, 1585–1638) were a relatively strict party of religious reform; the Molinists (from Luis Molina) were the party of the Jesuits. Their central issue of controversy was the relative importance of divine grace and human will to the salvation of man.

would have told me: 'It is true that I have been in love with Miss Cunégonde; but since seeing you, madame, I fear that I love her no longer.'

—Alas, ma'am, said Candide, I will answer any way you want.

—Your passion for her, said the marquise, began when you picked up her handkerchief; I prefer that you should pick up my garter.

—Gladly, said Candide, and picked it up.

—But I also want you to put it back on, said the lady; and Candide put it on again.

—Look you now, said the lady, you are a foreigner; my Paris lovers I sometimes cause to languish for two weeks or so, but to you I surrender the very first night, because we must render the honors of the country to a young man from Westphalia.

The beauty, who had seen two enormous diamonds on the two hands of her young friend, praised them so sincerely that from the fingers of Candide they passed over to the fingers of the marquise.

As he returned home with his Perigord abbé, Candide felt some remorse at having been unfaithful to Miss Cunégonde; the abbé sympathized with his grief; he had only a small share in the fifty thousand francs which Candide lost at cards, and in the proceeds of the two diamonds which had been half-given, half-extorted. His scheme was to profit, as much as he could, from the advantage of knowing Candide. He spoke at length of Cunégonde, and Candide told him that he would beg forgiveness from his beloved for his infidelity when he met her at Venice.

The Perigordian overflowed with politeness and unction, taking a tender interest in everything Candide said, everything he did, and everything he wanted to do.[2]

—Well, sir, said he, so you have an assignation at Venice?

—Yes indeed, sir, I do, said Candide; it is absolutely imperative that I go there to find Miss Cunégonde.

And then, carried away by the pleasure of talking about his love, he recounted, as he often did, a part of his adventures with that illustrious lady of Westphalia.

—I suppose, said the abbé, that Miss Cunégonde has a fine wit and writes charming letters.

2. Here ends the long passage interpolated by Voltaire in 1761, which began on p. 47. In the original version the transition was managed as follows. After the "commentator's" speech, ending: —Tomorrow I will show you twenty pamphlets written against him.

—Sir, said the abbé from Perigord, do you notice that young person over there with the attractive face and the delicate figure? She would only cost you ten thousand francs a month, and for fifty thousand crowns of diamonds . . .

—I could spare her only a day or two, replied Candide, because I have an urgent appointment at Venice.

Next night after supper, the sly Perigordian overflowed with politeness and assiduity.

—Well, sir, said he, so you have an assignation at Venice?

—I never received a single letter from her, said Candide; for, as you can imagine, after being driven out of the castle for love of her, I couldn't write; shortly I learned that she was dead; then I rediscovered her; then I lost her again, and I have now sent, to a place more than twentyfive hundred leagues from here, a special agent whose return I am expecting.

The abbé listened carefully, and looked a bit dreamy. He soon took his leave of the two strangers, after embracing them tenderly. Next day Candide, when he woke up, received a letter, to the following effect:

—Dear sir, my very dear lover, I have been lying sick in this town for a week, I have just learned that you are here. I would fly to your arms if I could move. I heard that you had passed through Bordeaux; that was where I left the faithful Cacambo and the old woman, who are soon to follow me here. The governor of Buenos Aires took everything, but left me your heart. Come; your presence will either return me to life or cause me to die of joy.

This charming letter, coming so unexpectedly, filled Candide with inexpressible delight, while the illness of his dear Cunégonde covered him with grief. Torn between these two feelings, he took gold and diamonds, and had himself brought, with Martin, to the hotel where Miss Cunégonde was lodging. Trembling with emotion, he enters the room; his heart thumps, his voice breaks. He tries to open the curtains of the bed, he asks to have some lights.

—Absolutely forbidden, says the serving girl; light will be the death of her.

And abruptly she pulls shut the curtain.

—My dear Cunégonde, says Candide in tears, how are you feeling? If you can't see me, won't you at least speak to me?

—She can't talk, says the servant.

But then she draws forth from the bed a plump hand, over which Candide weeps a long time, and which he fills with diamonds, meanwhile leaving a bag of gold on the chair.

Amid his transports, there arrives a bailiff followed by the abbé from Perigord and a strong-arm squad.

—These here are the suspicious foreigners? says the officer; and he has them seized and orders his bullies to drag them off to jail.

—They don't treat visitors like this in Eldorado, says Candide.

—I am more a Manichee than ever, says Martin.

—But, please sir, where are you taking us? says Candide.

—To the lowest hole in the dungeons, says the bailiff.

Martin, having regained his self-possession, decided that the lady who pretended to be Cunégonde was a cheat, the abbé from Perigord was another cheat who had imposed on Candide's innocence, and the bailiff still another cheat, of whom it would be easy to get rid.

Rather than submit to the forms of justice, Candide, enlightened by

Martin's advice and eager for his own part to see the real Cunégonde again, offered the bailiff three little diamonds worth about three thousand pistoles apiece.

—Ah, my dear sir! cried the man with the ivory staff, even if you have committed every crime imaginable, you are the most honest man in the world. Three diamonds! each one worth three thousand pistoles! My dear sir! I would gladly die for you, rather than take you to jail. All foreigners get arrested here; but let me manage it; I have a brother at Dieppe in Normandy; I'll take you to him; and if you have a bit of a diamond to give him, he'll take care of you, just like me.

—And why do they arrest all foreigners? asked Candide.

The abbé from Perigord spoke up and said: —It's because a beggar from Atrebatum listened to some stupidities; that made him commit a parricide, not like the one of May, 1610, but like the one of December, 1594, much on the order of several other crimes committed in other years and other months by other beggars who had listened to stupidities.[3]

The bailiff then explained what it was all about.[4]

—Foh! what beasts! cried Candide. What! monstrous behavior of this sort from a people who sing and dance? As soon as I can, let me get out of this country, where the monkeys provoke the tigers. In my own country I've lived with bears; only in Eldorado are there proper men. In the name of God, sir bailiff, get me to Venice where I can wait for Miss Cunégonde.

—I can only get you to Lower Normandy, said the guardsman.

He had the irons removed at once, said there had been a mistake, dismissed his gang, and took Candide and Martin to Dieppe, where he left them with his brother. There was a little Dutch ship at anchor. The Norman, changed by three more diamonds into the most helpful of men, put Candide and his people aboard the vessel, which was bound for Portsmouth in England. It wasn't on the way to Venice, but Candide felt like a man just let out of hell; and he hoped to get back on the road to Venice at the first possible occasion.

---

3. Atrebatum is the Latin name for the district of Artois, from which came Robert-François Damiens, who tried to stab Louis XV in 1757. The assassination failed, like that of Châtel, who tried to kill Henri Quatre in 1594, but unlike that of Ravaillac, who succeeded in killing him in 1610. 4. The point, in fact, is not too clear since arresting foreigners is an indirect way at best to guard against home-grown fanatics, and the position of the abbé from Perigord in the whole transaction remains confused. Has he called in the officer just to get rid of Candide? If so, why is he sardonic about the very suspicions he is trying to foster? Candide's reaction is to the notion that Frenchmen should be capable of political assassination at all; it seems excessive.

CHAPTER 23

Candide and Martin Pass the Shores of England; What They See There

—Ah, Pangloss! Pangloss! Ah, Martin! Martin! Ah, my darling Cunégonde! What is this world of ours? sighed Candide on the Dutch vessel.

—Something crazy, something abominable, Martin replied.

—You have been in England; are people as crazy there as in France?

—It's a different sort of crazy, said Martin. You know that these two nations have been at war over a few acres of snow near Canada, and that they are spending on this fine struggle more than Canada itself is worth.[5] As for telling you if there are more people in one country or the other who need a strait jacket, that is a judgment too fine for my understanding; I know only that the people we are going to visit are eaten up with melancholy.

As they chatted thus, the vessel touched at Portsmouth. A multitude of people covered the shore, watching closely a rather bulky man who was kneeling, his eyes blindfolded, on the deck of a man-of-war. Four soldiers, stationed directly in front of this man, fired three bullets apiece into his brain, as peaceably as you would want; and the whole assemblage went home, in great satisfaction.[6]

—What's all this about? asked Candide. What devil is everywhere at work?

He asked who was that big man who had just been killed with so much ceremony.

—It was an admiral, they told him.

—And why kill this admiral?

—The reason, they told him, is that he didn't kill enough people; he gave battle to a French admiral, and it was found that he didn't get close enough to him.

—But, said Candide, the French admiral was just as far from the English admiral as the English admiral was from the French admiral.

—That's perfectly true, came the answer; but in this country it is useful from time to time to kill one admiral in order to encourage the others.

Candide was so stunned and shocked at what he saw and heard, that he would not even set foot ashore; he arranged with the Dutch merchant (without even caring if he was robbed, as at Surinam) to be taken forthwith to Venice.

5. The wars of the French and English over Canada dragged intermittently through the eighteenth century till the peace of Paris sealed England's conquest (1763). Voltaire thought the French should concentrate on developing Louisiana, where the Jesuit influence was less marked.

6. Candide has witnessed the execution of Admiral John Byng, defeated off Minorca by the French fleet under Galisonnière and executed by firing squad on March 14, 1757. Voltaire had intervened to avert the execution.

The merchant was ready in two days; they coasted along France, they passed within sight of Lisbon, and Candide quivered. They entered the straits, crossed the Mediterranean, and finally landed at Venice.

—God be praised, said Candide, embracing Martin; here I shall recover the lovely Cunégonde. I trust Cacambo as I would myself. All is well, all goes well, all goes as well as possible.

CHAPTER 24

About Paquette and Brother Giroflée

As soon as he was in Venice, he had a search made for Cacambo in all the inns, all the cafés, all the stews—and found no trace of him. Every day he sent to investigate the vessels and coastal traders; no news of Cacambo.

—How's this? said he to Martin. I have had time to go from Surinam to Bordeaux, from Bordeaux to Paris, from Paris to Dieppe, from Dieppe to Portsmouth, to skirt Portugal and Spain, cross the Mediterranean, and spend several months at Venice—and the lovely Cunégonde has not come yet! In her place, I have met only that female pretender and that abbé from Perigord. Cunégonde is dead, without a doubt; and nothing remains for me too but death. Oh, it would have been better to stay in the earthly paradise of Eldorado than to return to this accursed Europe. How right you are, my dear Martin; all is but illusion and disaster.

He fell into a black melancholy, and refused to attend the fashionable operas or take part in the other diversions of the carnival season; not a single lady tempted him in the slightest. Martin told him: —You're a real simpleton if you think a half-breed valet with five or six millions in his pockets will go to the end of the world to get your mistress and bring her to Venice for you. If he finds her, he'll take her for himself; if he doesn't, he'll take another. I advise you to forget about your servant Cacambo and your mistress Cunégonde.

Martin was not very comforting. Candide's melancholy increased, and Martin never wearied of showing him that there is little virtue and little happiness on this earth, except perhaps in Eldorado, where nobody can go.

While they were discussing this important matter and still waiting for Cunégonde, Candide noticed in St. Mark's Square a young Theatine[7] monk who had given his arm to a girl. The Theatine seemed fresh, plump, and flourishing; his eyes were bright, his manner cocky, his glance brilliant, his step proud. The girl was very pretty, and singing aloud; she glanced lovingly at her Theatine, and from time to time pinched his plump cheeks.

7. A Catholic order founded in 1524 by Cardinal Cajetan and G. P. Caraffa, later Pope Paul IV.

—At least you must admit, said Candide to Martin, that these people are happy. Until now I have not found in the whole inhabited earth, except Eldorado, anything but miserable people. But this girl and this monk, I'd be willing to bet, are very happy creatures.

—I'll bet they aren't, said Martin.

—We have only to ask them to dinner, said Candide, and we'll find out if I'm wrong.

Promptly he approached them, made his compliments, and invited them to his inn for a meal of macaroni, Lombardy partridges, and caviar, washed down with wine from Montepulciano, Cyprus, and Samos, and some Lacrima Christi. The girl blushed but the Theatine accepted gladly, and the girl followed him, watching Candide with an expression of surprise and confusion, darkened by several tears. Scarcely had she entered the room when she said to Candide: —What, can it be that Master Candide no longer knows Paquette?

At these words Candide, who had not yet looked carefully at her because he was preoccupied with Cunégonde, said to her: —Ah, my poor child! so you are the one who put Doctor Pangloss in the fine fix where I last saw him.

—Alas, sir, I was the one, said Paquette; I see you know all about it. I heard of the horrible misfortunes which befell the whole household of my lady the Baroness and the lovely Cunégonde. I swear to you that my own fate has been just as unhappy. I was perfectly innocent when you knew me. A Franciscan, who was my confessor, easily seduced me. The consequences were frightful; shortly after my lord the Baron had driven you out with great kicks on the backside, I too was forced to leave the castle. If a famous doctor had not taken pity on me, I would have died. Out of gratitude, I became for some time the mistress of this doctor. His wife, who was jealous to the point of frenzy, beat me mercilessly every day; she was a gorgon. The doctor was the ugliest of men, and I the most miserable creature on earth, being continually beaten for a man I did not love. You will understand, sir, how dangerous it is for a nagging woman to be married to a doctor. This man, enraged by his wife's ways, one day gave her as a cold cure a medicine so potent that in two hours' time she died amid horrible convulsions. Her relatives brought suit against the bereaved husband; he fled the country, and I was put in prison. My innocence would never have saved me if I had not been rather pretty. The judge set me free on condition that he should become the doctor's successor. I was shortly replaced in this post by another girl, dismissed without any payment, and obliged to continue this abominable business which you men find so pleasant and which for us is nothing but a bottomless pit of misery. I went to ply the trade in Venice. Ah, my dear sir, if you could imagine what it is like to have to caress indiscriminately an old merchant, a lawyer, a monk, a gondolier, an abbé; to be subjected to every sort of insult and outrage; to be reduced, time and again, to borrowing a skirt in order to go have it lifted by some disgusting man; to be robbed by this fellow of what one has gained from that; to be shaken down by the police, and to have before one only the prospect of a hideous old age, a hospital, and a dunghill, you will conclude that I am one of the most miserable creatures in the world.

Thus Paquette poured forth her heart to the good Candide in a hotel room, while Martin sat listening nearby. At last he said to Candide: — You see, I've already won half my bet.

Brother Giroflée[8] had remained in the dining room, and was having a drink before dinner.

—But how's this? said Candide to Paquette. You looked so happy, so joyous, when I met you; you were singing, you caressed the Theatine with such a natural air of delight; you seemed to me just as happy as you now say you are miserable.

—Ah, sir, replied Paquette, that's another one of the miseries of this business; yesterday I was robbed and beaten by an officer, and today I have to seem in good humor in order to please a monk.

Candide wanted no more; he conceded that Martin was right. They sat down to table with Paquette and the Theatine; the meal was agreeable enough, and when it was over, the company spoke out among themselves with some frankness.

—Father, said Candide to the monk, you seem to me a man whom all the world might envy; the flower of health glows in your cheek, your features radiate pleasure; you have a pretty girl for your diversion, and you seem very happy with your life as a Theatine.

—Upon my word, sir, said Brother Giroflée, I wish that all the Theatines were at the bottom of the sea. A hundred times I have been tempted to set fire to my convent, and go turn Turk. My parents forced me, when I was fifteen years old, to put on this detestable robe, so they could leave more money to a cursed older brother of mine, may God confound him! Jealousy, faction, and fury spring up, by natural law, within the walls of convents. It is true, I have preached a few bad sermons which earned me a little money, half of which the prior stole from me; the remainder serves to keep me in girls. But when I have to go back to the monastery at night, I'm ready to smash my head against the walls of my cell; and all my fellow monks are in the same fix.

Martin turned to Candide and said with his customary coolness: — Well, haven't I won the whole bet?

Candide gave two thousand piastres to Paquette and a thousand to Brother Giroflée.

—I assure you, said he, that with that they will be happy.

8. His name means "gillyflower," and Paquette means "daisy." They are lilies of the field who spin not, neither do they reap.

—I don't believe so, said Martin; your piastres may make them even more unhappy than they were before.

—That may be, said Candide; but one thing comforts me, I note that people often turn up whom one never expected to see again; it may well be that, having rediscovered my red sheep and Paquette, I will also rediscover Cunégonde.

—I hope, said Martin, that she will some day make you happy; but I very much doubt it.

—You're a hard man, said Candide.

—I've lived, said Martin.

—But look at these gondoliers, said Candide; aren't they always singing?

—You don't see them at home, said Martin, with their wives and squalling children. The doge[9] has his troubles, the gondoliers theirs. It's true that on the whole one is better off as a gondolier than as a doge; but the difference is so slight, I don't suppose it's worth the trouble of discussing.

—There's a lot of talk here, said Candide, of this Senator Pococurante,[1] who has a fine palace on the Brenta and is hospitable to foreigners. They say he is a man who has never known a moment's grief.

—I'd like to see such a rare specimen, said Martin.

Candide promptly sent to Lord Pococurante, asking permission to call on him tomorrow.

CHAPTER 25

Visit to Lord Pococurante, Venetian Nobleman

Candide and Martin took a gondola on the Brenta, and soon reached the palace of the noble Pococurante. The gardens were large and filled with beautiful marble statues; the palace was handsomely designed. The master of the house, sixty years old and very rich, received his two inquisitive visitors perfectly politely, but with very little warmth; Candide was disconcerted and Martin not at all displeased.

First two pretty and neatly dressed girls served chocolate, which they whipped to a froth. Candide could not forbear praising their beauty, their grace, their skill.

—They are pretty good creatures, said Pococurante; I sometimes have them into my bed, for I'm tired of the ladies of the town, with their stupid tricks, quarrels, jealousies, fits of ill humor and petty pride, and all the sonnets one has to make or order for them; but, after all, these two girls are starting to bore me too.

---

9. I.e., supreme magistrate of Venice.   1. His name means "small care" or "Carelittle."

After lunch, Candide strolled through a long gallery, and was amazed at the beauty of the pictures. He asked who was the painter of the two finest.

—They are by Raphael,[2] said the senator; I bought them for a lot of money, out of vanity, some years ago; people say they're the finest in Italy, but they don't please me at all; the colors have all turned brown, the figures aren't well modeled and don't stand out enough, the draperies bear no resemblance to real cloth. In a word, whatever people may say, I don't find in them a real imitation of nature. I like a picture only when I can see in it a touch of nature itself, and there are none of this sort. I have many paintings, but I no longer look at them.

As they waited for dinner, Pococurante ordered a concerto performed. Candide found the music delightful.

—That noise? said Pococurante. It may amuse you for half an hour, but if it goes on any longer, it tires everybody though no one dares to admit it. Music today is only the art of performing difficult pieces, and what is merely difficult cannot please for long. Perhaps I should prefer the opera, if they had not found ways to make it revolting and monstrous. Anyone who likes bad tragedies set to music is welcome to them; in these performances the scenes serve only to introduce, inappropriately, two or three ridiculous songs designed to show off the actress's sound box. Anyone who wants to, or who can, is welcome to swoon with pleasure at the sight of a castrate wriggling through the role of Caesar or Cato, and strutting awkwardly about the stage. For my part, I have long since given up these paltry trifles which are called the glory of modern Italy, and for which monarchs pay such ruinous prices.

Candide argued a bit, but timidly; Martin was entirely of a mind with the senator.

They sat down to dinner, and after an excellent meal adjourned to the library. Candide, seeing a copy of Homer[3] in a splendid binding, complimented the noble lord on his good taste.

—That is an author, said he, who was the special delight of great Pangloss, the best philosopher in all Germany.

—He's no special delight of mine, said Pococurante coldly. I was once made to believe that I took pleasure in reading him; but that constant recital of fights which are all alike, those gods who are always interfering but never decisively, that Helen who is the cause of the war and then scarcely takes any part in the story, that Troy which is always under siege and never taken—all that bores me to tears. I have sometimes asked scholars if reading it bored them as much as it bores me; everyone

2. Raphael was widely reputed to be the supreme painter of the Italian Renaissance.
3. Since the mid-sixteenth century, when Julius Caesar Scaliger established the dogma, it had been customary to prefer Virgil to Homer. Voltaire's youthful judgments, as delivered in the *Essai sur la poésie épique* (1728), are here summarized with minor revisions—upward for Ariosto, downward for Milton.

who answered frankly told me the book dropped from his hands like lead, but that they had to have it in their libraries as a monument of antiquity, like those old rusty coins which can't be used in real trade.

—Your Excellence doesn't hold the same opinion of Virgil? said Candide.

—I concede, said Pococurante, that the second, fourth, and sixth books of his *Aeneid* are fine; but as for his pious Aeneas, and strong Cloanthes, and faithful Achates, and little Ascanius, and that imbecile King Latinus, and middle-class Amata, and insipid Lavinia, I don't suppose there was ever anything so cold and unpleasant. I prefer Tasso and those sleepwalkers' stories of Ariosto.[4]

—Dare I ask, sir, said Candide, if you don't get great enjoyment from reading Horace?

—There are some maxims there, said Pococurante, from which a man of the world can profit, and which, because they are formed into vigorous couplets, are more easily remembered; but I care very little for his trip to Brindisi, his description of a bad dinner, or his account of a quibblers' squabble between some fellow Pupilus, whose words he says *were full of pus,* and another whose words *were full of vinegar.*[5] I feel nothing but extreme disgust at his verses against old women and witches; and I can't see what's so great in his telling his friend Maecenas that if he is raised by him to the ranks of lyric poets, he will strike the stars with his lofty forehead. Fools admire everything in a well-known author. I read only for my own pleasure; I like only what is in my style.

Candide, who had been trained never to judge for himself, was much astonished by what he heard; and Martin found Pococurante's way of thinking quite rational.

—Oh, here is a copy of Cicero,[6] said Candide. Now this great man I suppose you're never tired of reading.

—I never read him at all, replied the Venetian. What do I care whether he pleaded for Rabirius or Cluentius? As a judge, I have my hands full of lawsuits. I might like his philosophical works better, but when I saw that he had doubts about everything, I concluded that I knew as much as he did, and that I needed no help to be ignorant.

—Ah, here are eighty volumes of collected papers from a scientific academy, cried Martin; maybe there is something good in them.

—There would be indeed, said Pococurante, if one of these silly

---

4. Pococurante mentions a lot of the minor characters in Virgil's *Aeneid*, to make clear that he is perfectly familiar with the book he despises. Tasso and Ariosto wrote in the sixteenth century "romantic," i.e., fantastic, epic poems often compared with those of their classical predecessors.

5. The reference is to Horace, *Satires* 1.7; Pococurante, with gentlemanly negligence, has corrupted Rupilius to Pupilus. Horace's poems against witches are *Epodes* 5, 8, 12; the one about striking the stars with his lofty forehead is *Odes* 1.1.

6. Cicero was the Roman lawyer, elocutionist, politician, and philosopher of the first century B.C. Since the sixteenth century "advanced" opinion had often dismissed him as a windbag, so Pococurante devotes little time to him.

authors had merely discovered a new way of making pins; but in all those volumes there is nothing but empty systems, not a single useful discovery.

—What a lot of stage plays I see over there, said Candide, some in Italian, some in Spanish and French.

—Yes, said the senator, three thousand of them, and not three dozen good ones. As for those collections of sermons, which all together are not worth a page of Seneca, and all these heavy volumes of theology, you may be sure I never open them, nor does anybody else.

Martin noticed some shelves full of English books.

—I suppose, said he, that a republican must delight in most of these books written in the land of liberty.

—Yes, replied Pococurante, it's a fine thing to write as you think; it is mankind's privilege. In all our Italy, people write only what they do not think; men who inhabit the land of the Caesars and Antonines dare not have an idea without the permission of a Dominican. I would rejoice in the freedom that breathes through English genius, if partisan passions did not corrupt all that is good in that precious freedom.

Candide, noting a Milton, asked if he did not consider this author a great man.

—Who? said Pococurante. That barbarian who made a long commentary on the first chapter of Genesis in ten books of crabbed verse? That clumsy imitator of the Greeks, who disfigures creation itself, and while Moses represents the eternal being as creating the world with a word, has the messiah take a big compass out of a heavenly cupboard in order to design his work? You expect me to admire the man who spoiled Tasso's hell and devil? who disguises Lucifer now as a toad, now as a pigmy? who makes him rehash the same arguments a hundred times over? who makes him argue theology? and who, taking seriously Ariosto's comic story of the invention of firearms, has the devils shooting off cannon in heaven? Neither I nor anyone else in Italy has been able to enjoy these gloomy extravagances.[7] The marriage of Sin and Death, and the monster that Sin gives birth to, will nauseate any man whose taste is at all refined; and his long description of a hospital is good only for a gravedigger. This obscure, extravagant, and disgusting poem was despised at its birth; I treat it today as it was treated in its own country by its contemporaries. Anyhow, I say what I think, and care very little whether other people agree with me.

Candide was a little cast down by these diatribes; he respected Homer, and had a little affection for Milton.

—Alas, he said under his breath to Martin, I'm afraid this man will have a supreme contempt for our German poets.

---

7. Voltaire, whose standards of classical correctness led him to find major flaws in Shakespeare, could not be expected to like *Paradise Lost*. But in the person of Pococurante he is satirizing the bored and superior esthete, as well as teasing respectable English taste, so he deliberately overstates his case.

—No harm in that, said Martin.

—Oh what a superior man, said Candide, still speaking softly, what a great genius this Pococurante must be! Nothing can please him.

Having thus looked over all the books, they went down into the garden. Candide praised its many beauties.

—I know nothing in such bad taste, said the master of the house; we have nothing but trifles here; tomorrow I am going to have one set out on a nobler design.

When the two visitors had taken leave of his excellency: —Well now, said Candide to Martin, you must agree that this was the happiest of all men, for he is superior to everything he possesses.

—Don't you see, said Martin, that he is disgusted with everything he possesses? Plato said, a long time ago, that the best stomachs are not those which refuse all food.

—But, said Candide, isn't there pleasure in criticizing everything, in seeing faults where other people think they see beauties?

—That is to say, Martin replied, that there's pleasure in having no pleasure?

—Oh well, said Candide, then I am the only happy man . . . or will be, when I see Miss Cunégonde again.

—It's always a good thing to have hope, said Martin.

But the days and the weeks slipped past; Cacambo did not come back, and Candide was so buried in his grief, that he did not even notice that Paquette and Brother Giroflée had neglected to come and thank him.

CHAPTER 26

About a Supper that Candide and Martin Had with Six Strangers, and Who They Were

One evening when Candide, accompanied by Martin, was about to sit down for dinner with the strangers staying in his hotel, a man with a soot-colored face came up behind him, took him by the arm, and said: —Be ready to leave with us, don't miss out.

He turned and saw Cacambo. Only the sight of Cunégonde could have astonished and pleased him more. He nearly went mad with joy. He embraced his dear friend.

—Cunégonde is here, no doubt? Where is she? Bring me to her, let me die of joy in her presence.

—Cunégonde is not here at all, said Cacambo, she is at Constantinople.

—Good Heavens, at Constantinople! but if she were in China, I must fly there, let's go.

—We will leave after supper, said Cacambo; I can tell you no more;

I am a slave, my owner is looking for me, I must go wait on him at table; mum's the word; eat your supper and be prepared.

Candide, torn between joy and grief, delighted to have seen his faithful agent again, astonished to find him a slave, full of the idea of recovering his mistress, his heart in a turmoil, his mind in a whirl, sat down to eat with Martin, who was watching all these events coolly, and with six strangers who had come to pass the carnival season at Venice.

Cacambo, who was pouring wine for one of the strangers, leaned respectfully over his master at the end of the meal, and said to him: — Sire, Your Majesty may leave when he pleases, the vessel is ready.

Having said these words, he exited. The diners looked at one another in silent amazement, when another servant, approaching his master, said to him: —Sire, Your Majesty's litter is at Padua, and the bark awaits you.

The master nodded, and the servant vanished. All the diners looked at one another again, and the general amazement redoubled. A third servant, approaching a third stranger, said to him: —Sire, take my word for it, Your Majesty must stay here no longer; I shall get everything ready.

Then he too disappeared.

Candide and Martin had no doubt, now, that it was a carnival masquerade. A fourth servant spoke to a fourth master: —Your majesty will leave when he pleases—and went out like the others. A fifth followed suit. But the sixth servant spoke differently to the sixth stranger, who sat next to Candide. He said: —My word, sire, they'll give no more credit to Your Majesty, nor to me either; we could very well spend the night in the lockup, you and I. I've got to look out for myself, so good-bye to you.

When all the servants had left, the six strangers, Candide, and Martin remained under a pall of silence. Finally Candide broke it.

—Gentlemen, said he, here's a strange kind of joke. Why are you all royalty? I assure you that Martin and I aren't.

Cacambo's master spoke up gravely then, and said in Italian: —This is no joke, my name is Achmet the Third.[8] I was grand sultan for several years; then, as I had dethroned my brother, my nephew dethroned me. My viziers had their throats cut; I was allowed to end my days in the old seraglio. My nephew, the Grand Sultan Mahmoud, sometimes lets me travel for my health; and I have come to spend the carnival season at Venice.

A young man who sat next to Achmet spoke after him, and said: — My name is Ivan; I was once emperor of all the Russias.[9] I was dethroned while still in my cradle; my father and mother were locked up, and I

8. His dates are 1673–1736; he was deposed in 1730.
9. Ivan VI reigned from his birth in 1740 till 1756, then was confined in the Schlusselberg, and executed in 1764.

was raised in prison; I sometimes have permission to travel, though always under guard, and I have come to spend the carnival season at Venice.

The third said: —I am Charles Edward, king of England;[1] my father yielded me his rights to the kingdom, and I fought to uphold them; but they tore out the hearts of eight hundred of my partisans, and flung them in their faces. I have been in prison; now I am going to Rome, to visit the king, my father, dethroned like me and my grandfather; and I have come to pass the carnival season at Venice.

The fourth king then spoke up, and said: —I am a king of the Poles;[2] the luck of war has deprived me of my hereditary estates; my father suffered the same losses; I submit to Providence like Sultan Achmet, Emperor Ivan, and King Charles Edward, to whom I hope heaven grants long lives; and I have come to pass the carnival season at Venice.

The fifth said: —I too am a king of the Poles;[3] I lost my kingdom twice, but Providence gave me another state, in which I have been able to do more good than all the Sarmatian kings ever managed to do on the banks of the Vistula. I too have submitted to Providence, and I have come to pass the carnival season at Venice.

It remained for the sixth monarch to speak.

—Gentlemen, said he, I am no such great lord as you, but I have in fact been a king like any other. I am Theodore; I was elected king of Corsica.[4] People used to call me *Your Majesty*, and now they barely call me *Sir*; I used to coin currency, and now I don't have a cent; I used to have two secretaries of state, and now I scarcely have a valet; I have sat on a throne, and for a long time in London I was in jail, on the straw; and I may well be treated the same way here, though I have come, like your majesties, to pass the carnival season at Venice.

The five other kings listened to his story with noble compassion. Each one of them gave twenty sequins to King Theodore, so that he might buy a suit and some shirts; Candide gave him a diamond worth two thousand sequins.

—Who in the world, said the five kings, is this private citizen who is in a position to give a hundred times as much as any of us, and who actually gives it?[5]

Just as they were rising from dinner, there arrived at the same estab-

---

1. This is the Young Pretender (1720–88), known to his supporters as Bonnie Prince Charlie. The defeat so theatrically described took place at Culloden, April 16, 1746.
2. Augustus III (1696–1763) elector of Saxony and king of Poland, dethroned by Frederick the Great in 1756.
3. Stanislas Leczinski (1677–1766), father-in-law of Louis XV, who abdicated the throne of Poland in 1736, was made duke of Lorraine and in that capacity befriended Voltaire.

4. Theodore von Neuhof (1690–1756), an authentic Westphalian, an adventurer and a soldier of fortune, who in 1736 was (for about eight months) the elected king of Corsica. He spent time in an Amsterdam as well as a London debtor's prison.
5. A late correction of Voltaire's makes this passage read: —Who is this man who is in a position to give a hundred times as much as any of us, and who actually gives it? Are you a king too, sir?
—No, gentlemen, and I have no desire to be.

lishment four most serene highnesses, who had also lost their kingdoms through the luck of war, and who came to spend the rest of the carnival season at Venice. But Candide never bothered even to look at these newcomers because he was only concerned to go find his dear Cunégonde at Constantinople.

CHAPTER 27

Candide's Trip to Constantinople

Faithful Cacambo had already arranged with the Turkish captain who was returning Sultan Achmet to Constantinople to make room for Candide and Martin on board. Both men boarded ship after prostrating themselves before his miserable highness. On the way, Candide said to Martin: —Six dethroned kings that we had dinner with! and yet among those six there was one on whom I had to bestow charity! Perhaps there are other princes even more unfortunate. I myself have only lost a hundred sheep, and now I am flying to the arms of Cunégonde. My dear Martin, once again Pangloss is proved right, all is for the best.

—I hope so, said Martin.

—But, said Candide, that was a most unlikely experience we had at Venice. Nobody ever saw, or heard tell of, six dethroned kings eating together at an inn.

—It is no more extraordinary, said Martin, than most of the things that have happened to us. Kings are frequently dethroned; and as for the honor we had from dining with them, that's a trifle which doesn't deserve our notice.[6]

Scarcely was Candide on board than he fell on the neck of his former servant, his friend Cacambo.

—Well! said he, what is Cunégonde doing? Is she still a marvel of beauty? Does she still love me? How is her health? No doubt you have bought her a palace at Constantinople.

—My dear master, answered Cacambo, Cunégonde is washing dishes on the shores of the Propontis, in the house of a prince who has very few dishes to wash; she is a slave in the house of a onetime king named Ragotski,[7] to whom the Great Turk allows three crowns a day in his

---

But this reading, though Voltaire's on good authority, produces a conflict with Candide's previous remark: —Why are you all royalty? I assure you that Martin and I aren't.

Thus, it has seemed better for literary reasons to follow an earlier reading. Voltaire was very conscious of his situation as a man richer than many princes; in 1758 he had money on loan to no fewer than three highnesses, Charles Eugene, duke of Wurtemburg; Charles Theodore, elector Palatine;

and the duke of Saxe-Gotha.

6. Another late change adds the following question: —What does it matter whom you dine with as long as you fare well at table?

I have omitted it, again on literary grounds (the observation is too heavy and commonplace), despite its superior claim to a position in the text.

7. Francis Leopold Rakoczy (1676–1735) who was briefly king of Transylvania in the early eighteenth century. After 1720 he was interned in Turkey.

exile; but, what is worse than all this, she has lost all her beauty and become horribly ugly.

—Ah, beautiful or ugly, said Candide, I am an honest man, and my duty is to love her forever. But how can she be reduced to this wretched state with the five or six millions that you had?

—All right, said Cacambo, didn't I have to give two millions to Señor don Fernando d'Ibaraa y Figueroa y Mascarenes y Lampourdos y Souza, governor of Buenos Aires, for his permission to carry off Miss Cunégonde? And didn't a pirate cleverly strip us of the rest? And didn't this pirate carry us off to Cape Matapan, to Melos, Nicaria, Samos, Petra, to the Dardanelles, Marmora, Scutari? Cunégonde and the old woman are working for the prince I told you about, and I am the slave of the dethroned sultan.

—What a lot of fearful calamities linked one to the other, said Candide. But after all, I still have a few diamonds, I shall easily deliver Cunégonde. What a pity that she's become so ugly!

Then, turning toward Martin, he asked: —Who in your opinion is more to be pitied, the Emperor Achmet, the Emperor Ivan, King Charles Edward, or myself?

—I have no idea, said Martin; I would have to enter men's hearts in order to tell.

—Ah, said Candide, if Pangloss were here, he would know and he would tell us.

—I can't imagine, said Martin, what scales your Pangloss would use to weigh out the miseries of men and value their griefs. All I will venture is that the earth holds millions of men who deserve our pity a hundred times more than King Charles Edward, Emperor Ivan, or Sultan Achmet.

—You may well be right, said Candide.

In a few days they arrived at the straits leading to the Black Sea. Candide began by repurchasing Cacambo at an exorbitant price; then, without losing an instant, he flung himself and his companions into a galley to go search out Cunégonde on the shores of Propontis, however ugly she might be.

There were in the chain gang two convicts who bent clumsily to the oar, and on whose bare shoulders the Levantine[8] captain delivered from time to time a few lashes with a bullwhip. Candide naturally noticed them more than the other galley slaves, and out of pity came closer to them. Certain features of their disfigured faces seemed to him to bear a slight resemblance to Pangloss and to that wretched Jesuit, that baron, that brother of Miss Cunégonde. The notion stirred and saddened him. He looked at them more closely.

—To tell you the truth, he said to Cacambo, if I hadn't seen Master

8. From the eastern Mediterranean.

Pangloss hanged, and if I hadn't been so miserable as to murder the baron, I should think they were rowing in this very galley.

At the names of 'baron' and 'Pangloss' the two convicts gave a great cry, sat still on their bench, and dropped their oars. The Levantine captain came running, and the bullwhip lashes redoubled.

—Stop, stop, captain, cried Candide. I'll give you as much money as you want.

—What, can it be Candide? cried one of the convicts.

—What, can it be Candide? cried the other.

—Is this a dream? said Candide. Am I awake or asleep? Am I in this galley? Is that my lord the Baron, whom I killed? Is that Master Pangloss, whom I saw hanged?

—It is indeed, they replied.

—What, is that the great philosopher? said Martin.

—Now, sir, Mr. Levantine Captain, said Candide, how much money do you want for the ransom of my lord Thunder-Ten-Tronckh, one of the first barons of the empire, and Master Pangloss, the deepest meta-physician in all Germany?

—Dog of a Christian, replied the Levantine captain, since these two dogs of Christian convicts are barons and metaphysicians, which is no doubt a great honor in their country, you will give me fifty thousand sequins for them.

—You shall have them, sir, take me back to Constantinople and you shall be paid on the spot. Or no, take me to Miss Cunégonde.

The Levantine captain, at Candide's first word, had turned his bow toward the town, and he had them rowed there as swiftly as a bird cleaves the air.

A hundred times Candide embraced the baron and Pangloss.

—And how does it happen I didn't kill you, my dear baron? and my dear Pangloss, how can you be alive after being hanged? and why are you both rowing in the galleys of Turkey?

—Is it really true that my dear sister is in this country? asked the baron.

—Yes, answered Cacambo.

—And do I really see again my dear Candide? cried Pangloss.

Candide introduced Martin and Cacambo. They all embraced; they all talked at once. The galley flew, already they were back in port. A jew was called, and Candide sold him for fifty thousand sequins a diamond worth a hundred thousand, while he protested by Abraham that he could not possibly give more for it. Candide immediately ran-somed the baron and Pangloss. The latter threw himself at the feet of his liberator, and bathed them with tears; the former thanked him with a nod, and promised to repay this bit of money at the first opportunity.

—But is it really possible that my sister is in Turkey? said he.

—Nothing is more possible, replied Cacambo, since she is a dish-washer in the house of a prince of Transylvania.

At once two more jews were called; Candide sold some more diamonds; and they all departed in another galley to the rescue of
Cunégonde.

CHAPTER 28

What Happened to Candide, Cunégonde, Pangloss, Martin, &c.

—Let me beg your pardon once more, said Candide to the baron,
pardon me, reverend father, for having run you through the body with
my sword.

—Don't mention it, replied the baron. I was a little too hasty myself,
I confess it; but since you want to know the misfortune which brought
me to the galleys, I'll tell you. After being cured of my wound by the
brother who was apothecary to the college, I was attacked and abducted
by a Spanish raiding party; they jailed me in Buenos Aires at the time
when my sister had just left. I asked to be sent to Rome, to the father
general. Instead, I was named to serve as almoner in Constantinople,
under the French ambassador. I had not been a week on this job when
I chanced one evening on a very handsome young ichoglan.[9] The evening was hot; the young man wanted to take a swim; I seized the occasion,
and went with him. I did not know that it is a capital offense for a
Christian to be found naked with a young Moslem. A cadi sentenced
me to receive a hundred blows with a cane on the soles of my feet, and
then to be sent to the galleys. I don't suppose there was ever such a
horrible miscarriage of justice. But I would like to know why my sister
is in the kitchen of a Transylvanian king exiled among Turks.

—But how about you, my dear Pangloss, said Candide; how is it
possible that we have met again?

—It is true, said Pangloss, that you saw me hanged; in the normal
course of things, I should have been burned, but you recall that a
cloudburst occurred just as they were about to roast me. So much rain
fell that they despaired of lighting the fire; thus I was hanged, for lack
of anything better to do with me. A surgeon bought my body, carried
me off to his house, and dissected me. First he made a cross-shaped
incision in me, from the navel to the clavicle. No one could have been
worse hanged than I was. In fact, the executioner of the high ceremonials
of the Holy Inquisition, who was a subdeacon, burned people marvelously well, but he was not in the way of hanging them. The rope was
wet, and tightened badly; it caught on a knot; in short, I was still breath-
ing. The cross-shaped incision made me scream so loudly that the
surgeon fell over backwards; he thought he was dissecting the devil, fled
in an agony of fear, and fell downstairs in his flight. His wife ran in, at
the noise, from a nearby room; she found me stretched out on the table

9. A page to the sultan.

with my cross-shaped incision, was even more frightened than her husband, fled, and fell over him. When they had recovered a little, I heard her say to him: 'My dear, what were you thinking of, trying to dissect a heretic? Don't you know those people are always possessed of the devil? I'm going to get a priest and have him exorcised.' At these words, I shuddered, and collected my last remaining energies to cry: 'Have mercy on me!' At last the Portuguese barber[1] took courage; he sewed me up again; his wife even nursed me; in two weeks I was up and about. The barber found me a job and made me lackey to a Knight of Malta who was going to Venice; and when this master could no longer pay me, I took service under a Venetian merchant, whom I followed to Constantinople.

—One day it occurred to me to enter a mosque; no one was there but an old imam and a very attractive young worshipper who was saying her prayers. Her bosom was completely bare; and between her two breasts she had a lovely bouquet of tulips, roses, anemones, buttercups, hyacinths, and primroses. She dropped her bouquet, I picked it up, and returned it to her with the most respectful attentions. I was so long getting it back in place that the imam grew angry, and, seeing that I was a Christian, he called the guard. They took me before the cadi, who sentenced me to receive a hundred blows with a cane on the soles of my feet, and then to be sent to the galleys. I was chained to the same galley and precisely the same bench as my lord the Baron. There were in this galley four young fellows from Marseilles, five Neapolitan priests, and two Corfu monks, who assured us that these things happen every day. My lord the Baron asserted that he had suffered a greater injustice than I; I, on the other hand, proposed that it was much more permissible to replace a bouquet in a bosom than to be found naked with an ichoglan. We were arguing the point continually, and getting twenty lashes a day with the bullwhip, when the chain of events within this universe brought you to our galley, and you ransomed us.

—Well, my dear Pangloss, Candide said to him, now that you have been hanged, dissected, beaten to a pulp, and sentenced to the galleys, do you still think everything is for the best in this world?

—I am still of my first opinion, replied Pangloss; for after all I am a philosopher, and it would not be right for me to recant since Leibniz could not possibly be wrong, and besides pre-established harmony is the finest notion in the world, like the plenum and subtle matter.[2]

---

1. The two callings of barber and surgeon, since they both involved sharp instruments, were interchangeable in the early days of medicine.
2. Rigorous determinism requires that there be no empty spaces in the universe, so wherever it seems empty, one posits the existence of the "plenum."

"Subtle matter" describes the soul, the mind, and all spiritual agencies—which can, therefore, be supposed subject to the influence and control of the great world machine, which is, of course, visibly material. Both are concepts needed to round out the system of optimistic determinism.

CHAPTER 29

How Candide Found Cunégonde and the Old Woman Again

While Candide, the baron, Pangloss, Martin, and Cacambo were telling one another their stories, while they were disputing over the contingent or non-contingent events of this universe, while they were arguing over effects and causes, over moral evil and physical evil, over liberty and necessity, and over the consolations available to one in a Turkish galley, they arrived at the shores of Propontis and the house of the prince of Transylvania. The first sight to meet their eyes was Cunégonde and the old woman, who were hanging out towels on lines to dry.

The baron paled at what he saw. The tender lover Candide, seeing his lovely Cunégonde with her skin weathered, her eyes bloodshot, her breasts fallen, her cheeks seamed, her arms red and scaly, recoiled three steps in horror, and then advanced only out of politeness. She embraced Candide and her brother; everyone embraced the old woman; Candide ransomed them both.

There was a little farm in the neighborhood; the old woman suggested that Candide occupy it until some better fate should befall the group. Cunégonde did not know she was ugly, no one had told her; she reminded Candide of his promises in so firm a tone that the good Candide did not dare to refuse her. So he went to tell the baron that he was going to marry his sister.

—Never will I endure, said the baron, such baseness on her part, such insolence on yours; this shame at least I will not put up with; why, my sister's children would not be able to enter the Chapters in Germany.[3] No, my sister will never marry anyone but a baron of the empire.

Cunégonde threw herself at his feet, and bathed them with her tears; he was inflexible.

—You absolute idiot, Candide told him, I rescued you from the galleys, I paid your ransom, I paid your sister's; she was washing dishes, she is ugly, I am good enough to make her my wife, and you still presume to oppose it! If I followed my impulses, I would kill you all over again.

—You may kill me again, said the baron, but you will not marry my sister while I am alive.

3. Knightly assemblies.

CHAPTER 30

Conclusion

At heart, Candide had no real wish to marry Cunégonde; but the baron's extreme impertinence decided him in favor of the marriage, and Cunégonde was so eager for it that he could not back out. He consulted Pangloss, Martin, and the faithful Cacambo. Pangloss drew up a fine treatise, in which he proved that the baron had no right over his sister and that she could, according to all the laws of the empire, marry Candide morganatically.[4] Martin said they should throw the baron into the sea. Cacambo thought they should send him back to the Levantine captain to finish his time in the galleys, and then send him to the father general in Rome by the first vessel. This seemed the best idea; the old woman approved, and nothing was said to his sister; the plan was executed, at modest expense, and they had the double pleasure of snaring a Jesuit and punishing the pride of a German baron.

It is quite natural to suppose that after so many misfortunes, Candide, married to his mistress, and living with the philosopher Pangloss, the philosopher Martin, the prudent Cacambo, and the old woman—having, besides, brought back so many diamonds from the land of the ancient Incas—must have led the most agreeable life in the world. But he was so cheated by the jews[5] that nothing was left but his little farm; his wife, growing every day more ugly, became sour-tempered and insupportable; the old woman was ailing and even more ill-humored than Cunégonde. Cacambo, who worked in the garden and went into Constantinople to sell vegetables, was worn out with toil, and cursed his fate. Pangloss was in despair at being unable to shine in some German university. As for Martin, he was firmly persuaded that things are just as bad wherever you are; he endured in patience. Candide, Martin, and Pangloss sometimes argued over metaphysics and morals. Before the windows of the farmhouse they often watched the passage of boats bearing effendis, pashas, and cadis into exile on Lemnos, Mytilene, and Erzeroum; they saw other cadis, other pashas, other effendis coming, to take the place of the exiles and to be exiled in their turn. They saw various heads, neatly impaled, to be set up at the Sublime Porte.[6] These sights gave fresh impetus to their discussions; and when they were not arguing, the boredom was so fierce that one day the old woman ventured to say: —I should like to know which is worse, being raped a hundred times by negro pirates, having a buttock cut off, running the gauntlet

---

4. A morganatic marriage confers no rights on the partner of lower rank or on the offspring. Pangloss always uses more language than anyone else to achieve fewer results.

5. Voltaire's anti-Semitism, derived from various unhappy experiences with Jewish financiers, is not

the most attractive aspect of his personality.

6. The gate of the sultan's palace is often used by extension to describe his government as a whole. But it was in fact a real gate where the heads of traitors, public enemies, and ex-officials were gruesomely exposed.

in the Bulgar army, being flogged and hanged in an auto-da-fé, being dissected and rowing in the galleys—experiencing, in a word, all the miseries through which we have passed—or else just sitting here and doing nothing?

—It's a hard question, said Candide.

These words gave rise to new reflections, and Martin in particular concluded that man was bound to live either in convulsions of misery or in the lethargy of boredom. Candide did not agree, but expressed no positive opinion. Pangloss asserted that he had always suffered horribly; but having once declared that everything was marvelously well, he continued to repeat the opinion and didn't believe a word of it.

One thing served to confirm Martin in his detestable opinions, to make Candide hesitate more than ever, and to embarrass Pangloss. It was the arrival one day at their farm of Paquette and Brother Giroflée, who were in the last stages of misery. They had quickly run through their three thousand piastres, had split up, made up, quarreled, been jailed, escaped, and finally Brother Giroflée had turned Turk. Paquette continued to ply her trade everywhere, and no longer made any money at it.

—I told you, said Martin to Candide, that your gifts would soon be squandered and would only render them more unhappy. You have spent millions of piastres, you and Cacambo, and you are no more happy than Brother Giroflée and Paquette.

—Ah ha, said Pangloss to Paquette, so destiny has brought you back in our midst, my poor girl! Do you realize you cost me the end of my nose, one eye, and an ear? And look at you now! eh! what a world it is, after all!

This new adventure caused them to philosophize more than ever.

There was in the neighborhood a very famous dervish, who was said to be the best philosopher in Turkey; they went to ask his advice. Pangloss was spokesman, and he said: —Master, we have come to ask you to tell us why such a strange animal as man was created.

—What are you getting into? answered the dervish. Is it any of your business?

—But, reverend father, said Candide, there's a horrible lot of evil on the face of the earth.

—What does it matter, said the dervish, whether there's good or evil? When his highness sends a ship to Egypt, does he worry whether the mice on board are comfortable or not?

—What shall we do then? asked Pangloss.

—Hold your tongue, said the dervish.

—I had hoped, said Pangloss, to reason a while with you concerning effects and causes, the best of possible worlds, the origin of evil, the nature of the soul, and pre-established harmony.

At these words, the dervish slammed the door in their faces.

During this interview, word was spreading that at Constantinople they had just strangled two viziers of the divan,[7] as well as the mufti, and impaled several of their friends. This catastrophe made a great and general sensation for several hours. Pangloss, Candide, and Martin, as they returned to their little farm, passed a good old man who was enjoying the cool of the day at his doorstep under a grove of orange trees. Pangloss, who was as inquisitive as he was explanatory, asked the name of the mufti who had been strangled.

—I know nothing of it, said the good man, and I have never cared to know the name of a single mufti or vizier. I am completely ignorant of the episode you are discussing. I presume that in general those who meddle in public business sometimes perish miserably, and that they deserve their fate; but I never listen to the news from Constantinople; I am satisfied with sending the fruits of my garden to be sold there.

Having spoken these words, he asked the strangers into his house; his two daughters and two sons offered them various sherbets which they had made themselves, Turkish cream flavored with candied citron, orange, lemon, lime, pineapple, pistachio, and mocha coffee uncontaminated by the inferior coffee of Batavia and the East Indies. After which the two daughters of this good Moslem perfumed the beards of Candide, Pangloss, and Martin.

—You must possess, Candide said to the Turk, an enormous and splendid property?

I have only twenty acres, replied the Turk; I cultivate them with my children, and the work keeps us from three great evils, boredom, vice, and poverty.

Candide, as he walked back to his farm, meditated deeply over the words of the Turk. He said to Pangloss and Martin: —This good old man seems to have found himself a fate preferable to that of the six kings with whom we had the honor of dining.

—Great place, said Pangloss, is very perilous in the judgment of all the philosophers; for, after all, Eglon, king of the Moabites, was murdered by Ehud; Absalom was hung up by the hair and pierced with three darts; King Nadab, son of Jeroboam, was killed by Baasha; King Elah by Zimri; Ahaziah by Jehu; Athaliah by Jehoiada; and Kings Jehoiakim, Jeconiah, and Zedekiah were enslaved. You know how death came to Croesus, Astyages, Darius, Dionysius of Syracuse, Pyrrhus, Perseus, Hannibal, Jugurtha, Ariovistus, Caesar, Pompey, Nero, Otho, Vitellius, Domitian, Richard II of England, Edward II, Henry VI, Richard III, Mary Stuart, Charles I, the three Henrys of France, and the Emperor Henry IV? You know . . .

—I know also, said Candide, that we must cultivate our garden.

---

7. Intimate advisers of the sultan. The divan is a council of state; a mufti is an expounder of Mohammedan law. Everyone who takes part in affairs of state, whether civil or religious, dies, sooner or later, an atrocious death.

—You are perfectly right, said Pangloss; for when man was put into the garden of Eden, he was put there *ut operaretur eum*, so that he should work it; this proves that man was not born to take his ease.

—Let's work without speculating, said Martin; it's the only way of rendering life bearable.

The whole little group entered into this laudable scheme; each one began to exercise his talents. The little plot yielded fine crops. Cunégonde was, to tell the truth, remarkably ugly; but she became an excellent pastry cook. Paquette took up embroidery; the old woman did the laundry. Everyone, down even to Brother Giroflée, did something useful; he became a very adequate carpenter, and even an honest man; and Pangloss sometimes used to say to Candide: —All events are linked together in the best of possible worlds; for, after all, if you had not been driven from a fine castle by being kicked in the backside for love of Miss Cunégonde, if you hadn't been sent before the Inquisition, if you hadn't traveled across America on foot, if you hadn't given a good sword thrust to the baron, if you hadn't lost all your sheep from the good land of Eldorado, you wouldn't be sitting here eating candied citron and pistachios.

—That is very well put, said Candide, but we must cultivate our garden.

BACKGROUNDS

Candide is at the same time a novel of abstract ideas with long, complex histories and a highly personal book, into which Voltaire poured an immense amount of himself—his experiences, his enmities, his learning, his desires, his anguish. Two sorts of preliminary background material are therefore pretty much indispensable: one a background of intellectual history, the other a background of personal history. The following section contains materials toward the construction of these two backgrounds. Especially in constructing the background of eighteenth-century philosophical optimism, it is hoped that brief notices of Saint Augustine, the Manichees, Leibniz, Pope, and Bayle, with the major concepts in which they were involved (original sin, the natural goodness of man, the role of evil in the world), will prove useful.

ROBERT M. ADAMS

Summary: The Intellectual Backgrounds

There is no ultimate answer to the question why an omniscient, omnipotent, benevolent God made a world with a great deal of evil in it; but, like most insoluble questions, this one has proved hard for mankind to set aside. It was present to human consciousness long before the eighteenth century, and before the Christian religion itself—an essential part of which is a story designed to answer this very question. The stories of the fall of Satan and of the linked, analogous fall of the human race, growing as they do out of the daily perception of evil in the world, are narratives framed to provide an answer to the query, How did things get this way? But when we phrase the question logically instead of historically, even these answers become subject to question. How did God, omnipotent, omniscient, and good, shape man in such a way that he would fall—without Himself incurring responsibility for that fall? If He had the making of all things, including Satan, and knew when He framed him that immense evil would result—how can He be absolved of the charge of deliberate malice toward His creatures? These are challenges that have confronted every thoughtful Christian believer since the faith began. They are the core of the Book of Job, in which man challenges God's apparent injustice most directly and audaciously.

The orthodox answer to the problem of evil is to assert freedom of the will in God's creatures, to say that He made them (Satan and Adam alike) sufficient to stand but free to fall; therefore the fall is the fault of the creatures and not of the Creator. But a belief in original sin, if it is not to be totally despairing, requires a complementary belief in vicarious atonement (i.e., that Christ's death on the cross atoned at least partially for Adam's fall); it also implies a belief in the existence of a Christian church and the value of its sacraments, a belief in the Last Judgment, and in reward or punishment in an afterlife. A classic expression of this view is Milton's *Paradise Lost*; it is perfectly congruent (so far as these general outlines are concerned) with that found in Saint Augustine's *City of God*.

But in the late seventeenth and early eighteenth centuries another doctrine began to be heard. By analogy with previous heresies, it was sometimes known as "Pelagianism" or "Socinianism"; more often it was called "deism," "rational Christianity," or "natural religion"; it had close affinities with "philosophical optimism" and "systematic idealism." Though differently colored in each of these manifestations, the new assumption which underlay all of them consisted essentially of a tendency to deny or minimize the fall of man. Theologically it tended to resemble modern Unitarianism; but its social application (like that of many other skeptical movements) was strongly conservative. One reason why it is hard to define is its transitional, provisional nature; its exponents were often trying to justify social attitudes like submission and benevolence without recourse to the theological sanctions which had been traditional. They aimed at a secular, social ethic which could be defended "by reason," i.e., without appeal to supernatural revelation, and which would therefore be universal and secure. The consequences for traditional theology were so revolutionary that it is not altogether easy to see why the new tone in philosophy won acceptance as placidly as it did. For if the entire human race did not fall with Adam, then it did not have to be redeemed by Christ, does not have to belong to the true church wherever that may be found, does not have to partake of supernatural faith, will not be judged after death and devoted to salvation or damnation. Perhaps the new mood in philosophy drew tacit support from the great achievements in psychology and physics of John Locke and Isaac Newton. Having explained so much in the universe on the basis of the three laws of motion and the rational understanding of material evidence, people felt more ready to dispense with theological hypotheses. Partly too, no doubt, the way had been cleared for optimism by the great war of sects which accompanied the Puritan revolution. With fifty squabbling sects, all believing in the Bible, all interpreting it differently, and all denouncing one another as heretical, a civilized man could be excused for doubting if any of them knew a safe way to salvation—and if nobody knew, why bother? All parties to the English revolutions of 1640 and 1688 emerged from them relatively disillusioned with, and skeptical of, the social influence of the clergy—doubtful of their social wisdom, contemptuous of their social power. Under the circumstances, the separation of ethics from its previous reliance on theology seems to have appeared a thoroughly prudent and conservative step.

Whatever the reasons, one finds in eighteenth-century Europe increasing readiness to doubt man's fallen condition and to question the absolute need of supernatural revelation or inspired faith. In a familiar metaphor, God is now a remote clock-maker, an artisan or an artist; the natural universe is his masterpiece; and man best fulfills the divine purpose by accepting gratefully, unquestioningly, whatever role has been assigned to him in its operation. He must not set himself up as private judge of the social forms, must not become so inflamed with the private spirit of religious enthusiasm (the pursuit of individual salvation, in other words) that he questions or rebels against the rational arrangements of society. He should submit to the rules of social convenience, even— *especially*—if they inconvenience him, in the full assurance that he is thereby fulfilling the larger will of God as well as that of man. For no religious duties are demanded of him as indispensably necessary to salvation which are incompatible with common sense and the general reason.

Inevitably, this new philosophy of social optimism and rational religion raised afresh the old question of evil. If the universe, or society, was a divinely planned unity, with an overriding welfare of its own to which individual men must conform and submit, one had to be sure it was not malfunctioning. But everyday experience showed that it did malfunction, regularly, horribly—in wars and diseases and natural catastrophes and the daily terrible toll of pointless misery and injustice. What then to do, what to think? It is this central question with which *Candide* (and in fact much of Voltaire's intellectual life) was concerned. Almost all the classic positions in the immemorial debate over the origins of evil are represented in *Candide*—represented, if not endorsed. For the better understanding of the book and its counterpointed ideas there follows a list, in rough chronological order, of these classic positions and their exponents:

1. THE MANICHEES were a sect of heretic Christians, of Near-Eastern origin, with deep pre-Christian roots. They limited the omnipotence of God by proclaiming that He ruled only half the universe. He ruled it, of course, for good, but He was incapable of controlling the operations of the Devil, who ruled, with absolute authority and for his own dark ends, the other half. The Manichees thus disposed of the origin of evil by saying that it had no origin, it had always been there in the original constitution of the universe; and they impugned one of the Christian God's most cherished attributes, his omnipotence. They flourished from the third to the fifth centuries A.D.; their reappearance in modern controversy was largely due to Pierre Bayle—see 4 below.

2. SAINT AUGUSTINE, whose *City of God* was completed in 426, is included here as a representative of orthodox Catholic Christianity; it was his view that God originally created the universe entirely good, but that owing to a spontaneous act of Satan's will evil entered the world. God can, and someday will destroy Satan and evil altogether; meanwhile, however, man with the aid of Christ and His church is to struggle in dubious battle with the forces of darkness and to earn, as a result of his good or evil service, salvation or damnation.

3. BLAISE PASCAL, whose *Pensées* were first published in mutilated form in 1670, eight years after his death, saw the presence of evil in the world as evidence of man's radically flawed nature. Being so faulty, so limited, and so corrupt, man is unable to perceive God's justice in the world, but instead thinks it injustice and evil. Therefore he must believe in an afterlife, where justice will be done and the nature of God's earthly justice will at last be understood. The very desperation of man's condition on earth constitutes a motive for him to believe in a better sphere and the possibility of a clearer vision elsewhere.

4. PIERRE BAYLE in his *Dictionnaire historique et critique* (1697) undertook to argue for religious toleration by showing that theologians had been largely unable to agree among themselves on any single version of the truth. Among the great religious questions which he described as unsolved was that of the origin of evil; having shown how most of the proposed solutions impugned either God's goodness, His intelligence, or His power, he concluded that the question was insoluble, and that the Manichees, who in effect begged it, had come closest to a solution. Bayle was one of the first modern authors to revive Manicheism from its resting-place among the forgotten heresies.

5. GOTTFRIED WILHELM VON LEIBNIZ published his *Théodicée* in 1710; he described the world as organized, according to a preestablished harmonious plan, in a series of ascending "monads" or indivisible unities, of which the highest was God. This system, having been created by the loftiest and most benevolent of minds, must be, taken as a whole, the best of all possible systems; within it, all events are linked by a chain of cause and effect, and what looks to our limited view like evil and injustice will, when the web of cause and effect is unravelled, be found to cause greater compensating goods. Leibniz died in 1716, an unhappy and neglected man; but CHRISTIAN WOLFF (1679–1754), his most energetic and vociferous disciple, though he added nothing to the structure of Leibniz's system, did much to render it popularly accessible.

6. ANTHONY ASHLEY COOPER, THIRD EARL OF SHAFTESBURY, whose works were collected in three volumes under the unpromising title *Characteristics of Men, Manners, Opinions, and Societies* (1711), discounted all metaphysics and supernatural dogmas, but disliked also a certain cold, selfish pursuit of interest which he thought was inculcated by Thomas Hobbes and Locke. Instead, he tried to elaborate a system of virtue founded on natural principles and dedicated to benevolence. Suspicious of religious enthusiasm and enthusiasts, he invoked an earnest but somewhat vague optimism regarding the power of man to derive a "moral sense" from his natural instincts. Since Shaftesbury saw human nature as naturally good and naturally attuned to God, it followed that for him the world is "governed, ordered, or regulated for the best by a designing principle or mind necessarily good and permanent." In other words, he agreed with Leibniz's conclusions without knowing his arguments.

7. BERNARD MANDEVILLE published in 1704 and 1715 a *Fable of the Bees* in rough, witty doggerel verse; the second edition added a prose commentary which directly attacked Shaftesbury's doctrine of the "moral sense," arguing instead that man is inherently vicious and selfish, and that most virtues are simply well-disguised and publicly-approved vices. We note with edification that as soon as morality is rooted in the ways of the world, clever rascals like Mandeville become better casuists than men of high-minded good will like Shaftesbury.

8. HENRY ST. JOHN VISCOUNT BOLINGBROKE was an English grandee and statesman who during the 1720s, after his return from exile in France, began to philosophize in the vein of a Shaftesbury somewhat toughened by reading Mandeville. His own work is languid and textureless, and he is best known for his influence on Pope's *Essay on Man*, much of which was written in consultation with him. Too skeptical to build a "system," he thought sensible men could reach all the truth they needed by studying natural religion without the help of the clergy. They would thus arrive at the religious view which all sensible men share (total skepticism) and which they are too sensible ever to admit.

9. ALEXANDER POPE, in his poem *Essay on Man* (1733–34), emphasized the duty of man to "submit" because "whatever is is right" and everything which seems like "partial evil" is really "universal good." In Pope's poem the principle that nature must contain a plenum, or full range of creatures from the lowest to the highest, no longer serves merely to justify the existence of creatures with various imperfections; it bears witness to God's surpassing excellence, which could only have been manifested in the full diapason of the creatures. But for man as he finds himself the lesson of submission is explicit; he cannot ask (judging matters according to his lowly "scale of sense") for greater powers or more commodity, lest he disturb the order of the universe and cast doubt on the workings of Providence. The disasters which occasionally afflict him are caused by general laws, beneficent in their overall character, at whose working in specific instances he must not repine. In asking that things be differently and more conveniently arranged, man reveals himself a creature of madness, pride, and impiety; for, given his necessary degrees of blindness and weakness, things in general are quite as good as they can be.

10. JEAN-JACQUES ROUSSEAU addressed his "Letter on Providence" to Voltaire (August 18, 1756) in response to Voltaire's poem on the Lisbon earthquake. Rousseau argued that God was not to blame for natural disasters like the earthquake, or for the presence of evil in the world. Man has brought many misfortunes on himself by crowding into cities when he should have been living naturally and safely in the country. Indeed, says Rousseau, there may have been individuals in Lisbon to whom sudden death was a blessing in disguise. In any event, Providence works, not for the benefit of this or that individual, but through general laws to which we must reverentially submit.

11. THE MARQUIS DE SADE comes too late, historically, to influence Voltaire (most of his work was published in the 1790s), but he supplies one clear terminus of the argument over evil. He accepts the two fundamental dogmas of the age, that evil exists in the world and that God is all-powerful, but he draws the unwelcome conclusion which everyone had been trying to dodge: *therefore* God is malignant and brutish, and the way for man to serve Him is to imitate Him by being as natural, as

cruel, and as vicious as possible. With a single stroke of thought, de Sade escaped all the tensions of two incompatible beliefs. It would be interesting to compare him with William Blake, who also, and at the same time, but to very different effect, stood the eighteenth-century world on its head by asserting that Satanic energy was good and divine conformity evil.

VOLTAIRE

Well, Everything Is Well†

I beg of you, gentlemen, explain for me this phrase, *all is well*, I don't understand it.

Does it mean, *everything is arranged, everything is ordered,* according to the laws of moving bodies? I understand, I agree.

Or do you mean by it that everyone is well off, that he has the means of living well, that nobody suffers? You know how false that is.

Is it your idea that the lamentable calamities which afflict the earth are good, in relation to God, and please him? I don't believe this horrible idea, nor do you.

So please, explain this phrase *all is well*. Plato the philosopher deigned to allow God the freedom of creating five worlds, for the reason, as he said, that there are only five regular bodies in geometry: the tetrahedron, cube, hexahedron, dodecahedron, and icosahedron.[1] But why restrict divine power in this way? Why not allow him the sphere, which is even more regular, and even the cone, the pyramid with various faces, the cylinder, and so on?

God chose, according to Plato, the best of possible worlds. This concept has been embraced by various Christian philosophers, though it seems repugnant to the doctrine of original sin; for our globe, after that transgression, is no longer the best of globes; it was before, and could be again, but now plenty of people think it the worst of worlds instead of the best.

Leibniz, in his *Theodicy*, took the part of Plato. Many a reader has complained of being able to understand one no more than the other. For our part, having read both of them more than once, we avow our ignorance, according to our custom; and since the Evangelist has re-

† Voltaire's essay appeared under the title "Bien, Tout est Bien" as an entry in the *Dictionnaire Philosophique* (1764). This large collection of Voltaire's miscellaneous thoughts had been many years in the gathering; it contained mostly articles of religious or philosophical interest, with of course

a strong leaning toward skeptical rationalism. Translation by Robert M. Adams.
1. In Plato's *Timaeus*, for reasons that the present editor undertands no better than Voltaire, these five geometrical forms are said to be the building blocks of the universe.

vealed nothing to us on this score,[2] we remain without regret in our shadows.

Leibniz, who speaks of everything, has spoken of original sin as well; and as every man with a system gets into his scheme everything that contradicts it, he imagined that man's disobedience to God, and the shocking evils which ensued, were integral parts of the best of worlds, necessary ingredients of the highest possible felicity. *Calla calla señor don Carlos; todo che se haze es por su ben.*[3]

What! to be driven out of a delightful garden where one could have lived forever if one hadn't eaten an apple! What! to give birth in anguish to miserable and sinful children, who will suffer everything themselves and make everyone else suffer! What! to experience every sickness, feel every grief, die in anguish, and then in recompense to be roasted for eternity! This fate is really the best thing possible? It's not too good for us; and how can it be good for God?

Leibniz sensed there was nothing to be said in reply; and so he made big fat books in which he confused himself.

A denial that evil exists: it can be made in jest, by a Lucullus[4] in good health, who is eating a fine dinner with his friends and his mistress in the hall of Apollo; but let him stick his head out the window, he'll see miserable people; let him catch a fever, he'll be miserable himself.

I don't like to quote—it's a prickly job at best, for one leaves out what precedes and follows one's chosen passage, and thus lies exposed to a thousand complaints. But I must cite Lactantius, father of the church, who in Chapter XIII of his treatise *On the Wrath of God* makes Epicurus talk in this fashion:[5]

---

2. The Evangelist is no doubt St. John, who wrote the book of Revelation. Short of divine inspiration neither Plato nor Leibniz can be understood.
3. The first eight paragraphs of the article as printed in the text were compressed in a later edition into the following passages:

"It made a great noise in the schools and even among thinking people, when Leibniz, paraphrasing Plato, constructed his edifice of the best of all possible worlds and imagined that everything was for the best. He asserted, in the north of Germany, that God could make only a single world. Plato had allowed Him at least the liberty of making five, because there are only five solid regular bodies: tetrahedron, or pyramid with three faces and an equal base: cube, hexahedron, dodecahedron, and icosahedron. But as our world isn't in the shape of any one of the five bodies of Plato, one ought to allow God a sixth way of building it.

"Let's leave the divine Plato there. Leibniz, who was certainly a better geometrician and a more profound metaphysician, did the human race this service, of letting us see that we should be very contented, and that God could not do any more for us; that he had necessarily chosen, among all the possible options, the best one conceivable.

" 'What happens to original sin?' they asked him. 'Let it look after itself,' said Leibniz and his friends; but in public he wrote that original sin necessarily entered into the best of possible worlds."

The earlier version is reprinted in the text because it makes livelier reading. The quotation in Spanish means "Peace, peace, señor don Carlos; everything which is being done is for your good": it no doubt comes from one of a dozen or so dramas inspired by the insanity and death of unhappy Don Carlos, prince of Asturias and son of Philip II (1545–68).
4. Lucullus was a famous Roman gourmand who retired from the ungrateful demands of public service to cultivate the richer possibilities of food and drink.
5. Epicurus is the Greek philosopher who placed the true end of life in pleasure; Lactantius, a Church father known as "the Christian Cicero," wrote his treatise *On the Wrath of God* in the early fourth century. Voltaire's skepticism was more erudite than the faith of most true believers.

Either God wants to remove evil from the world and cannot;
or he can and does not want to; or he cannot and does not
want to, either one; or else, finally, he wants to and can. If
he wants to and cannot, that is impotence, which is contrary
to the nature of God; if he can and does not want to, that is
malice, which is equally contrary to his nature; if he neither
wants to nor can, that is malice and impotence at the same
time; if he wants to and can (and this is the only one of the
alternatives that is consistent with all the attributes of God),
then where does all the evil of the world come from?

The argument is pressing; and Lactantius gets out of it very awkwardly,
by saying that God wishes the evil but that he has given us the wisdom
to acquire good. The answer, it must be confessed, is less potent than
the objection, for it supposes that God could give wisdom only by
producing evil; and thus, what a pleasant wisdom we have!

The origin of evil has always been a pit of which nobody could see
the bottom. This is what reduced so many philosophers and legislators
to positing two principles, one good and the other bad. Typhon was the
bad principle for the Egyptians; Arimane for the Persians.[6] As is known,
the Manichees adopted this theology; but as they never had conversations
with either the good principle or the bad, one needn't take it on their
word.

Among the absurdities with which the world is choked, and which
one can include among our evils, it is not a trifling achievement to have
predicated a pair of all-powerful beings fighting over which of the two
should put most of himself into the world, and making a treaty like
Molière's two doctors: let me have the emetic, and you can have the
bleeding-cup.[7]

After the Platonists, Basilides pretended in the first centuries of the
church that God had allotted the making of our world to his latest angels
and that they, not being very skilful, made things as we see them. This
theological fable crumbles to dust before the terrible objection that it is
not in the nature of an omnipotent, omniscient Deity to have a world
built by architects who don't know their trade.

Simon,[8] who felt the force of this objection, tried to forestall it by
saying that the angel who supervised the workshop is damned for botch-
ing his work; but burning that angel does us no good.

The Greek story about Pandora meets the objection no better. The

---

6. Typhon, a mythical monstrous deity usually
represented as a crocodile, was held responsible for
the death and dismemberment of his brother the
good Osiris; Arimane was the principle of darkness
in the Zoroastrian philosophy, who opposes Mazda
or Ormuzd, the god of light.

7. The Molière play in question is *L'Amour Mé-
decin*. Basilides was a subtle Alexandrian Christian
of the second century, and a celebrated gnostic.
8. Voltaire's knowledge of that shadowy figure Simon the Samaritan probably came from Irenaeus's
treatise *Against the Heretics*, 1.23.

box in which all the evils are hidden, and at the bottom of which rests hope, is a charming allegory; but this Pandora was made by Vulcan only to be revenged on Prometheus, who had formed a man from clay.[9]

The Indians have not succeeded either. God, having created man, gave him a drug to keep him healthy forever; the man loaded the drug on his donkey, the donkey got thirsty, the serpent told him of a spring, and while he was drinking, the serpent took the drug for himself.

The Syrians imagined that when man and woman were created in the fourth heaven, they decided to eat a cake instead of the ambrosia which was their natural diet. The ambrosia they could exhale through their pores; but after eating the cake, they had to go to the toilet. Man and woman together asked an angel where were the facilities.—Look ye, says the angel, see that little planet down there, no bigger than a minute, some sixty million leagues from here? That's the privy for the whole universe; now get there right away.—So they went, and were left there; and that's why, ever since, our world has been what it is.

Of course you can ask the Syrians why God let man eat the cake and allowed such a swarm of evils to follow from his doing so.

I pass quickly from this fourth heaven to Lord Bolingbroke, to keep from being bored. This man, who no doubt had a great genius, gave the celebrated Pope his idea for "all is well," which can be found word for word in the posthumous works of Lord Bolingbroke, and which Lord Shaftesbury had formerly inserted in his *Characteristics*. Read in Shaftesbury the chapter on the Moralists, and you will find these words:

> Much is alleged in answer to show why Nature errs, and how she came thus impotent and erring from an unerring hand. But I deny she errs. . . . 'Tis from this order of inferior and superior things that we admire the world's beauty, founded thus on contrarieties, whilst from such various and disagreeing principles a universal concord is established. . . . The vegetables by their death sustain the animals, and animal bodies dissolved enrich the earth, and raise again the vegetable world. . . . The central powers, which hold the lasting orbs in their just poise and movement, must not be controlled to save a fleeting form, and rescue from the precipice a puny animal, whose brittle frame, however protected, must of itself soon dissolve.

Bolingbroke, Shaftesbury, and Pope, who gave their ideas a shape, resolve the question no better than their predecessors; their *all is well* means nothing but that all is directed by unchangeable law. Who doesn't know that? You teach us nothing when you tell us, what every little

9. Prometheus's stupid brother Epimetheus opened the box that Zeus gave Pandora—with deplorable results, to be read in the world around us.

child knows, that flies are born to be eaten by spiders, spiders by swallows, swallows by shrikes, shrikes by eagles, eagles to be killed by men, men to kill one another, and to be eaten by worms and then by devils—at least a thousand of them for every one who meets another fate.

There, now, is an order, neat and regular, among the animals of every species; there is order everywhere. When a stone forms in my bladder, it's an admirable mechanism; various chalky deposits assemble in my blood, pass through my kidneys, descend the urethra, and deposit themselves in my bladder, assembling there in an excellent demonstration of Newtonian attraction.[1] The pebble forms, grows, I suffer pains a thousand times worse than death, through the most elegant arrangement in the world. A surgeon, having perfected the art invented by Tubal Cain,[2] comes to stick a sliver of sharp steel through my perinaeum; he grasps the stone in his pincers, it breaks under the pressure by a necessary mechanism, and by the same necessity I die in horrible torments. All this is well, it is all the evident consequence of unalterable physical principles, I agree; and I knew it just as well as you did.

If we were insentient beings, there would be nothing to say to this physics. But that's not the question; we ask you if there are not sensible evils, and if there are, where they come from. Pope says in his Fourth Epistle, There are no evils; if there are private evils, they compose the universal good.[3]

This implies a remarkable definition of private, including the stone, the gout, all the crimes, all the sufferings of mankind, death, and damnation.

The fall of man is the plaster we put on all these individual maladies of soul and body which make up the general health. Shaftesbury and Bolingbroke dared to attack original sin directly; Pope doesn't talk about it; but it is clear that their system undermines the very foundations of the Christian religion, and explains nothing at all.

Yet this system has since won the approval of several theologians who cheerfully accept contradictions; and in fact one shouldn't grudge anyone the consolation of accounting as he can for the flood of evils that overwhelm us. It's only fair to let men who are desperately sick eat whatever they want. Some have gone so far as to pretend that the system is consoling. God, says Pope,

> sees with equal eye, as God of all,
> A hero perish, or a sparrow fall;
> Atoms or systems into ruins hurled,

1. I.e., the law of gravity (very loosely speaking).
2. Tubal Cain was the world's first metalworker, Genesis 4.22.
3. The passage Voltaire paraphrases partially and inaccurately must be this one:
   "What makes all physical or moral ill? / There deviates nature, and here wanders will. / God sends not ill; if rightly understood, / Or partial ill is universal good, / Or change admits, or nature lets it fall, / Short, and but rare, till man improved it all" (Essay on Man 4.111–16).

And now a bubble burst, and now a world.
Essay on Man, 1. 87–90

Here, I confess, is a pleasant consolation; don't you find great comfort in Lord Shaftesbury's remark that God isn't going to disturb his eternal laws for a miserable little animal like man? But you must grant this miserable little animal the right to exclaim humbly and to seek, as he exclaims, why these eternal laws are not made for the well-being of each individual.

This system of *all is well* represents the author of all nature as a potent, malicious king, who never worries if his designs mean death for four or five hundred thousand of his subjects, and poverty and tears for the rest, as long as they gratify him.

Far from consoling, the *best of all possible worlds* doctrine is a doctrine of despair for those who embrace it. The question of good and evil remains an insoluble chaos for those who seek in good faith for an answer; it's a joke only for those who debate over it, they are slave-laborers who play with their chains. As for thoughtless people, they are like fish carried from a river to a tank; they don't suspect that they are there only to be eaten next Friday. Just so, we too know nothing at all, by our unaided powers, of the causes of our destiny.

Let us put, at the end of almost all these chapters of metaphysics, the two letters that Roman judges used when they couldn't understand a case: NL, *non liquet*, it's not clear. Let us above all impose silence on the rascals who, even as they are overwhelmed, like the rest of us, by the sheer weight of human calamity, add to it the furious rage of calumny. Let us confound their execrable impostures by appealing to faith and Providence.

Some logicians have pretended that it isn't in the nature of the Being of all beings that things should be other than they are. It's an audacious assertion; I don't know enough even to dare examine it.

GUSTAVE LANSON

Voltaire at *Les Délices* and at Ferney†

Philosophers have to have two or three underground burrows to escape
from the dogs that chase them.

Tavernier . . . , asked by Louis XIV why he had chosen a home in
Switzerland, answered as you know: *Sire, I very much wanted to have
something which belonged just to me.*[1]

It was with much these feelings that Voltaire, escaped from Berlin and
thoroughly scarmentado,[2] leased at Monrion, on the slope between
Lausanne and the lake, a winter-house well protected from the cold
north wind. And for the summers, he acquired, at a price of 87,000
francs, a property near Geneva, at Saint-Jean, which he named *Les
Délices*; from it, he could see at a glance "Geneva, the lake, the Rhône,
another river [the Arve], some fields, and the Alps."[3] A little later, as
Monrion had neither garden nor adequate heating, he rented at Lausanne, for nine years, a large and comfortable house, with fifteen front
windows looking out over the lake and the Alps of Savoy.

A delightful sense of ease and well-being pervaded his spirit. He looked
with charmed eyes on the elegant yet grandiose landscape of lake and
mountains; before the beauty of the Alpine countryside he recalled, with
unaccustomed enthusiasm, the heroic stories of Swiss liberty. He was
exalted nearly to lyricism.

But he did not fall to dreaming. Action caught him up, as soon as
he felt himself safe. He built, planted, and gardened at *Les Délices*. He
had his six mares serviced—vainly, alas—by a too-elderly Danish stal-
lion. He gave dinners to all the most distinguished company of the
district; he received all the notable travelers who came through Lausanne
and Geneva—Palissot, Lekain, Mmes. d'Epinay and du Bocage, the
English philosopher Gibbon, the Italian Jesuit Bettinelli. He took great
pains to disavow *La Pucelle*,[4] overwhelmed his secretary Collini with

---

† From Gustave Lanson, *Voltaire* (Paris, 1906).
Translation by Robert M. Adams. Lanson's note
gives the following references: Longchamp et Wagnière, *Mémoires sur Voltaire et ses ouvrages*, 1825,
2 vols.; Desnoiresterres, V–VIII; Perey et Maugras,
Voltaire aux Délices et à Ferney, 1885; Maugras,
Voltaire et Jean-Jacques Rousseau, 1886; L. Fois-
set. *Voltaire et le Président de Brosses*, 1858; H.
Tronchin, *Le Conseiller François Tronchin et ses
amis*, 1895; E. Asse, *Lettres de Mmes. de Graffigny, d'Epinay, Suard*, etc. (sur leur séjour auprés
de Voltaire), 1878: *Zeitschrift für franz. Spr. und
Litt.* (Stengel, "Lettres de Voltaire et de Mme. de
Gallatin au Landgrave de Hesse-Cassel"), 1887,
vol. VII; *Revue de Paris*, 1905 (H. Jullemier).

1. Moland XXXIX, 198; Besterman 6519. [All references are to the Moland edition of the *Complete
Works* (Garnier, 1877–85); all cross-references to
the Besterman edition of the *Correspondence*, are
by the editor.]
2. From the hero of Voltaire's novel of the same
name; embittered and disillusioned, Scarmentado
settles down, is married, cuckolded, and happy.
Used in the sense here of "back from one's travels
and rather disillusioned by them" [*Editor*].
3. Moland XXXVIII. 390; Besterman 5640.
4. Published in 1755, this poem was Voltaire's
most disastrous failure to estimate public taste; it
is a bawdy, mock-heroic poem about Joan of Arc
[*Editor*].

dictation and copying chores, reworked his *Essai sur les moeurs*, wrote a Chinese tragedy,[5] disputed with Providence and Leibniz over the Lisbon disaster, deplored the war which broke out in 1756, made up with the king of Prussia while still keeping one fang bared for him, tried to take a hand in peace negotiations, wrote to England on behalf of Admiral Byng, took service with the *Encyclopédie*, exchanged insults with Grasset, squabbled with Haller,[6] went to visit the Elector Palatine, bemoaned the Margrave of Bayreuth, prodded d'Alembert into writing for the *Encyclopedia* an article on "Geneva" full of praise for reasonable Christianity, the pure deism of the modern Calvinists, and then urged him to refuse the Genevan pastors the retraction which, for political or pious reasons they demanded.

The storm which blew up over the article on "Geneva" gave him pause for reflection. Gradually he came to sense the incompatibilities of temper and outlook between himself and the Genevans.[7] The Magnificent Council forbade the citizens and merchants to take part in, or even attend, theatrical performances at Voltaire's residences; Voltaire himself was told not to sponsor a playhouse within the borders of the Christian republic. He evaded the ruling by "playing the actor" in his house at Lausanne, or at Monrepos, estate of the Marquis of Gentil. But at Lausanne still other points of Calvinist zeal disturbed him.

He returned then to French soil. He bought, in the district of Gex a half-hour from Geneva, the estate of Fernex (he always wrote it Ferney, as it is pronounced); and he rented for life, from the Président de Brosses, the estate of Tournay. This time he was safe on all sides, with his forefeet, as he said, at Lausanne and Geneva, and his back feet at Ferney and Tournay. He could erect his stages at Ferney, and especially at Tournay, in his lobby, defying the Magnificent Council, the Consistory, and all the preachers; and if the sky looked dark over Paris or Versailles, a short ride on horseback would put him over the border, thumbing his nose at the ministry, the Parlement, and the church. Only once, in 1766, after the death of the Chevalier de la Barre,[8] was he seriously scared, and indulged the momentary fantasy of going off to found a colony of philosophers, a "truth factory," with a printing press in the country of Cleves which belonged to the king of Prussia.

After 1760, he resided ordinarily at Ferney, where he had built up a

---

5. *L'Orphelin de la Chine* (1755) [*Editor*].

6. François Grasset was an irresponsible bookseller and printer, who put out an inopportune collection of Voltaire's polemics; Albert von Haller, a botanist and philosopher of some distinction, was understood to have supported Grasset against Voltaire's demands for drastic punishment [*Editor*].

7. Geneva had received, under John Calvin in the sixteenth century, the tone of austere sobriety and prudence which it still, in part, retains. By the eighteenth century most of the persecuting and some of the censorious tendencies of the city had

melted away, but the Consistory of preachers and the Magnificent Council of city fathers kept an eye out for evidences of flagrant scandal—in close proximity to which they usually discovered M. de Voltaire [*Editor*].

8. A young man of Abbéville, the Chevalier de la Barre was accused with four others of mutilating a crucifix. He was convicted, tortured, and executed July 1, 1766; a copy of the *Philosophical Dictionary* was found in his library and burnt with his corpse [*Editor*].

splendid establishment. His fortune was immense and steadily increasing. He had investments in trade, in banks,[9] at Cadiz, Leipzig, and Amsterdam. But he generally placed his liquid capital in annuities, at such profitable rates as would make his old age comfortable and keep his "complexion clear."[1] Among his debtors were noblemen of France and princes of Germany, marshal Richelieu, the Elector Palatine, and the Duke of Wurtenburg; though often careless about their payments, they were men who wound up paying in the end, with whom one lost no more than one would with Jews and bankers, and who atoned for the lateness of their payments with publicity and protection. Voltaire's bookkeeper told Collé in 1768 that his employer had 80,000 francs in annuities, 40,000 francs in income from real estate, and 60,000 francs in portfolio investments. In 1775 an authentic summary mentions 177,000 francs of income, over and above 235,000 of liquid assets.

Expenses at Ferney were enormous. The manor built by Voltaire was small but elegant. The staff was considerable; over and above the regular residents, on days when a play was produced, supper was served to sixty or eighty special guests. In 1768, after an energetic reform of his household, Voltaire established the budget for Ferney at 4,000 francs a year, for the support of a dozen horses and sixteen persons.

Habitual guests at Ferney were fat Mme. Denis,[2] who spent her time arguing and making up with her uncle,[3] the faithful secretary Wagnière, who succeeded Collini, and to whom were added, in 1763, the copyist Simon Bigex, and Father Adam, a Jesuit whom Voltaire picked up to play chess with. From 1760 to 1763, it was the great granddaughter of Pierre Corneille, little dark Marie, ugly but with big beautiful black eyes, whom he raised and supplied with a dowry;[4] later, Mlle. de Varicourt, "beautiful and good,"[5] to whom he gave no dowry because the Marquis de Villette, who married her, was rich and needed no more money.

Always some visitor was in residence at Ferney, for weeks or months; it might be the other niece, Mme. de Fontaine, with the Marquis de Florian, her second husband, and pretty little "Florianet." Or it was cousin Daumart, musketeer to the king, or supple Ximenès, or little LaHarpe and his wife, or poor Durey de Morsan, after his ruin.[6] It

9. Moland XXXVIII. 189; Besterman 5071.

1. *Memoirs of Collini.*

2. Asse, *Lettres de Mme. de Graffigny*, etc., p. 263.

3. Moland XXXVIII, 186–87; Besterman 5067.

4. Fréron, with his usual gift for malignant insinuation, spread dark rumors about the fate of Mlle. Corneille; but in fact she was the idol of the household at Ferney, and the patriarch himself took time out from his furious schedule of work to correct her themes. Pierre Corneille (1606–84) was the great French dramatist of an earlier age; when Voltaire learned that the family was in misery, he adopted little Marie [*Editor*].

5. Voltaire's nickname for her was "Belle et Bonne" [*Editor*].

6. Durey de Morsan was a ne'er-do-well of good family, whom Voltaire salvaged from the scrap heap and housed for a while; LaHarpe was the critic and poet, who could get along with no one else, but knew Voltaire as "papa grand homme"; while the Marquis of Ximenès, though he had stolen a MS from Voltaire and been driven from the house for it, re-established himself with a set of satiric letters on the *New Heloïse*. Does not this little group of damaged derelicts remind one of Candide's collection? [*Editor*].

might be the Duc de Villars, passionately devoted to the tragic stage.[7] A crowd of Genevans made themselves at home with Voltaire, coming and going continually between town and Ferney; they were like members of his family, rather than friends. All the Tronchins, the household of Rilliet, the two Cramers, Mme. Gallatin, Huber the clever snipper of silhouettes which sometimes infuriated the patriarch; and let's not forget "Monsieur the fornicator" Covelle.[8]

And what visitors, of every class, of every nation! Voltaire was a European curiosity, whom one simply had to see. Ferney was the spot to which free spirits and sensitive hearts made pilgrimage. Through its doors filed D'Alembert, Turgot, the Abbé Morellet, the royal musician and *valet de chambre* Laborde, the Chevalier de Boufflers, Chabanon, Grétry, the Englishmen Sherlock and Moore, the prince of Brunswick, the Margrave of Hesse, Mme. Suard, the Marquis de Villette—and so many more, one would never finish naming them.[9] It was a declaration of principles and a personal affront when the Count of Falkenstein, one day to be [the Holy Roman Emperor] Joseph II, chose *not* to go out of his way to visit Ferney.

Some of the visitors have left their impressions. They allow us to see this lean old skeleton with the sparkling eyes, wrapped in his blue dressing-gown, or else, on special days, in his full dress suit of reddish-brown velvet, with a huge wig, and lace at the wrists falling to his fingertips; cleanly, erect, dry, quick, abstemious, taking only a few cups of coffee with cream; always perishing of some ailment, always taking medicine, working in bed part of every day and receiving visitors there; very much the lord of the manor, conscious of his rights and his honors, a landowner to the bottom of his soul, proud of his buildings, his plantings, his herds, his church, eager to close a deal for the sale of watches or silk stockings made in his factories; lordly and gracious with the friends and vassals who celebrated his birthdays with triumphal arches, fireworks, and adulatory verses; always wild for the theater, for poetry, and for wit, a delightful talker with the gift of charming gaiety; but capricious, fantastic, irritable, a despot; generous to all who cajoled him, stingy or tricky with anyone to whom he took a dislike; peddling a hunting knife at an outrageous price, or going to law with the Président de Brosses over a few sticks of wood, which he was enraged to have to pay for; a haggler and petty bargainer, greedy and intriguing in all affairs involving Geneva;

7. Unimportant son of a famous father, the duc de Villars was not even a good actor; Voltaire once said drily he played an impassioned rôle "like a duke and a peer of the realm" [*Editor*].

8. Something of a simpleton. Covelle was summoned before the ecclesiastical court at Geneva on charges of fornication, and condemned to beg pardon on his knees. He admitted the fact but refused to perform the public act of contrition; and for his successful act of defiance (in which he was abetted by Voltaire), he became as it were a household pet at Ferney under the title of "M. le fornicateur." All the servants announced him in this sonorous way, to whatever company; and Voltaire wrote a mock-heroic poem about his story, *The Civil Wars at Geneva* [*Editor*].

9. For all these characters and their relations with Voltaire, see Gustave Desnoiresterres, *Voltaire et la Société au XVIIIe Siècle*, in eight volumes [*Editor*].

and mad to make fun of everyone, always being bitten and biting back, dragging after him a whole swarm of enemies to whom he added at his pleasure, Fréron, La Beaumelle, Chaumeix, the Pompignans, Nonnotte, Patouillet, Larcher, Cogé;[1] never at rest, always wanting to have the last blow, whether with words or deeds, a diabolical torturer of unhappy Jean-Jacques[2] whom he would cheerfully receive in his house, blackening at every opportunity the name of the great Montesquieu,[3] whom he had defended during his lifetime, an unwearied prober after the weak spots of those he detested and sometimes of those he did not detest; not always malicious against those whom he withered under his deadly sarcasms, often reconciled by an advance or a bit of fair dealing, and so making up with Trublet, with Buffon;[4] without rancor, even against the friends or disciples who betrayed him, who robbed him, so long as they did not brag of it; at war with the parish priest and the bishop, and highly amused to talk them into giving him absolution unintentionally;[5] not a mean man at heart, nor a stingy one; indulgent, liberal, generous to his nieces and Marie Corneille; and hospitable, rescuing, protecting, and encouraging I know not how many people; reconciling Champfleur the younger with his father, paying for the journey of a little Pichon or the marriage of a pregnant daughter in the same way as he conducted the campaign for Calas[6] or the war against Fréron; a Paris street urchin, a brat spoiled to the absolute limit, all self-esteem and nerves, and never, in his follies, doing anyone else as much harm as he did himself.[7]

From his little kingdom at Ferney he exchanges truths and claw-scratches with Frederick, whom he knows down to the ground, and who knows him; he trades philosophy and compliments with the Empress Catherine, who perhaps pulls the wool over his eyes a bit in the matter

1. Fréron we have seen before, an implacable, malicious, and skilful publicist, who never missed a chance to wound or insult Voltaire. LaBeaumelle had criticized "The Century of Louis XIV," Larcher "The Philosophy of History." Patouillet wrote as an avowed polemicist for the Society of Jesus; the Pompignans, Jean-Jacques a nobleman and Jean-Georges a bishop, were ardent supporters of the church and enemies of the philosophers. Chaumeix, Nonnotte, and Cogé were miscellaneous volunteer enemies of Voltaire. M. Charles Nisard has described, in a well-populated volume, *Les Ennemis de Voltaire* (Paris, 1853) [*Editor*].

2. Jean-Jacques Rousseau.

3. Distinguished eighteenth-century philosopher, author of the *Lettres Persanes* and *Esprit des Lois*.

4. The abbé Trublet had simply said that Voltaire's epic poem on Henri IV, the *Henriade*, made him yawn; with Buffon, the celebrated naturalist, Voltaire's quarrel was even more trifling.

5. Banned from the sacraments by the bishop of

Annecy for a burlesque sermon on theft delivered from the pulpit of "his" church (it bore the inscription *Deo Erexit Voltaire*, Voltaire Built it for God), Voltaire took cruel revenge. He feigned mortal illness, and by a series of bluffs, threats, bribes, pretences, and bullyings, extorted from the parish priest an absolution for his sins to which he was not entitled and in which he did not believe. This whole game against the clergy was played in a spirit of malicious irreverence deeply humiliating to the churchmen involved [*Editor*].

6. Jean Calas, a Protestant merchant of Toulouse, was hideously tortured and executed in 1762 for a crime he did not commit; religious prejudice was largely responsible. Voltaire undertook to rehabilitate his good name, and in 1765, after a vigorous and skilful campaign in which many people were involved, the sentence was revoked [*Editor*].

7. See *Lettres de Mme. de Graffigny*, pp. 247–483, and Bibliothèque Nationale manuscript 12 285, the notebook of Voltaire, especially p. 21.

of Poland.[8] He flirts with all sorts of kings and princes. He engages in political dalliance with the court of France; he flatters and teases the Pompadour[9] during her lifetime, without suspecting the incurable wound he inflicted with a passing phrase in the dedication of *Tancrède*. He draws what he can from his old and uncertain friend, Marshal Richelieu, as also from the passing parade of ministers; he repays them lavishly in adulation: Babet the flowergirl—that is, Cardinal Bernis— the Duc de Choiseul, the Duc D'Aiguillon, Maupeou, and finally Turgot, the real minister after his heart, and the only one for whom his compliments were never insincere.[1] Of all of them he asked not only protection, favors for himself, for Ferney, and for the philosophers; he wanted reforms, encouraged them, and supported them whenever they were attempted.

That is the spectacle which, from *Les Délices* and Ferney, for twenty-three years, Voltaire displayed to a Europe alternately enthusiastic and scandalized, but always amused. For twenty-three years he succeeded in this miracle, of being the news of the day, of providing the last word, comic or serious but always unexpected, which filled the public ear. His Easter duties and his indigestions, *Tancrède* or *La Pucelle*, the adoption of Marie Corneille, a letter to the king of Prussia, the dismissal or return of Mme. Denis, a generous effort in behalf of Calas or LaBarre, a salvo of malicious jokes on LaBeaumelle or Jean-Jacques, all the flowers of good sense and humanity, all the stenches of filth and impiety—he was capable of all this; and of this amazing mixture he emitted something every day, and never the same thing two days in a row. For twenty-three years, Voltaire's was the noisiest toy trumpet in Europe.

No doubt noise was agreeable to him and popular applause necessary. He never worried if there was a little contempt in the laughter of the gallery; he had never donned the stiff armor of moralism, the shell of dignity which makes the vainest and most ambitious of men preserve the postures of decorum. Having the glories of wit and beneficence, he did not disdain those won by contortions and grimaces. But in all his harlequinades he had his idea, which never quitted him any more than his self-esteem. He wanted to improve the social order. After 1755, and above all from 1760 to his death, one may say he never wrote a single page which did not criticize an abuse or propose a reform, which is not

8. Empress Catherine II (the Great) of Russia was a German adventuress who, after many lofty philosophic professions of liberalism, ruthlessly partitioned Poland with the help of Frederick (also the Great) in 1772 [*Editor*].
9. Madame de Pompadour was the mistress of Louis XV, but also the most influential and best informed of his ministers. Voltaire had said "If some censorious person disapproves of the homage I render you, he must have been born with a hard,

ungrateful heart." Some poison-pen letter writer at court told Mme. de Pompadour that the mere supposition implied disrespect, and she believed it [*Editor*].
1. Of these various ministers of Louis XV, the duc de Choiseul and Turgot were the most consistently sympathetic to the party of the philosophers. Cardinal Bernis was known as "Babet la Bouquetière" because of some dainty verses he had indiscreetly made in his youth [*Editor*].

an appeal to the government or the public against one and for the other. At eighty years of age, he was as violent in his feelings as at sixty. One must be blind with prejudice not to sense the profound and disinterested conviction which lies behind his principal attitudes.

He had returned from Germany at the moment when the enlightened nation, despairing at last of the king and the court, was becoming impatient before the problem of social evil; when the war-machine of the *Encyclopédie*,[2] around which free thought organized itself into a party, was just being mounted; when, alongside the old religious factions (Jansenists and defenders of the bull *Unigenitus*)[3] groups of men were forming with the intention of expanding enlightenment and contributing to the general welfare—philosophers, economists, *patriots*; when all the individual voices of reason and liberty were certain of rousing widespread echoes in every state and province; when men who had the gift of expression felt themselves more and more lifted to the forefront by it, drawn by the crowd which was ready to hear them.

The forces of conservatism were powerful; more than the court, irregular and erratic, the Sorbonne and the Parlement of Paris opposed to "reason" a resistance of which the principal episodes were the condemnation of the thesis of the Abbé of Prades (1752), the condemnation of *L'Esprit des Lois* (1758), the condemnation of *Emile* (1762), the suppression and suspension of the *Encyclopédie* (1752 and 1758), and the censure of *Bélisaire* (1767).[4]

Voltaire threw himself furiously into the fight. He is "the man who laughs at all the trifling stupidities and tries to correct those which are cruel."[5] Disillusioned himself, he wanted to disillusion other people; and he boiled with impatience at the idea that progress might well take two or three hundred years to achieve.[6] He fought, by no means heroically, but stubbornly, seeking to obtain the maximum results with the minimum risk. He knew the terrain as well as the enemy, and showed himself a wonderful tactician.

He knew that neither immunity nor tacit permission was to be expected. Underground printing, in France or abroad, and above all in Geneva, saved him the bother of dealing with censors, but it brought

---

2. The immense project of writing a new encyclopedia of human knowledge, which originated with a cartel of Paris booksellers, brought together all the liveliest pens in France, and provided a rallying-point for the party of the *philosophes*. But if it was actually a war-machine (the phrase was originated by Desnoiresterres), the *Encyclopédie* was such a cumbersome, many-handed, ill-directed machine that a full and adequate history of its operation has yet to be written. Voltaire's relations with the apparatus have been studied by Raymond Naves, *Voltaire et l'Encyclopédie* (Paris,

1938) [*Editor*].
3. Clement XI promulgated this bull on September 8, 1713; it declared heretical more than a hundred doctrines [*Editor*].
4. In all these controversies the party of repression was the Church, particularly the Jesuit wing of it, acting against the "philosophes" and their friends. For a compact history of these events, see Léon Cahen, *Les querelles religieuses et parlementaires sous Louis XV* (Paris, 1913) [*Editor*].
5. Moland XLIII, 104; Besterman 10830.
6. Moland XXV, 344, 318; Besterman XXVI, 95.

close to him all the dangers of smuggling and dealing fraudulently in forbidden merchandise. Serious punishments were decreed for authors, booksellers, and traffickers in forbidden books. The latter were almost the only ones ever caught, and for these poor devils it was chains, the galleys, and the branding-iron. The writer who got himself caught might be let off with a humiliating retraction; but it would have been imprudent to count on this resource.

Voltaire took cover. His position on the border, supplemented by anonymity, pseudonyms, and categorical denials of authorship, kept him safe. Formal justice paused before denials which never deceived the public and often amused it.

To block the men of ill-will and prevent the *lettres de cachet*[7] which were always possible, to ensure a free circulation for his pamphlets, he cultivated friendships at court—Bernis and Choiseul, Richelieu, Villars, and LaVallière—and made use of them to cool off the zeal of their subordinates. He scarcely needed Malesherbes, director of the Louvre library and the censorship; but he tried to stand well with police lieutenants, postal inspectors, district supervisors, and undersecretaries. The postal official Damilaville, first secretary of the twentieth precinct, maintained for some years a correspondence with Ferney as one of the curiosities of the postal service. Finally, Voltaire had as accomplices the entire public, all travelers returning from abroad, the ambassadors and their staffs, the officers of the army, who arrived at Paris with suitcases full of Voltaire's "scandal-sheets"[8] even before "the man named Huguet and the woman known as Léger"[9] had received their supply for clandestine distribution.

As long as he had the public on his side, he was sure to get around all the spiritual and temporal powers. And this public, he knew how to get hold of it; a public intelligent and fickle, inquisitive and sophisticated, whom one trifle would displease and another trifle amuse, a public with a narrow and delicate taste, with a short attention-span, which one must constantly catch and intrigue. Every single day for twenty-three years he served up to it the sauce of wit, satire, jokes, and smut with which it was necessary to season his ideas.

Above all, he wrote clear, short, and quick. No more big works. Little twelve-page tracts, leaflets a couple of pages long. "Twenty volumes in folio," he said, thinking of the *Encyclopédie*," will never make a revolution; it's the little pocket-volumes at thirty cents apiece that have to

---

7. *Lettres de cachet* could be obtained from the king, upon presentation to him of a grievance or an alleged grievance; the recipient was ordered forthwith to jail, house arrest, or exile. No process of law protected the victim [*Editor*].

8. Gustave Lanson, "Quelques Documents Inédits" in *Annales de la Société Jean-Jacques Rous-*seau, I (Genève, 1905), 129.

9. Huguet and Léger, denominated in contemporary police papers as suspected distributors of subversive books, were respectively a bookseller living in the Temple and the wife of a bookbinder living in the Rue Chartière [*Editor*].

be watched. If the New Testament had cost 4,200 sesterces, the Christian religion would never have taken root."[1] These "little pot-pies," these portable scandal-sheets, easy to read, and continuously exciting, came out of the factory at Ferney for twenty-three years; they emerged in all forms, on all subjects, in verse, in prose, dictionaries, stories, tragedies, diatribes, extracts on history, literature, metaphysics, religion, the sciences, politics, legislation, Moses, snails, Shakespeare, and notes written by a gentleman. In reality, dearly as he prized the arts of literature and poetry, they became nothing more for him than a means to an end. Tragedies and verses served to hasten the spread of his ideas.

He repeated himself, he went over the same ground again and again. He was aware of it, and started the same old ideas on still another round. For he knew that ideas enter the public mind only by dint of repetition. But the seasoning must be varied, to prevent disgust; and at that art he was a past master.

He has all the qualities, with many of the faults, of the journalist, above all the gift of the immediate, and the penetrating voice which carries and fixes our attention through the noisy confusion of life. But it is not enough to say Voltaire is a journalist; all by himself he is a journal, a great journal. He does the whole thing himself, the serious articles, the spot-reporting, the gossip column, the funny-papers, the crossword puzzles. He is a journal, but also a review, an encyclopedia; all the jobs of popularization, propaganda, polemic, and information fall together in his hands. This quick old man is a whole press, a complete popular library.

Finally, by means of his innumerable letters, which reached people of every rank and every nation—the king of Prussia, the Empress Catherine, German princes, Russian or Italian gentlemen, English thinkers, ministers, courtiers, provincials, judges, comedians, abbés, men of letters, administrators, merchants, lawyers, women of the world—by these thousands of letters, of which there is not so to speak one which does not contain a compliment to the addressee's self-esteem, a joke for his amusement, and a thought for him to mull over, Voltaire interested I know not how many individuals in the success of his propaganda. He made them carriers, voluntary and uncontrollable, of his ideas. He strengthened, he doubled, by means of his correspondence, the effect of his pamphlets.

1. Moland XXXXIII, 520; Besterman 12362.

HAYDN MASON

[Gestation: *Candide* Assembling Itself]†

[Monsieur Lanson's enchanting picture of Voltaire's little *"metairie"* (farm) at Ferney—busy and prosperous, playful yet disciplined, cozy and intimate yet engaged in a vast semiclandestine conspiracy—had yet another aspect. In those hundreds of letters that Voltaire dispatched all across Europe, he accumulated (almost surely without realizing it) phrases and formulas and turns of thought that after lying dormant in his mind would emerge coated with crystals of Voltairean wit and anger to form part of *Candide*. Whether this material amounted in the end to a private language addressed to a special group of Voltairean *initiés* may be debated; the case is proposed by Geoffrey Murray in *Voltaire's Candide: The Protean Gardener*, published as volume 69 (1970) of *Studies on Voltaire*. Without getting into that argument, one can say that the materials assembled by Mr. Mason clearly demonstrate the inchoate preexistence of the book in Voltaire's mind and imply its assemblage, more abrupt than gradual, into the sparkling coherence we know. Where Mason does not do so, I have translated into English the French materials cited in the body of the text.]

* * *

Let us return to an examination of Voltaire's own attitudes as they evolved in the period immediately preceding *Candide*. That *conte*,[1] considered by general consent to be Voltaire's masterpiece, is a kind of summation of Voltaire's views in the late 1750s on the human condition, beset by suffering and wickedness yet not wholly without scope for initiative and improvement. This is not the place for an analysis of Voltaire's tale; but no biography of the *philosophe* can reasonably neglect a close look at the way his mind came to absorb and shape materials from the world around him and from his own reading. Such a consideration, involving as it does a careful review of detailed, even minute, matters, inevitably calls for a certain rigour of attention; yet without it we cannot hope to understand very much about the genesis of Voltaire's greatest work.

As we have seen, the news of the Lisbon earthquake in 1755 played an important rôle. Voltaire's immediate reaction is one of horror: 'One hundred thousand ants, our neighbours, crushed all of a sudden in our ant-heap, half of them perishing doubtless in inexpressible anguish.' The sole consolation is that the Jesuit Inquisitors of Lisbon will have disappeared with the rest. That, concludes Voltaire, should teach men not to persecute men, 'for while a few confounded rascals are burning a few fanatics the earth is swallowing up both' (D6597, 24 November [1755]).[2] Already the ironic perspective that informs Chapter VI of *Can-*

---

† From *Voltaire* (London, 1975) 79–92. Reprinted by kind permission of Curtis Brown Ltd., London.
1. For a formal definition of the distinctly informal term *conte*, see below, p. 129.

2. D preceding a number indicates the position of a letter in the immense Besterman edition of Voltaire's correspondance.

dide on the Lisbon auto-da-fé has been glimpsed. Such expressions of horror resound through letters of succeeding days. The very size of the catastrophe is 'a terrible argument against Optimism' (D6605). Confronted by it, Voltaire feels his own problems shrink to such petty dimensions that he is ashamed of them (D6605, 6607). This attitude is somewhat reminiscent of the way his hero Zadig in an earlier *conte* had forgotten his own miseries in contemplation of the infinite heavens. But there is a sombre difference; Zadig's vision was sublimely consoling, whereas Voltaire's merely confirms the awful destructiveness latent in physical nature.

It is clear that the *Poème sur le désastre de Lisbonne* constituted an almost instinctive response. However, less attention has been paid to the fact that once the poem is completed Voltaire's attitudes are swiftly transmuted into a rather different stance. In a letter to the Protestant pastor Allamand on 16 December 1755 he writes: 'I pity the Portuguese, like you, *but men do still more harm to each other on their little molehill than nature does to them.* Our wars massacre more men than are swallowed up by earthquakes. If we had to fear only the Lisbon adventure in this world, we should still be tolerably well off' (D6629: my italics). Two new notes are struck. Despondent alarm at the earthquake has given way to a more detached attitude; and the physical evils of the universe are set in a context in which man's wickedness to man, particularly in wars, looms far greater. Even in his very first letter after learning of the earthquake (D6597) he had, as we saw, found space to think also of the persecutions inflicted by the Inquisitors. It is this kind of consideration which, with more time for reflection, becomes paramount. Physical suffering, it is true, is a sufficient refutation of the belief that 'all is well'; but the true horror lies in the spectacle of what men do to one another. The same evolution of attitudes can also be glimpsed in the *Poème sur le désastre*, which begins with the actual catastrophe at Lisbon but then opens out onto a wider scene in which 'tout est en guerre.'[3]

Reasons to support this new-found awareness that war is the supreme evil were soon to be sadly abundant in the world around. On 29 August 1756 Frederick the Great invaded Saxony, thereby precipitating the Seven Years War. It accords well with Voltaire's darkening mood. In early 1756 he had passed from specific concern with the Lisbon earthquake to a more general brooding on the problem of evil. He tells Elie Bertrand (another of the Genevan clergy) in February that the myth of the Fall of Man, whether Christian or otherwise, is more reasonable in human terms than the Optimism of Leibniz and Pope, which beneath the disguise of a consoling name simply removes all hope: 'if *all is well*, how do the Leibnizians admit of a better?' (D6738: author's italics) It is the fatalistic quality of Optimism that is so cruel, for it invites man to

3. Everything is at war.

acquiesce and therefore give up all striving for improvement. As we have seen, in the desolate picture Voltaire paints of the human condition, he allows man one single consolation: hope. Otherwise, the pessimism is general, and indeed increasing in the author's view of the world. He begins to become more interested in Manichean beliefs, according to which evil has a life of its own quite independent of the forces of good in the universe. A letter to Mme du Deffand in May 1756 talks of Jupiter's two casks, one for good and another, bigger, for evil. Not only does he pose the basic question—Why so? More daringly, he wonders whether the evil cask could have constructed itself. Here are the seeds of an outlook voiced in *Candide* by the self-styled Manichean Martin.

However, this increasingly sombre view of the world does not relate to a personal crisis as is sometimes claimed. Apart from worries over such matters as the widespread circulation, despite his efforts to the contrary, of his notorious mock-epic *La Pucelle*, Voltaire is by and large happily established in Geneva. Les Délices has needed some improvements and from the early weeks he is busy planting, furnishing, building. Claude Patu, a visitor in autumn 1755, speaks wonderingly of Voltaire's vigour: 'Imagine, together with the air of a dying man, all the fire of first youth, and the brilliance of his attractive stories!' Never has one seen better fare or more engaging manners; the whole of Geneva is delighted to have him there and is doing all it can to keep him (D6562). The picture, in short, is not far short of idyllic. True, Voltaire looks like a corpse, as another visitor confirms (D6646). But the sense of returning vitality and purpose flows from the correspondence as it must have done at the dinner table. In 1758 Mme d'Epinay was also to find the *philosophe* full of gaiety and cheerfulness (D7704). Even the references to ill-health become less common. Voltaire has found 'a port after weathering so many storms' (D6842). To Thieriot he makes the touching confession that he is writing about the sufferings of his fellow-men out of pure altruism, for 'I am so happy that I am ashamed of it' (D6875, 27 May [1756]).

Yet this state of personal contentment in no way precludes a total divorce with the philosophy of Optimism, and from its outset the Seven Years War is invoked as a decisive refutation (e.g., D7001). To his friend the Duchess of Saxe-Gotha, who is to find herself in the thick of the battle, he never ceases to point up the absurd horror of it all, using the War polemically to express disagreement with her adherence to Optimism (e.g., D7023). To his more intimate acquaintance Thieriot, he voices an attitude of indifference: 'Happy is he who lives in tranquillity on the edge of his lake, far from the throne, and far from envy' (D7028). To the duc de Richelieu, also a friend but more distant as being of high rank and politically influential, another side appears. Richelieu being in charge of the larger of the two French armies, Voltaire turned to him to advocate his invention of an armed chariot which, he reckoned, would kill many Prussians, indeed would knock out everyone it met, so that two of the machines would be enough against a battalion and squadron combined (D7043, 7293). This particular notion (which the French Government did not take up) should of itself dispose of two long-standing myths about Voltaire: that he was a total pacifist, and lacked all sense of patriotism. Generally pacifist in outlook, he nevertheless was forced to accept the realities of preparing a military defence against the aggression of Prussia on land and the British at sea. Both countries fill him with consternation, though for rather different reasons.

He is appalled by the desolation wrought by Frederick's armies in central Europe, once they had won the decisive engagement at Rossbach on 5 November 1757. But prior to that he had been moved by compassion for the Prussian King, who had intimated that he was contemplating suicide (D7373). Voltaire replied in urgent tones dissuading him from such a course, pointing out that it would dismay his supporters and give joy only to his enemies. Instead, Frederick should seek an honourable peace (D7400), show he is a *philosophe* and live for all the good things still remaining to him: possessions, dignities, friends (D7419). A further plea follows on 13 November (D7460). Ironically, it is written after Rossbach, which is Frederick's contemptuous reply to Voltaire's advice (the King had already expressed his scorn in a letter to his sister Wilhelmina, D7414, Commentary). The news of that Prussian victory reverses Voltaire's attitude. A despairing Frederick gains immediate access to his warm sympathy. Yet at the same time he is hoping for revenge over Frederick for the humiliating moment at Frankfurt when four bayonets had menaced Mme Denis, and he is disappointed when Frederick triumphs (D7471). His feelings towards the Prussian King are as strongly ambivalent as ever. Richard Phelps, a British visitor at this time, acutely observed: 'He was the most inconsistent, whenever he talked of the King of Prussia.'

By contrast, Voltaire's views on the British Navy are unequivocal. He fears their superior numbers (D7210) and wants to see their piratical ways punished (D7491). The British were exercising a direct influence upon Voltaire's life. Not only were they likely by their hostile actions and blockades to cause the price of sugar to rise (D7131, 7901). They were, more gravely, capturing French vessels in which the writer had considerable investments, especially the fleet sailing from Cadiz (D5719), and at times the Cadiz mercantile trade was to give him much cause for concern (e.g., D6811). Besides, the British Government had provided one of the more signal instances of horrible folly during the Seven Years War by the execution of Admiral Byng for failing to relieve Minorca against the duc de Richelieu's forces at Port-Mahon in May 1756. Voltaire and Richelieu had both intervened on Byng's behalf in the court-martial following the engagement, but to no avail; Byng was sentenced on 27 January 1757 to be shot, the sentence being carried out on 14 March. André-Michel Rousseau, providing a comprehensive account of the affair, sees it as Voltaire's baptism as champion of the oppressed. This time he was to gain nothing, save the achievement of making Byng, through his appearance in *Candide*, far more famous in death than he ever was in life and of turning the ironic remark that he had been executed 'pour encourager les autres'[4] into one of the very few phrases from French literature to have gained a proverbial currency in the English language.

After the outbreak of the Seven Years War, Voltaire's sense of the absurd aspect of warfare evolves considerably. Tales in that vein from the Duchess of Saxe-Gotha (D7040) might have heightened that impression, just as the Byng episode undoubtedly did. By February 1757 the acid tones of *Candide* are evident in a letter to the Englishman George Keate when Voltaire writes à propos of Byng: 'Your sailors are not polite', going on: 'If you want to see some fine battles, Germans killed by Germans and a few towns pillaged, it is up to you to enjoy this little entertainment in the spring' (D7162). In June 1757 the same spirit of sarcasm appears in a letter to the Duchess of Saxe-Gotha. There would be much unhappiness, he tells her, if the warring armies did not destroy at least fifty towns, reduce some fifty thousand families to beggary, and kill four or five hundred thousand men. 'We cannot yet say "All is well" but it is not going badly, and with time Optimism will be conclusively proven' (D7297).

In early 1757, then, the essential tone of *Candide* is already present in Voltaire's mind. Other details too are beginning to appear in his letters. The final destination of Candide and his little band in the garden outside Constantinople is already foreshadowed in March 1757, when Voltaire cites a comparison between the view he has over the lake from Lausanne with a similar outlook in Constantinople (D7213). The writer who had drawn this parallel, so suggestive to Voltaire's imagination, was the seventeenth-century explorer Jean-Baptiste Tavernier, who had travelled widely in the East before retiring to Switzerland not far from Voltaire's house in Lausanne. Louis XIV had been offended that Tavernier had settled in Switzerland, to which he had replied that he wanted to own something that belonged entirely to him. Not surprisingly, Voltaire felt a kinship with this earlier Frenchman who had also shaken the dust of France from off his feet in order to find genuine independence; he adds that 'I am finishing up as he did' (D7215). One sees here a complex interweaving of elements. Lausanne view = Constantinople view, thanks to Tavernier. As Voltaire is retired and free outside France, so too Candide in his final retreat in Turkey. Whether yet consigned to paper, the lineaments of the *dénouement* to the *conte* are all mentally in place by March 1757.

On 26 October 1757 Voltaire laments the death of Patu, who had

---

4. To encourage others.

visited him two years before. His obituary notice is simple and touching: 'il aimait tous les arts, et son âme était candide' (D7434).[5] Thus appears our hero's name. When Voltaire introduces it at the beginning of the *conte* the conjunction is much the same: 'Sa physionomie annonçait son âme . . . on le nommait Candide'.[6] A vital step in the creation of the *conte* is prefigured here. Shortly afterwards on 9 November 1757 Thieriot is writing to Voltaire saying that they are as ignorant as 'des souris dans un vaisseau de l'intention de ceux qui le conduisent' (D7456).[7] This, as we have seen, is not the first time the image has come to Voltaire's mind, as he had himself used a similar expression to Frederick in 1736. But Thieriot probably refreshed Voltaire's memory at a crucial moment, and his influence is seen in one of the most trenchant observations in *Candide* about divine Providence: 'Quand Sa Hautesse envoie un vaisseau en Egypte, s'embarrasse-t-elle si les souris qui sont dans le vaisseau sont à leur aise ou non?'[8]

Another important detail is added to the genesis of Voltaire's *conte* at the end of November 1757 when he receives a letter from the Margravine of Bayreuth describing the battle of Rossbach. She wrote:

> Cette armée [i.e., prussienne] . . . fut rangée en ordre de bataille sur une ligne. Alors l'artillerie fit un feu si terrible que des Français . . . disent que chaque coup tuait ou blessait huit ou neuf personnes. La mousqueterie ne fit pas moins d'effet. Les Français avançaient toujours en colonne pour attaquer avec la baïonnette . . . L'infanterie . . . fut taillée en pièces et entièrement dispersé.
>
> (This [Prussian] army was drawn up in battle order along a line. Then the artillery laid down such a terrible barrage that Frenchmen say . . . each shot killed or wounded eight or nine people. The musketry was no less efficacious. The French were still advancing in columns to attack with the bayonet . . . The infantry . . . were cut to pieces and totally scattered.
>   (D7477)

This must surely be at the origin of Voltaire's account in *Candide* of the battle between the Bulgares and the Abares:

> Rien n'était si beau, si leste, si brillant, si bien ordonné que les deux armées. . . . Les canons renversèrent d'abord à peu près six mille hommes de chaque côté; ensuite la mousqueterie

5. He loved the arts, and his soul was candid.
6. His features admirably expressed his soul . . . they called him Candide.
7. as ignorant as mice in a ship of the intentions of those controlling her.
8. When His Highness sends a ship to Egypt, does he worry whether the mice on board are comfortable or not?

ôta du meilleur des mondes environ neuf à dix mille coquins
qui en infectaient la surface. La baïonnette fut aussi la raison
suffisante de la mort de quelques milliers d'hommes.

(Nothing was as beautiful, as sprightly, as well ordered as the
two armies. . . . The cannon first of all knocked over about
six thousand men on either side; next the musketry removed
from the best of worlds around nine to ten thousand rascals
who were infecting its surface. The bayonet was also the sufficient cause of the deaths of a few thousand men.)

The order of details is the same: the military line-up, the artillery,
musketry, bayonet. Voltaire simply transforms an honest and poignant
account into a display of ironic brilliance. The rôles are similarly dis-
tributed in both passages, and the overall effect of utter devastation is
the same. But at Rossbach only the French were routed. It is part of
Voltaire's strategy to ensure that both sides in his absurd and horrible
battle are shot to pieces. The Margravine is able to offer further help a
week later when writing to Voltaire about the starving soldiers who have
fled after the defeat at Rossbach and are now wandering about everywhere
(D7483). This time the impact upon *Candide* is less impressive, but it
is true that Candide too flees without direction and runs out of food.

Such are the details that have begun to accumulate by the beginning
of December 1757. At the turn of the year the number of parallels
increases strikingly. Voltaire's bitter memory of the Frankfurt incident
where his niece had 'Four bayonets . . . in the stomach' (D7521) is
renewed, as we have noticed, after Frederick had triumphed at Rossbach.
This may be the starting point for the knife wound which the heroine
of the *conte* Cunégonde receives in the side (Chapter VIII) or the account
of her disembowelling by Bulgarian soldiers (Chapter IV). Voltaire ad-
vises the Genevan clergy not to react to the *Encyclopédie* article 'Genève':
'Que faut-il donc faire? Rien, se taire, vivre en paix . . .' (D7536, 27
December [1757]).[9] The similarity is close with the dervish's brusque
reply to Pangloss, who wants to know the truths of metaphysics: 'Que
faut-il donc faire? dit Pangloss.—Te taire, dit le derviche.'[1] In January
1758 Voltaire is telling the Duchess of Saxe-Gotha that Prussians and
the like are 'the children of the evil principle' (D7554); we see here a
further premonition of the Manichean Martin in *Candide*, who believes
that God has abandoned this world to some evil being and cites war as
one of his strongest arguments for believing so. At the same time Voltaire
is working on his history the *Essai sur les moeurs*. The topics to which
he specifically refers include the English colonies in America and the
Jesuits in Paraguay (D7559). Both enter into the make-up of *Candide*,

9. What to do then? Nothing, keep quiet, live in   1. 'What shall we do then? asked Pangloss.—Hold
peace . . .   your tongue, said the dervish.'

Paraguay directly (Chapter XIV) and the State of Pennsylvania in the disguise of Eldorado (Chapter XVIII), that Utopia where, as in Pennsylvania, there are no judges, doctors or priests. Just as, in Eldorado, the natives build a machine 'pour guinder [to hoist]' Candide and his companion Cacambo out of Eldorado, so too does Voltaire on 26 January 1758 use the same somewhat uncommon verb in writing that 'we would hoist' a visitor over the mont Cenis to Turin if he should wish to pass by Geneva (D7603).

On 8 January 1758 a reference to the efficient manoeuvres of Frederick's troops, including 'le pas redoublé [at the double]' (D7565), compares with the well-drilled Bulgar in *Candide* who also knew how to 'doubler le pas' (Chapter II). Reference to the auto-da-fé recurs in a letter of 12 January (D7579). On the 15th mention is made of the mosques in Constantinople, as too of the Sultan's officers with the exotic title of 'azamoglans' (D7584); Cunégonde's brother is sent to the galleys for being found bathing with 'un jeune icoglan', and Pangloss for making advances to a pretty girl in a Constantinople mosque (Chapter XXVIII). On 29 January Voltaire sympathises with d'Alembert's problems over the *Encyclopédie*, adding that his colleague is a victim of the publishers: 'Vous avez travaillé pour des libraires' (D6708). So too in *Candide* has Martin suffered, and acquired his gloomy outlook on life, as the 'pauvre savant qui avait travaillé dix ans pour les libraires . . .'[2] Just as the 'Protestant ministers' of Surinam persecute Martin because they take him for a Socinian, so too d'Alembert suffers persecution because his article 'Genève' had suggested that the Genevan pastors were Socinian. On 12 February Voltaire writes that the War is a labyrinth from which one can hardly escape except over dead bodies, and he expresses regret that the nations must fight so ruinously for 'quelques arpents de glace en Acadie [a few acres of ice in Acadia]', a reference to the battles between the French and English in North America (D7630). Candide leaves his own battle by crossing over heaps of dead (Chapter III), while Martin represents Voltaire's feeling of folly that England and France are at war for 'quelques arpents de neige vers le Canada'.[3] The next day Voltaire compares working on the *Encyclopédie* to rowing in the galleys (D7632); this latter occupation is what we find Pangloss and Cunégonde's brother doing near the end of the *conte*. Finally, Voltaire refers on 3 March to 'La canaille de vos convulsionnaires'[4] when writing of the odious Jansenist fanatics who went into convulsions (D7660); 'la canaille convulsionnaire' is known to Martin also.

These details, by their nature fragmentary, need to be assembled if one is to obtain a comprehensive view of Voltaire's state of mind during the period between late October 1757 and early March 1758. His letters,

2. poor scholar who had worked ten years for the booksellers . . .

3. a few acres of snow near Canada.

4. The rabble of your convulsionaries.

we can see, are full of allusions that are taken up, often without any virtual reworking, in *Candide*. The *conte* must have been taking shape in his mind during those months. More specifically, the passages cluster around certain areas of the story: the opening, and particularly the battle; the Eldorado episode; the appearance of Martin soon afterwards; and the concluding sections in and around Constantinople. Equally interesting, direct echoes of *Candide* more or less vanish from Voltaire's correspondence after the beginning of March 1758 and do not reappear until he pays a visit to the Elector Palatine at Schwetzingen four months later.

This visit, which takes him away from Geneva in July 1758 for about five weeks, appears to coincide with a change in Voltaire's mood that has not been sufficiently noted by his biographers. Until his departure he had led a relatively contented existence. A visitor to Geneva just before he left remarks on how he seemed younger, happier, healthier than before his stay in Prussia (D7784). But even so, a period is coming to an end in Voltaire's life. The disappointments with the Genevan clergy have had their effect and he wishes to leave the territory where they hold sway. The search is on once more to find a property which combines the maximum of security and independence. He thinks of Lorraine, which he had last seen at the time of Mme du Châtelet's death; as he writes to Saint-Lambert from Schwetzingen, he would like to place himself under the protection of King Stanislas (D7795). But though the latter appears to have been personally sympathetic to the proposal, he was well aware that he could not afford to sanction it without first seeking the approval of his son-in-law Louis XV (cf. D7787). The latter was to reply in August to Stanislas, clearly intimating his coolness on the matter (D7787, Commentary); and Voltaire thereafter was to look elsewhere for a home.

The visit to Schwetzingen, reluctantly undertaken, was made apparently with business in mind in order to invest money for optimum benefit. Perhaps Voltaire's maritime losses through the activities of the British Navy had made the excursion indispensable. However, the journey permitted him also to sound out a number of influential people about returning to Lorraine or France, and this in the end may have been the more important reason. Whatever the precise motives, it is clear that uncertainty about his future has re-entered Voltaire's life. For a period he is transported back to the climate of insecurity that prevailed during the years immediately preceding installation at Les Délices. Hopes of a return to Paris flicker briefly, and for that he is willing to do obeisance to the French King (e.g. D7762). But the nomadic life no longer brings him any pleasure at all. Although well fêted at Schwetzingen, he is also miserable and lonely. One of his letters to Mme Denis[5] is a *cri de coeur* such as has not been heard in his correspondence

5. His niece but also his mistress.

for some years: 'No letters from you, it is heart-breaking, it is abominable. I write to you daily, and you abandon me. I have never missed you so much and never been so angry with you' (D7803). It is the eloquent complaint of a man homesick for Les Délices and above all for the one person there whose company is essential to him.

Was *Candide* elaborated under such unhappy circumstances? Did Voltaire perhaps take with him a sketch, drafted out some months before, such as we now know preceded the composition of *L'Ingénu?* If so, he had probably written at least some sections in greater detail, as we have seen. But the composition of *Candide* may essentially date from the visit, when ample leisure time would have been available for it. It seems quite possible, as Voltaire's secretary appears to have made the first copy of the *conte* while at the château, the author then presenting it to his host. But the work was not necessarily finished even then, and one biography of Voltaire recounts an incident, which must remain unverifiable, to the effect that it was completed in three days' concentrated work back at Les Délices. However, Schwetzingen would seem to mark an important milestone in the genesis of the tale. When Voltaire wrote to Countess Bentinck in mid-August on his return journey that he had much to tell her when he saw her, adding that 'notre roman est singulier' (D7825)[6] he may well have been referring obliquely to *Candide* as much as to personal experiences. At any rate, the phrase he uses: 'nous re-prendrons le fil de nos aventures [we shall pick up the thread of our adventures]' is echoed by Voltaire's observation in *Candide* about Cu-négonde's narration of her own troubles: 'Elle reprit ainsi le fil de son histoire.'[7]

Unless *Candide* were virtually finished before Voltaire's visit to Schwetzingen, which appears unlikely, one must view it as written not simply in a state of ambivalent feelings about Paris and Geneva nor as a work of detached irony by a happy man but as the composition of someone who was once more plunged into despairing gloom. When he returned to Geneva he received definitive news from d'Argental that Mme de Pompadour had declared him *persona non grata* at Court. Besterman rightly notes: 'it is from this moment that can be dated his spiritual severance from his fatherland' (D7836, Commentary). A gen-uine sadness prevails in this letter, betokening the same kind of personal vulnerability as he had shown at Schwetzingen regarding Mme Denis. The buoyancy which had been uppermost even when he was deploring the horrors of the War has vanished. Comments are more direct, less ironic: 'tout le monde est ruiné. . . . Ah quel siècle!' (D7842, 2 September 1758). 'Quel triste siècle' (D7846, 3 September 1758); 'Le nauf-rage paraît universel' (D7848, 5 September 1758). To the theme of shipwreck is added the despairing note: 'Une planche, vite . . . !' (D7839,

---

6. Our story is unusual.   7. So she took up the thread of her tale.

2 September 1758).[8] It is the dark mood of the Lisbon storm, when the one selfless man in *Candide,* Jacques, is drowned, while the sailor who murdered him swims to safety (Chapter V).

One general factor must also not be overlooked in this pessimism. Voltaire is disheartened by the decline of French prestige and influence in the world. Concern is often expressed about cultural and military affairs together, as in a letter to d'Argental in March where he bewails the fact that since the battle of Rossbach 'everything has been in decline in our armies, as in the fine arts in Paris' (D7676). The *philosophe* had long been persuaded that *belles-lettres* in France were degenerating and that the French were living on past credit. This kind of comment proliferates in 1758. Voltaire notes that every French play now is hissed in Europe (D7836). The observation about living off the glory of the previous century returns in a letter where the author links together a series of charges against the French: a shortage of talent in every field; a profusion of writings on war, the navy and trade, yet French ruin and defeat on land and sea; a plethora of mediocre minds who possess a little wit, but not a genius anywhere; persecution and calumny as the lot of any man of merit who appears in France (D7846). Voltaire's professed response is to turn his back on all these lamentable happenings and enjoy the asylum he has discovered. But the very intensity of his reactions indicates a man who once again feels the need to be *engagé,* even if as yet he has no clear idea whether or how he will achieve. When he eventually undertook negotiations to buy the Châteaux of Tournay and subsequently of Ferney, both just outside Geneva on the French-Swiss border, was his only idea, as he put it to the vendor of Tournay (President de Brosses), 'to die perfectly free' (D7871)? Or did he already have some inkling of what his new life would bring?

Be that as it may, the depressed tones of August and early September are closely related to the search for a new home. Voltaire approached de Brosses about Tournay on 9 September (D7853). A month later he has bought that château and, more important still for his future life, is about to buy the one at Ferney (D7896). He has taken a new decision, to renounce urban life (D7936). The tone of contentment begins to return to the correspondence. To his friend Formont he writes: 'I do not know of any situation preferable to mine' (D7888, [*c.* 3 October 1758]). True, he protests perhaps too much in his fulminations against a Paris that he can no longer hope to see; but elsewhere, too, the sense that the life of philosophers is much better than that of kings (D7936) and that he can now cultivate his garden in tranquillity (D7943) emerges clearly.

Thus far one might say that Voltaire is merely repeating in 1758 the search previously undertaken in 1755. But a remarkable letter of 18

8. the whole world is ruined. . . . Ah, what an age!—What a gloomy age.—The shipwreck seems universal.—A plank, quickly!

November, the importance of which Besterman has rightly stressed, marks the beginning of a new and final period in Voltaire's life. He has been inspecting his new estate at Ferney and finding that there is more involved than the cultivation of plants. He has acquired peasants who depend on him. What is the state of the community? Half the land lies fallow, the *curé* has celebrated no marriages in seven years, the countryside is depopulated as people rush to nearby Geneva. Taxation (especially the salt-tax) destroys those who remain; either the peasants pay and are reduced to abject poverty, or they evade payment and are clapped in jail. 'It is heart-breaking to witness so many misfortunes. I am buying the Ferney property simply in order to do a little good there. . . . The prince who will be my liege lord should rather help me to drag his subjects out of the abyss of poverty, than profit from his ancient feudal rights ['du droit goth et visigoth des lods et ventes']⁹ (D7946, 18 November 1758).

This is a new voice in Voltaire's letters. We have seen how many times he had sought to intervene on the social or political scene and been frustrated. Here at last the right opportunity in time and place comes to hand. By acquiring seigneurial rights he is freer, he says, than when he possessed only his house in Lausanne and his 'country cottage [guinguette]' in Geneva, where the people were 'a little arrogant' and the priests 'a little dangerous'; Ferney and Tournay have added 'deux grands degrés'¹ to his happiness (D7976). The rôles of 'maçon' and 'jardinier'² which he has long since arrogated to himself are now supplemented by a new one: 'seigneur' (D7985). Once again, as in 1755 (D6214), he claims that he is becoming a patriarch (D7970); this time the claim will have a firmer grounding. Already before he is even installed at Ferney he has taken up the cudgels against the *curé* of Moëns, who is the malefactor extorting moneys from Voltaire's peasants and forcing them to sell their own lands. His appeal to the diocesan bishop at Annecy (D7981, 16 December 1758) marks the beginning of a long campaign against the priest.

This note of social concern enters into *Candide*, but only just. From late August 1758 another spate of parallels with the *conte* is to be found in the correspondence: Westphalia (D7838); shipwreck (D7839, 7848, 7862); the earth covered with corpses and beggars (D7852) reminding us of Chapters III–IV; the cultivation of pineapples in India (D7875), as in Turkey in Chapter XXX; *te deums* as thanksgiving after battle (D7890, 7908, 7928): these and other phrases reminiscent of the *conte* suggest that the latter was in the forefront of Voltaire's mind up to early November. But most of these are not new and indicate no more than elaboration of the finished product. However, one episode, that of the

9. from the gothic and visigothic rights of dues and fines.

1. Two great rises.
2. Mason; gardener.

black slave in Chapter XIX, is more important, because we now know that it did not figure in the earliest manuscript version of *Candide*. René Pomeau has shown that the source for this passage lies in Voltaire's reading of Helvétius's *De l'esprit*, which contains strikingly similar references to slavery, around 18 October 1758 (cf. D7912). Not that Voltaire was unaware of the horrors occurring to blacks in the colonies; he had already written about them in the *Essai sur les moeurs* the previous January. But Helvétius recalled the institution of slavery to mind as one of the horrors which no comprehensive account of the world's evils should ignore. It also linked up for Voltaire with his new experiences as *seigneur de Ferney*.

This passage in *Candide* is surely the one where the most direct assault is made on the reader's conscience: 'This is the price you pay for eating sugar in Europe.' It also leads to one of *Candide*'s few impassioned outbursts against Optimism. But it is poorly integrated into the plot, as was almost inevitable given the date of its interpolation, and has no direct impact upon anything subsequent to it. An element of hesitation can be discerned on the author's part. It relates to the ambiguity of Voltaire's views on social commitment in the *conte*. The Ferney epoch with all its glorious activities in social protest and reform is only just opening after virtually the whole of *Candide* has been completed. One of the reasons for the unique tragi-comic quality of the tale must surely be sought in its period of gestation: the relative contentment of the Geneva years is beginning to dissolve as Voltaire begins work on it, a sharp decline in morale accompanies the Schwetzingen phase when it is generally thought to have been for the most part composed, and the prospect of a new era opening out, as yet full of possibility but of uncertainty too, is descried as it is finished. No biography of a writer can, or should, attempt to explain his art through his life. Voltaire's *Candide*, infinitely complex, savagely lucid, is the author's most brilliant of his innumerable attacks on the strongholds and methods of obscurantism. Like all such creations, it will not yield its ultimate secrets. The biographer, confronted by such mysteries, has but one useful function. By delineating the area where echoes from the world of *Candide* overlap into the world of Voltaire's daily life, he may hope to catch an element that went into the amalgam of forces creating the *conte*.

At the end of 1758, Voltaire tells d'Argental with pride that he has created for himself 'a rather nice kingdom' (D7988). At last he has his own principality: he is now both *roi* and *philosophe*. His installation at Tournay on Christmas Eve 1758 was of fitting dignity and pomp, with sound of cannon, fife and drum, all the peasants bearing arms and girls presenting flowers to his two diamond-bedecked nieces. 'M. de Voltaire', writes a spectator, 'was very pleased and full of joy . . . He was, believe me, very flattered' (D7998). Henceforth rank and authority will be used to advance social good. By the New Year Voltaire sees this as involving the overthrow of superstition (D8029); it is the tone of 'écrasez l'infâme', and the famous phrase itself will make its appearance in 1760 (D9006).[3] As *Candide* begins to enjoy, a few weeks later, the success which has never since deserted it, so too does Voltaire enter at last into his kingdom. In his sixty-fifth year, François-Marie Arouet has finally realised himself as M. de Voltaire.[4]

ENGLISH VISITORS TO FERNEY: A SAMPLING

Especially after he settled down in and near Geneva, fabulously rich and famous, witty and wicked, despised by half Europe and lionized by the other half, it became the thing for visitors passing in the neighborhood or on the "Grand Tour" to visit M. de Voltaire if they could wangle an invitation or permission for a brief visit. Not altogether to his own satisfaction, Voltaire had become a "sight." Visitors approached him with trepidation; they interrupted his work; they asked silly questions or aired silly notions of their own. Then, afterward, in their hotel rooms, they wrote long letters home, describing the man, his habits, and what they thought were his ideas.

Five of these "reports from Ferney" are represented here, from the much fuller collection assembled by Sir Gavin de Beer and André-Michel Rousseau. The heading of the volume is *Voltaire's British Visitors*. Copious and entertaining as this collection is, one shouldn't forget that Britons comprised only one strain of visitors to Ferney: German, French, Spanish, Italian, Russian, and visitors from the far corners of the earth came to see the patriarch of Ferney.

The five visitors represented here include some people who were or were to become well known in their own right. Edward Gibbon was the historian whose masterpiece is *The Decline and Fall of the Roman Empire*. His frail health, dislike of Oxford, and possession of an independent income made him a regular visitor and then a permanent resident of Switzerland, where, inevitably, he encountered Voltaire.

At the age of twenty-four, James Boswell was a Scottish laird of passage, who had not yet settled on Samuel Johnson as the focus of the great biography he already intended to write. As he would do later with Johnson, he tried during his visit to Ferney to provoke Voltaire into revealing his "true self." He was very good at this sort of thing, but one may suspect there's a good deal of Boswellian flash and exaggeration in his story, at the expense of some dry Voltairean wit.

The Reverend Norton Nicholls never actually visited Voltaire, for reasons described in his letter; but the superstitious hostility that kept him away and the extraordinary conviction that this one diabolically intelligent man had

3. "Ecrasez l'infâme" is a slogan many times repeated by Voltaire in the course of his crusades against bigotry, intolerance, and cruelty in the church of his day. "Wipe out the disgrace" is a literal translation, but the phrase implies much more. See Pater Gay's acute analysis of the word "infâme," below p. 183.

4. François-Marie Arouet is the name of an insignificant Paris bourgeois; M. de Voltaire (wherever his name comes from) is a gentleman, a seigneur, a person of European repute.

changed fundamentally, and for the worse, the course of European history are curious elements of the Voltaire mystique.

Charles Burney was a musicologist, father of Frances (Fanny) Burney the novelist-diarist. Doctor Burney was traveling in Europe to do research on the present state of music there, a study preliminary to his general *History of Music* (1776–89); his observations of Voltaire are acute and fair-minded. We are specially in his debt for description of the gallows standing before the house at Ferney. No doubt it was an instrument more for show than for use, but its presence is revelatory.

Doctor John Moore, a Scottish physician drawn into service abroad by the army, spent most of his life there, and wrote an important book of observations, first published in 1783 but then extended to cover events of the French Revolution. Perhaps because he was the least eminent of Voltaire's visitors, he was one of the most careful observers.

Edward Gibbon, August 1763

Gibbon to Mrs. Gibbon,[1] *Lausanne 6 August 1763*, 'I made a little excursion some days ago to Geneva, not so much for the sake of the town which I had often seen before, as for a representation of Monsieur de Voltaire's. He lives now entirely at Fernay, a little place in France, but only two Leagues from Geneva. He has bought the estate, and built a very pretty tho' small house upon it. After a life passed in courts and Capitals, the Great Voltaire is now a meer country Gentleman, and even (for the honor of the profession) sometimes of a farmer. He says he never enjoyed so much true happiness. He has got rid of most of his infirmities, and tho' very old and lean, enjoys a much better state of health than he did twenty years ago. His playhouse is very neat and well contrived, situated just by his Chappel, which is far inferior to it, tho', he says himself, *que son Christ est du meilleur faiseur, de tout le pays de Gex.*[2]

The play they acted was my favourite *Orphan of China*. Voltaire himself acted Gengis and Madame Denys Idamé; but I do not know how it happened: either my taste is improved or Voltaire's talents are impaired since I last saw him. He appeared to me now a very ranting unnatural performer. Perhaps indeed as I was come from Paris, I rather judged him by an unfair comparison, than by his own independent value. Perhaps too I was too much struck with the ridiculous figure of Voltaire at seventy acting a Tartar Conqueror with a hollow broken voice, and making love to a very ugly niece of about fifty. The play began at eight in the evening and ended (entertainment and all) about half an hour after eleven. The whole Company was asked to stay and set Down about twelve to a very elegant supper of a hundred Covers

---

1. Mrs. Gibbon is the stepmother of the historian; he never married [*Editor*].

2. I.e., that his Christ is by the best sculptor in the entire district of Gex [*Editor*].

[places]. The supper ended about two, the company danced till four, when we broke up, got into our Coaches and came back to Geneva, just as the Gates were opened. Shew me in history or fable, a famous poet of Seventy who has acted in his own plays, and has closed the scene with a supper and ball for a hundred people. I think the last is the more extraordinary of the two.'[3]

James Boswell, December 1764

James Boswell to William Temple, Ferney, 28 December 1764,[4] . . . I returned yesterday to this enchanted castle. The magician appeared a very little before dinner. But in the evening he came into the drawing-room in great spirits. I placed myself by him. I touched the keys in unison with his imagination. I wish you had heard the music. He was all brilliance. He gave me continued flashes of wit. I got him to speak English, which he does in a degree that made me now and then start up and cry, "Upon my soul this is astonishing!" When he talked our language he was animated with the soul of a Briton. He had bold flights. He had humour. He had an extravagance; he had a forcible oddity of style that the most comical of our *dramatis personae* could not have exceeded. He swore bloodily, as was the fashion when he was in England. He hummed a ballad; he repeated nonsense. Then he talked of our Constitution with a noble enthusiasm. I was proud to hear this from the mouth of an illustrious Frenchman. At last we came upon religion. Then did he rage. The company went to supper. Monsieur de Voltaire and I remained in the drawing-room with a great Bible before us; and if ever two mortal men disputed with vehemence, we did. Yes, upon that occasion he was one individual and I another. For a certain portion of time there was a fair opposition between Voltaire and Boswell. The daring bursts of his ridicule confounded my understanding. He stood like an orator of ancient Rome. Tully[5] was never more agitated than he was. He went too far. His aged frame trembled beneath him. He cried,

---

3. *Letters of Edward Gibbon,* ed. J. E. Norton (London, 1956), 1.154–55.

The italic material that follows is by the editors of *Voltaire's British Visitors:*

One thing which Gibbon does not relate in his letter to his stepmother, is that among the company was Suzanne Curchod. This fact would not be known but for her letter to Gibbon of 21 September, 1763, "Intimidée et accablée à Fernex par le jeu continuel d'une gayeté forcée et par la dureté de vos réponses, mes lèvres tremblantes refusèrent absolument de me servir" (Journal de Gibbon à Lausanne, pub. G. Bonnard (Lausanne 1945), p. 302). (Intimidated and overwhelmed by the continual play of strained wit and by the harshness of your replies, my trembling lips absolutely refused to serve me.)

Suzanne Curchod was the girl to whom Gibbon had been engaged until his father forced him to break off the connection. Mlle. Curchod, though she appears rather forlorn here, got her revenge by marrying the very next year Jacques Necker, the affluent banker and distinguished finance minister of France [Editor].

4. From *Voltaire's British Visitors,* ed. Sir Gavin De Beers and Andre Michel Rousseau, *Studies on Voltaire* 49 (1967): 89–90.

5. I.e., Marcus Tullius Cicero [Editor].

"Oh, I am very sick; my head turns round," and he let himself gently fall upon an easy chair. He recovered. I resumed our conversation, but changed the tone. I talked to him serious and earnest. I demanded of him an honest confession of his real sentiments. He gave it me with candour and with a mild eloquence which touched my heart. I did not believe him capable of thinking in the manner that he declared to me was "from the bottom of his heart". He expressed his veneration—his love—of the Supreme Being, and his entire resignation to the will of Him who is All-wise. He expressed his desire to resemble the Author of Goodness by being good himself. His sentiments go no farther. He does not inflame his mind with grand hopes of the immortality of the soul. He says it may be, but he knows nothing of it. And his mind is in perfect tranquillity. I was moved; I was sorry. I doubted his sincerity. I called to him with emotion, "Are you sincere? are you really sincere?" He answered, "Before God, I am". Then with the fire of him whose tragedies have so often shone on the theatre of Paris, he said, "I suffer much. But I suffer with patience and resignation; not as a Christian— but as a man".'

Rev. Norton Nicholls, August 1771

In his reminiscences of Thomas Gray, Nicholls wrote:[6] 'The great object of his detestation was *Voltaire,* whom he seemed to know even beyond what had appeared of him, and to see with the eyes of a prophet in his future mischiefs.[7] He said to me, "No one knows what mischief that man will do". When I took my leave of him, and saw him for the last time, in his lodgings in Jermyn Street, before I went abroad, in the beginning of June, 1771, he said, "I have one thing to beg of you, which you must not refuse." I replied, "You know you have only to command; what is it?" "Do not go to see Voltaire"; and then he added what I have written above. I said, "Certainly I will not; but what could a visit from me signify?" "Every tribute to such a man signifies." This was when I was setting out for Switzerland, to pay a visit to Mons. de Bonstetten, in which he would have accompanied me if his health had permitted. I kept my word, for I passed a month at the Chateau d' Aubonne, near Lausanne, with Mons. de Tscharner, bailif of the district, and did not go to Ferney'.

6. *Correspondence of Thomas Gray and the Rev. Norton Nicholls,* ed. the Rev. John Mitford (London, 1843) 32.
7. The "future mischiefs" attributed to Voltaire are, evidently, the French Revolution, for which some people to this day hold Voltaire and/or Rousseau responsible [*Editor*].

Charles Burney, July 1770

'The going to M. Fritz[8] at the time above-mentioned, broke into a plan I had formed of visiting M. de Voltaire at the same hour, with some other strangers, that were then going to Ferney; but to say the truth, besides the visit to Fritz being more *my business*, I did not much like going with these people, who had only a Bookseller to introduce them, & I had heard that some English had lately met with a rebuff from Voltaire by going without any letter of recommendation, or anything to recommend themselves. They were asked by him what they wanted. Upon their replying they wished only to see so extraordinary a man, he said—Well, gentlemen, you now see me, and did you take me to be a wild beast or a Monster that was fit only to be stared at, as a show? This story very much frighted me; for not having any intention of going to Geneva, when I left London, or even Paris, I was quite unprovided with a pass-port, however I was determined to see his place (which I took to be—Cette maison d'Aristippe, ces jardins d'Epicure: to which he retired in 1755, but was mistaken).[9] I drove to it alone, after I left Fritz. His house is 3 or 4 miles from Geneva, but near the lake, & I approached it with reverence, and a curiosity of the most minute kind. I enquired *when* I first trod on his domain; I had an intelligent and talkative coachman, who answered all my questions very satisfactorily. His estate is very large here, and he is building pretty farm-houses upon it. He has a quadrangular *justice*, or gallows, to show that he is the *seigneur*. One of his farms, or rather manufacturing houses (for he is establishing a manufacture upon his estate) was so handsome that I thought it was his *château*, but we drove to Ferney, through a charming country, covered with corn and vines, with a view of the lake and mountains above described. On the left hand, approaching the house, is a neat chapel with this inscription:—

DEO

EREXIT

VOLTAIRE

MDCCLXI[1]

This seems a little ostentatious in one who has as little religion of any sort perhaps as may fall to the share of a thinking man. I wanted to write two lines of Pope used in the Inscript.

---

8. Burney's business on the Continent was to investigate the state of music; apart from that M. Fritz is unidentified [*Editor*].

9. I.e., "this house of Aristippus, these gardens of Epicurus." The phrase is from Voltaire's poem on his first arrival in Switzerland; the two ancient philosophers alluded to were famous for their quiet good taste. For Voltaire's first residences in Switzerland see above, Lanson, p. 90.

1. Voltaire Raised It to God 1761 [*Editor*].

Who builds a Church to God & not to Fame
Ne'er mars the Building with the Donor's name.'

[*Another manuscript gives the following paragraph in place of the last*:
'When this building was constructed, M. de Voltaire gave a curious
reason for placing upon it this inscription. He said it was high time to
dedicate *one church to God*, after so many had been dedicated to Saints.']

I sent in to enquire whether a stranger might be allowed to see the
house & was answered in the affirmative. The servant soon came &
conducted me into the cabinet or closet where his master had just been
writing, which is never shown when he is at home; but being walked
out, I was allowed that privilege. From thence to the library. Not a very
large one, but well filled. Here I found a whole length figure in marble
of himself recumbent in one of the windows; & many curiosities in
another room a bust of himself not 2 years since; his mother's picture;
that of his niece, Mad. Denis; her brother, M. Dupuis; the Calas family,
&c &c. It is a very neat and elegant house, not large, or affectedly
decorated. I should have said, that close to the chapel, between that
and the house, is the theatre, he built some years ago in which he treated
his friends with some of his own tragedies: it is now only used as a
receptacle for wood and lumber, there having been no play acted in it
these 4 years. The servant told me his master was 78, but very well. His
words were these Il travaille pendant dix heures chaque jour. He studies
ten hours every day; writes constantly without spectacles, and walks out
with only a domestic, very often a mile or two—"Et le voilà, là bas!"[2]

He was going to his workmen. My heart leaped at the sight of so
extraordinary a man. He had just then quitted his garden, and was
crossing the court before his house. Seeing my chaise, and me on the
point of mounting it, he made a sign to his servant, who had been my
Cicerone,[3] to go to him, in order, I suppose, to enquire who I was. After
they had exchanged a few words together, he approached the place where
I stood, motionless, in order to contemplate his person as much as I
could when his eyes were turned from me; but on seeing him move
towards me, I found myself drawn by some irresistible power towards
him; and, without, knowing what I did, I insensibly met him half way.
It is not easy to conceive it possible for life to subsist in a form so nearly
composed of mere skin and bone, as that of M. de Voltaire. He complained of decrepitude, and said he supposed I was curious to form an
idea of the figure of one walking after death. However his eyes and whole
countenance are still full of fire; and though so emaciated, a more lively
expression cannot be imagined. He enquired after English news, and
observed that poetical squabbles had given way to political ones; but
seemed to think the spirit of opposition as necessary in poetry as in

2. And there he is, right there! [*Editor*].
3. Literally, guide, but with a joke on the Italian

form of Cicero, i.e., an orator or elocutionist
[*Editor*].

politics. "Les querelles d'auteurs sont pour le bien de la littérature, comme dans un gouvernement libre, les querelles des grands, et les clameurs des petits sont nécessaires à la liberté". (Disputes among authors are of use to literature; as the quarrels of the great, and the clamours of the little, in a free government, are necessary to liberty.) And added, "When critics are silent, it does not so much prove the age to be correct as dull". He enquired what poets we had now; and I told him we had Mason and Gray.[4] They write but little, said he, and you seem to have no one who lords it over the rest like Dryden, Pope and Swift. I told him that it was, perhaps, one of the inconveniences of periodical journals, however well executed, that they often silenced modest men of genius, while impudent blockheads were impenetrable, and unable to feel the critic's scourge: that Mr. Gray and Mr. Mason had both been illiberally treated by mechanical critics, even in newspapers; and added, that modesty and love of quiet seemed in these gentlemen to have got the better even of their love of fame. During this conversation, we approached the buildings he was constructing near the road to his *château*. These, said he, pointing to them, are the most innocent, and, perhaps, the most useful of all my works. I observed that he had other works, which were of far more extensive use, and would be much more durable than those. He was so obliging as to show me several farmhouses he had built, and the plans of others; after which I took my leave, for fear of breaking in upon his time, being unwilling to rob the public of things so precious as the few remaining moments of this great and universal genius."[5]

John Moore and Douglas Hamilton (Eighth Duke of Hamilton), July 1772

Dr. John Moore to baron Mure, ' Geneva, Monday, Aug 3, 1772,[6] 'We were visiting Voltaire, a privilege granted to very few. He was particularly attentive to the duke [of Hamilton], and, speaking of Mr. Hume, he said to me in English, "you mos write him that I am hees great admeerer; he is a very great onor to Ingland, and abofe all to Ecosse".[7] The Duke, Mr. Mallet, and I am to sup and stay all night sometime this week with Voltaire; his vivacity and spirit is amazing; he is writing and publishing

4. William Mason was a friend and associate of Thomas Gray (best known for the *Elegy Written in a Country Churchyard*); neither man was very prolific [*Editor*].
5. Brit. Mus., Add. MSS.35122, ff. 26–27; printed in *London magazine* (1771).
6. From John Moore, A *View of society and manners in France, Switzerland, and Germany* (London, 1783) 1:261–85. Since Moore's extended

account of Voltaire was written over several days, each day's entry in his notebook is marked by the renewed indication "Geneva," to make clear that he is still in the same spot [*Editor*].
7. David Hume, as a vigorously sceptical philosopher, naturally appealed to Voltaire, who called him (as here) an honor to "Ecosse" (Scotland) [*Editor*].

every day; and I do believe he is not without hopes that the Christian religion will die before him'.

'Geneva. I am not surprised that your inquiries of late entirely regard the philosopher of Ferney. This extraordinary person has contrived to excite more curiosity, and to retain the attention of Europe for a longer space of time, than any other man this age has produced, monarchs and heroes included.—Even the most trivial anecdote relating to him seems, in some degree, to interest the Public.

Since I have been in this country, I have had frequent opportunities of conversing with him, and still more with those who have lived in intimacy with him for many years; so that, whatever remarks I may send you on this subject, are founded either on my own observation, or on that of the most candid and intelligent of his acquaintance.

He has enemies and admirers here, as he has every where else; and not unfrequently both united in the same person.

The first idea which has presented itself to all who have attempted a description of his person, is that of a skeleton. In as far as this implies excessive leanness, it is just; but it must be remembered, that this skeleton, this mere composition of skin and bone, has a look of more spirit and vivacity, than is generally produced by flesh and blood, however blooming and youthful.

The most piercing eyes I ever beheld are those of Voltaire, now in his eightieth year. His whole countenance is expressive of genius, observation, and extreme sensibility.

In the morning he has a look of anxiety and discontent; but this gradually wears off, and after dinner he seems cheerful:—yet an air of irony never entirely forsakes his face, but may always be observed lurking in his features, whether he frowns or smiles.

When the weather is favourable, he takes an airing in his coach, with his niece, or with some of his guests, of whom there is always a sufficient number at Ferney. Sometimes he saunters in his garden; or if the weather does not permit him to go abroad, he employs his leisure-hours in playing at chess with Pere Adam;[8] or in receiving the visits of strangers, a continual succession of whom attend at Ferney to catch an opportunity of seeing him; or in dictating and reading letters; for he still retains correspondents in all the countries of Europe, who inform him of every remarkable occurrence, and send him every new literary production as soon as it appears.

By far the greater part of his time is spent in his study; and whether he reads himself, or listens to another, he always has a pen in his hand, to take notes, or make remarks.

8. Père Adam was a Jesuit priest whom Voltaire kept in the house to say the occasional mass but mostly as an antagonist over the chessboard. See Lanson, above, p. 92 [Editor].

Composition is his principal amusement. No author who writes for daily bread, no young poet ardent for distinction, is more assiduous with his pen, or more anxious for fresh fame, than the wealthy and applauded Seigneur of Ferney.

He lives in a very hospitable manner, and takes care always to keep a good cook. He has generally two or three visitors from Paris, who stay with him a month or six weeks at a time. When they go, their places are soon supplied; so that there is a constant rotation of society at Ferney. These, with Voltaire's own family, and his visitors from Geneva, compose a company of twelve or fourteen people, who dine daily at his table, whether he appears or not. For when engaged preparing some new production for the press, indisposed or in bad spirits, he does not dine with the company; but satisfies himself with seeing them for a few minutes, either before or after dinner.

All who bring recommendations from his friends, may depend upon being received, if he be not really indisposed.—He often presents himself to the strangers, who assemble almost every afternoon in his antechamber, although they bring no particular recommendation. But sometimes they are obliged to retire without having their curiosity gratified.

As often as this happens, he is sure of being accused of peevishness; and a thousand ill-natured stories are related, perhaps invented, out of revenge, because he is not in the humour of being exhibited like a dancing-bear on a holiday. It is much less surprising that he sometimes refuses, than that he should comply so often. In him, this complaisance must proceed solely from a desire to oblige; for Voltaire has been so long accustomed to admiration, that the stare of a few strangers cannot be supposed to afford him much pleasure.

His niece, Madame Denis, does the honours of the table, and entertains the company, when her uncle is not able, or does not choose to appear. She is a well disposed woman, who behaves with good-humour to every body, and with unremitting attention and tenderness to her uncle.

The forenoon is not a proper time to visit Voltaire. He cannot bear to have his hours of study interrupted. This alone is sufficient to put him in bad humour; besides, he is then apt to be queruious, whether he suffers by the infirmities of age or from some accidental cause of chagrin. Whatever is the reason, he is less an optimist at that part of the day than at any other.—It was in the morning, probably, that he remarked,—que c'étoit domage que le quinquina se trouvoit en Amérique, et la fièvre en nos climats.[9]

Those who are invited to supper, have an opportunity of seeing him in the most advantageous point of view. He then exerts himself to entertain the company, and seems as fond of saying, what are called

9. that it's too bad quinine is found in America and fever in our part of the world [Editor].

good things, as ever:—and when any lively remark or bon mot comes from another, he is equally delighted, and pays the fullest tribute of applause.—The spirit of mirth gains upon him by indulgence.—When surrounded by his friends, and animated by the presence of women, he seems to enjoy life with all the sensibility of youth. His genius then surmounts the restraints of age and infirmity, and flows along in a fine strain of pleasing, spirited observation, and delicate irony.

He has an excellent talent of adapting his conversation to his company.—The first time the D[uke] of H[amilton] waited on him, he turned the discourse on the ancient alliance between the French and Scotch nations.—Reciting the circumstance of one of his Grace's predecessors having accompanied Mary Queen of Scots, whose heir he at the time was, to the court of France,—he spoke of the heroic characters of his ancestors, the ancient Earls of Douglas—of the great literary reputation of some of his countrymen, then living; and mentioned the names of Hume and Robertson in terms of high approbation.

A short time afterwards, he was visited by two Russian noblemen, who are now at Geneva. Voltaire talked to them a great deal of their Empress, and the flourishing state of their country.—Formerly, said he, your countrymen were guided by ignorant priests,—the arts were unknown, and your lands lay waste;—but now the arts flourish, and the lands are cultivated.—One of the young men replied, That there was still a great proportion of barren land in Russia.—At least, said Voltaire, you must admit, that of late your country had been very *fertile in laurels*.

His dislike to the clergy is well known.—This leads him to join in a very trite topic of abuse with people who have no pretension to that degree of wit which alone could make their railings tolerable.—The conversation happening to turn into this channel, one person said, If you subtract pride from priests, nothing will remain.—Vous comptez donc, Monsieur, la gourmandise pour rien,[1] said Voltaire.

He approves much more of Marmontel's Art of Poetry, than of any poems of that author's composition. Speaking of these, he said that Marmontel, like Moses, could guide others to the Holy Land, though he was not allowed to enter it himself.[2]

Voltaire's unbecoming allusions to the Sacred Writings, and his attempts to turn into ridicule some of the most venerable characters mentioned in them, are notorious.

A certain person, who stammered very much, found means to get himself introduced at Ferney.—He had no other recommendation than the praises he very liberally bestowed on himself.—When he left the room, Voltaire said, he supposed him to be an aventurier, un impos-

---

1. Then, Sir, you consider gluttony nothing? [Editor].

2. Though a prolific and various writer, and a long-time member of the Académie Française, Marmontel never rose on the literary scale above the mediocre [Editor].

teur.—Madame Denis said, Imposters never stammer:—To which
Voltaire replied—Moise, ne begayoit-il pas?[3]

You must have heard of the animosity which has long subsisted between Voltaire and Freron the Journalist at Paris. The former was walking one day in his garden with a gentleman from Geneva. A toad crawled
across the road before them:—The gentleman, to please Voltaire, said
pointing at the toad,—There is a Freron.—What can that poor animal
have done to you, replied the Wit, to deserve such a name?

He compared the British nation to a hogshead of their own strong
beer; the top of which is froth, the bottom dregs, the middle excellent.

A friend of Voltaire's having recommended to his perusal a particular
system of metaphysics, supported by a train of reasonings, by which the
author displayed his own ingenuity and address, without convincing the
mind of the reader, or proving any thing besides his own eloquence
and sophistry, asked, sometime after, the critic's opinion of this performance?

Metaphysical writers, replied Voltaire, are like minuet-dancers; who
being dressed to the greatest advantage, make a couple of bows, move
through the room in the finest attitude, display all their graces, are in
continual motion without advancing a step, and finish at the identical
point from which they set out.

This I hope will satisfy you for the present; in my next, I shall send
you what farther particulars I think worth your notice concerning this
singular man'.

'Geneva. Considered as a master, Voltaire appears in a very amiable
light. He is affable, humane, and generous to his tenants and depen-
dants. He loves to see them prosper; and takes part in their private and
domestic concerns, with the attention of a patriarch.—He promotes
industry and manufactures among them, by every means he can devise:
by his care and patronage alone, Ferney, from a wretched village, whose
inhabitants were sunk in sloth and poverty, is become a flourishing and
commodious little town.

That acrimony, which appears in some of Voltaire's works, seems to
be excited only against rival wits, and contemporary writers, who refuse
him that distinguished place on Parnassus,[4] to which his talents entitle
him.

If he has been the author of severe satire, he has also been the object
of a great deal. Who has been the aggressor, it would be difficult to
determine; but it must be confessed, that where he has not been irritated
as a writer, he appears a good-humoured man; and, in particular instances, displays a true philanthropy.—The whole of his conduct re-

---

3. Wasn't Moses a stutterer? [Editor].   4. The mountain of the muses, i.e., the world of
                                                letters [Editor].

specting the Calas[5] family;—his protection of the Sirvens, his patronage of the young lady descended from Corneille, and many examples, which might be mentioned, are all of this nature.

Some people will tell you, that all the bustle he made, on these, and similar occasions, proceeded from vanity; but in my mind, the man who takes pains to justify oppressed innocence, to rouse the indignation of mankind against cruelty, and to relieve indigent merit, is in reality benevolent, however vain he may be of such actions.—Such a man is unquestionably a more useful member of society, than the humblest monk, who has no other plan in life, than the working out his own salvation in a corner.

Voltaire's criticisms on the writings of Shakespear do him no honour; they betray an ignorance of the author, whose works he so rashly condemns. Shakespear's irregularities, and his disregard for the unities of the drama, are obvious to the dullest of modern critics; but Voltaire's national prejudices, and his imperfect knowledge of the language, render him blind to some of the most shining beauties of the English Poet; his remarks, however, though not always candid nor delicate, are for the most part lively.

One evening, at Ferney, the conversation happening to turn on the genius of Shakespear, Voltaire expatiated on the impropriety and absurdity of introducing low characters and vulgar dialogue into Tragedy; and gave many instances of the English bard's having offended in that particular, even in his most pathetic plays. A gentleman of the company, who is a great admirer of Shakespear, observed, by way of palliation, that though those characters were low, yet they were natural (dans la nature, was his expression). Avec permission, Monsieur, replied Voltaire, mon cul est bien dans la nature, et cependant je porte de culottes.[6]

Voltaire had formerly a little theatre at his own house, where dramatic pieces were represented by some of the society who visited there, he himself generally taking some important character; but by all accounts this was not his forte, nature having fitted him for conceiving the sentiments, but not representing the actions of a hero.

Mr. Cramer of Geneva sometimes assisted upon these occasions. I have often seen that gentleman act at a private theatre in that city with deserved applause. Very few of those who have made acting the study and business of their lives, could have represented the characters in which he appeared, with more judgment and energy.

The celebrated Clairon[7] herself has been proud to tread Voltaire's domestic theatre, and to display at once his genius and her own.

These dramatic entertainments at Ferney, to which many of the in-

---

5. Calas and Sirven were two of many victims of religious bigotry in France, on whose behalf Voltaire exercised all his powers of satirical protest. On little Marie Corneille, see Lanson, above, p. 92 [Editor].

6. Begging your pardon, Sir, my butt is perfectly natural, and yet I wear trousers [Editor].

7. Claire Leris, known as Clairon, was the preeminent tragic actress of her day on the French stage [Editor].

habitants of Geneva were, from time to time, invited, in all probability increased their desire for such amusements, and gave the hint to a company of French comedians, to come every summer to the neighborhood.

As the Syndics and Council did not judge it proper to license their acting, this company have erected a theatre at Chatelaine, which is on the French side of the ideal line which separates that kingdom from the territories of the Republic, and about three miles from the ramparts of Geneva.

People come occasionally from Savoy and Switzerland to attend these representations; but the company on which the actors chiefly depend, are the citizens of Geneva. The play begins at three or four in the afternoon, that the spectators may have time to return before the shutting of the gates.

I have been frequently at this theatre. The performers are moderately good. The admired Le Kain,[8] who is now at Ferney, on a visit to Voltaire, sometimes exhibits:—but when I go, my chief inducement is to see Voltaire, who generally attends when Le Kain acts, and when one of his own tragedies is to be represented.

He sits on the stage, and behind the scenes; but so as to be seen by a great part of the audience. He takes as much interest in the representation, as if his own character depended on the performance. He seems perfectly chagrined and disgusted when any of the actors commit a mistake; and when he thinks they perform well, never fails to make his approbation with all the violence of voice and gesture.

He enters into the feigned distresses of the piece with every symptom of real emotion, and even sheds tears with the profusion of a girl present for the first time at a tragedy.

I have sometimes sat near him during the whole entertainment, observing with astonishment such a degree of sensibility in a man of eighty. This great age, one would naturally believe, might have considerably blunted every sensation, particularly those occasioned by the fictitious distresses of the drama, to which he has been habituated from his youth.

The pieces represented having been wrote by himself, is another circumstance which, in my opinion, should naturally tend to prevent their effect on him. Some people indeed assert that this, so far from diminishing, is the real cause of all his sensibility; and they urge, as a proof of this assertion, that he attends the theatre only when some of his own pieces are to be acted.

That he should be better pleased to see his own tragedies represented than any others, is natural; but I do not readily comprehend, how he can be more easily moved and deceived, by distresses which he himself invented. Yet this degree of deception seems necessary to make a man

8. Henri Louis Cain (Le Kain), originally a protégé of Voltaire's, achieved great success in his own right as a tragic actor [Editor].

shed tears. While these tears are flowing, he must believe the woes he weeps are real: he must have been so far deceived by the cunning of the scene, as to have forgot that he was in a playhouse. The moment he recollects that the whole is fiction, his sympathy and tears must cease.

I should be glad, however, to see Voltaire present at the representation of some of Corneille or Racine's tragedies, that I might observe whether he would discover more or less sensibility than he has done at his own. We should then be able to ascertain this curious, disputed point, whether his sympathy regarded the piece of the author.

Happy, if this extraordinary man had confined his genius to its native home, to the walks which the muses love, and where he has always been received with distinguished honour, and that he had never deviated from these, into the thorny paths of controversy. For while he attacked the tyrants and oppressors of mankind, and those who had perverted the benevolent nature of Christianity to the most selfish and malignant purposes, it is for ever to be regretted, that he allowed the shafts of his ridicule to glance upon the Christian religion itself.

By persevering in this, he has not only shocked the pious, but even disgusted infidels, who accuse him of borrowing from himself, and repeating the same argument in various publications; and seem as tired of the stale sneer against the Christian doctrines, as of the dullest and most tedious sermons in support of them.

Voltaire's behaviour during sickness has been represented in very opposite lights. I have heard much of his great contrition and repentance, when he had reason to believe his end approaching. These stories, had they been true, would have proved, that his infidelity was affectation, and that he was a believer and Christian in his heart.

I own I could never give any credit to such reports; for though I have frequently met with vain young men, who have given themselves airs of free-thinking, while in reality they were even superstitious, yet I never could understand what a man like Voltaire, or any man of common understanding, could propose to himself by such absurd affectation. To pretend to despise what we really revere, and to treat as human, what we believe to be divine, is certainly, of all kinds of hypocrisy, the most unpardonable.

I was at some pains to ascertain this matter; and I have been assured, by those who have lived during many years in familiarity with him, that all these stories are without foundation. They declare, that although he was unwilling to quit the enjoyment of life, and used the means of preserving health, he seemed no way afraid of the consequences of dying. That he never discovered, either in health or sickness, any remorse for the works imputed to him against the Christian religion.—That, on the contrary, he was blinded to such a degree, as to express uneasiness at the thoughts of dying before some of them, in which he was at that time engaged, were finished.

Though this conduct is not to be justified upon any supposition, yet there is more consistency, and, in my opinion, less wickedness in it, if we admit the account which his friends give, than there would be in his writing at once against the established opinions of mankind, the conviction of his own conscience, and the inspirations of the Deity, merely to acquire the applause of a few mistaken infidels.

However erroneous he may have been, I cannot suspect him of such absurdity. On the contrary, I imagine, that as soon as he is convinced of the truths of Christianity, he will openly avow his opinion, in health as in sickness, uniformly, to his last moment.

＊　＊　＊

CRITICISM

ROBERT M. ADAMS

The *Conte* Defined

Formal critical appreciation of *Candide* as a work of literary art does not have a very long history. For its own age it was too light and unpretentious a book, too "easy" to need any sort of formal study. The usual eighteenth- or nineteenth-century discussion touches on the pace and rhythm of its prose, the gaiety of its ridicule—and then gets on to the more satisfying question of its morality or immorality. But recently, the book has come to seem less simple than it once did—perhaps because Voltaire's irony, for all its swiftness and levity, appears to have a destructive power that is hard to limit. Hence the opening up of some interesting questions about how the book should be read—on which the following pages present a scattering of views.

In order to render more accessible the discussions, it seems useful to prefix a technical definition, as well as a brief list of Voltaire's major works, other than *Candide*, to which the various essayists refer. A *conte*, therefore, is in set, formal terms, an account of an anecdote or adventure, marvelous or otherwise, told for purposes of amusement. A *conte* can be what we in English would call a short story, but it can also be a very short parable, a fable, or a novelette (like *Candide*). As they grow longer, more substantial in their social renderings, and more serious in their moral tonality, *contes* tend to be called *nouvelles*, as *nouvelles*, by heightening these qualities still further, turn into *romans*. *Contes* are the slightest, lightest, and least pretentious of prose narratives.

At the beginning of his career, when he was devoted to the "noble" genres (tragedy and epic), Voltaire himself despised these trivialities of fiction. But in the course of his philosophic arguments he always told illustrative stories and sketched dramatic vignettes. While living at Cirey in the deep country with Madame du Chatelet (1734–45), he often entertained the household and their visitors with comic stories and one-man sketches (sometimes illustrated with magic-lantern slides). Thus, gradually, he came to see that serious thoughts could be mixed with the funny business. And so was born the special Voltairean form of the *conte*—which, in familiar words, floats like a butterfly and stings like a bee.

A Checklist of the *Contes* of Voltaire, and Related Writings

A complete listing of Voltaire's publications constitutes in itself a volume of several hundred pages. The present short list aims merely to name those of his works that are most often mentioned in connection with *Candide*, to translate the title where possible, indicate the genre and date, and with respect to a few of the most important, to give summary indication of the contents.

Aventure Indienne ("An Indian Adventure"), 1766, conte.
Babouc (see *Le Monde comme il va*).
Cosi-Sancta, 1784, conte.
Le Crocheteur borgne ("The One-Eyed Porter"), 1774, conte.
Les Deux Consolés ("The Two Who Were Comforted"), 1756, conte.

Dialogue entre un Bramin et un Jésuite ("Dialogue Between a Brahmin and a Jesuit"), 1756, philosophical dialogue.
Dialogue entre Lucrèce et Posidone ("Dialogue Between Lucretius and Posidonius"), 1756, philosophical dialogue.
Dictionnaire Philosophique ("Philosophical Dictionary"), 1764. The many short articles and satiric definitions of this one-man encyclopedia give it stature as one of Voltaire's most implacable and weighty assaults on "l'infâme."
Discours en Vers sur l'Homme ("Discourses on Man"), 1738, poem. Inspired by Pope's "Essay on Man," these six discourses try similarly to sum up an attitude toward human life.
Eléments de la Philosophie de Newton ("Elements of Newton's Philosophy"), 1738, prose exposition.

Epître à Uranie ("Epistle to Urania"), 1722, poem.
Essai sur les moeurs ("Essay on Customs," also sometimes known as the "Universal History"), 1756, an essay in history, folklore, and comparative anthropology. The omnivorous reading that Voltaire did for this immense survey of human behavior-patterns is particularly reflected in the cosmopolitan perspectives of *Candide*.
Fragments sur l'Inde ("Fragments on India"), 1773, polemic on aspects of British rule.
La Henriade—originally *La Ligue ou Henri le Grand* ("The Henriad") published 1723 under one title and 1728 under the other, an epic poem on Henry IV.
Histoire d'un bon Bramin ("The Story of a Good Brahmin"), 1761, conte.

L'Histoire de Jenni ("Jenny's Story"), 1775, conte.
Histoire des voyages de Scarmentado ("The Travels of Scarmentado"), 1756, conte. A rascal from Crete, Scarmentado gyrates rapidly through the world, from one scrape to another, finally returns home, and settles into complacent domesticity.

Homélies prononcées à Londres en 1765 ("Homilies delivered in London in 1765"), 1767, lay sermons, on atheism, superstition, and the Old and New Testaments. They were not, of course, delivered at London.

L'Homme aux quarante écus ("The Man with Forty Pounds a Year"), 1768, conte. A sensible, simple, middle-of-the-road fellow, the man with forty pounds a year wanders about, discussing with various frauds he meets such disagreeable eventualities as taxation, syphilis, and war. He has read *Candide*, cites it frequently, and finds it a useful guide to things as they are.

Il faut prendre un parti ("One Must Take Sides"), 1772, polemic.

L'Ingénu ou le Huron ("Simplicity"), 1767, conte. A man brought up among the Mohawk Indians returns to France and finds he is the son of a French couple; his simplicity suffers all sorts of checks and frustrations in adapting to the sophistications and corruptions of French society.

Jeannot et Colin ("Johnny and Colin"), 1764, conte. A morality on social arrogance.

Lettres d'Amabed ("Letters from Amabed"), 1769, conte. An innocent Brahmin wanders into Europe and describes its peculiar institutions.

Lettres Philosophiques ("Philosophic Letters"), 1733–34, essays largely descriptive of English culture and thought.

Memnon, 1749, conte. (Not to be confused with *Zadig*, which originally appeared under this title.)

Micromégas, 1752, conte. An inhabitant of Sirius, who is immense, and his friend from Saturn, who, though still immense by human standards, is a dwarf compared to the Sirian, go adventuring through the universe.

Le Mondain ("The Worldly Man"), 1736?, poem. A defence of luxury.

Le Monde comme il va ("The World As It Is"), 1748, conte.

Les Oreilles du Comte de Chesterfield ("Lord Chesterfield's Ears"), 1775, conte. Chesterfield was deaf; but his ears have almost nothing at all to do with this discussion of whether and in what sense man is a machine.

L'Orphelin de la Chine ("The Chinese Orphan"), 1755, tragedy.

Le Pauvre Diable ("The Poor Devil"), 1758, verse satire.

Poème sur le Désastre de Lisbonne ("Poem on Lisbon"), 1756, philosophical poem.

Précis de l'Ecclésiaste ("Ecclesiastes Abridged"), 1759, verse translation.

La Princesse de Babylone ("The Princess of Babylon"), 1768, conte. Amazan, in love with Formosanta, Princess of Babylon, travels round the world in search of her—meanwhile furnishing Voltaire with opportunities for witty comment and satire.

La Pucelle ("The Maid"), 1755, mock-heroic poem, in more than dubious taste, on Joan of Arc.

Questions sur L'Encyclopédie ("Questions on the Encyclopedia"), 1770–72, commentary and criticism in nine volumes.

Le Siècle de Louis XIV ("The Century of Louis XIV"), 1751, history—social, intellectual, and cultural, as well as diplomatic and military.

Tancrède, 1760, tragedy. Love and misunderstanding in XI-century Sicily, with a noble corsair for a hero, a noble young lady for *ingenue*, and a ridiculous plot.

Le Taureau blanc ("The White Bull"), 1774, conte.

Traité de métaphysique ("Treatise on Metaphysics"), 1734, philosophy.

Zadig ou la destinée, 1747, conte. Persecuted by persistent ill fortune, Zadig after many trials, and with the help of illumination from an angel named Jesrad, finally wins the hand of Queen Astarte.

Zaïre, 1732, tragedy.

ERICH AUERBACH

[Tone, Pace, Insinuation]†

[Voltaire's prose, which at first glance looks like a simple taut string on which to hang a set of one-liners, is a great deal more complex and interesting than that. Nobody has been more deft and patient at unraveling the way a piece of writing actually works than Erich Auerbach, the much-admired German humanist, whose classic *Mimesis* traces through European literature the way in which a thread of social realism intertwines with other themes and literary modes, bending syntax subtly to its purposes.

The chapter dealing with Voltaire begins by discussing a passage from the Abbé Prévost's novel *Manon Lescaut* (1731). Here the surface of things is colorful, varied, lively, and graphic; the feelings depicted, on the other hand, are serious, almost tragic. Yet the language is almost invariably charming and elegant. Very different is the manner cultivated by Voltaire in one of his *Lettres Philosophiques*, then in a late verse narrative, and finally in *Candide*.]

*   *   *

Quite different is the stylistic level of the realistic texts which serve the propaganda purposes of the Enlightenment. Examples are to be found from the Regency on, and in the course of the century they become more frequent and increasingly aggressive polemically. The master of the game is Voltaire. As a first example we choose a fairly

† From Erich Auerbach, *Mimesis: The Representation of Reality in Western Literature*, tr. Willard Trask. Copyright 1953 Princeton University Press.

early piece, from the sixth of the Philosophical Letters, which deal with his impressions of England.[1]

> Entrez dans la bourse de Londres, cette place plus respect-able que bien des cours; vous y voyez rassemblés les députés de toutes les nations pour l'utilité des hommes. Là, le juif, le mahométan et le chrétien traitent l'un avec l'autre comme s'ils étaient de la même religion, et ne donnent le nom d'in-fidèles qu'à ceux qui font banqueroute; là, le presbytérien se fie à l'anabaptiste, et l'anglican reçoit la promesse du quaker. Au sortir de ces pacifiques et libres assemblées, les uns vont à la synagogue, les autres vont boire; celui-ci va se faire baptiser dans une grande cuve au nom du Père, par le Fils, au Saint-Esprit; celui-là fait couper le prépuce de son fils et fait mar-motter sur l'enfant des paroles hébraïques qu'il n'entend point; ces autres vont dans leurs églises attendre l'inspiration de Dieu leur chapeau sur la tête, et tous sont contents.

> (Enter the London stock exchange, that more respectable place than many a court; you will see the deputies of all nations gathered there for the service of mankind. There the Jew, the Mohammedan, and the Christian deal together as if they were of the same religion, and apply the name of infidel only to those who go bankrupt; there the Presbyterian trusts the An-abaptist, and the Anglican accepts the Quaker's promise. On leaving these peaceful and free assemblies, some go to the synagogue, others go to drink; one goes to have himself bap-tized in the name of the Father, through the Son, to the Holy Ghost; another has his son's foreskin cut off and Hebrew words mumbled over him which he does not understand; others go to their church to await the inspiration of God with their hats on their heads; and all are content.)

This description of the London exchange was not really written for a realistic purpose. What goes on there, we are told only in a general way. The purpose is much rather to insinuate certain ideas, which in their crudest and driest form would run as follows: "Free international business as dictated by the egotism of individuals is beneficial to human society; it unites men in common pacific activities. Religions, on the other hand, are absurd. Their absurdity needs no proof beyond the observation that they are very numerous while each claims to be the only true one, and

1. Voltaire's involuntary visit to England lasted three years (1726–29) and put the finishing touches on his literary and political education. The *Philosophical Letters on the English*, which ap- peared in 1733, were powerful and important in themselves and laid the foundations of many of Voltaire's future attitudes [*Editor*].

that their dogmas and ceremonies are nonsensical. However, in a country where they are very many and very different, so that they are forced to put up with one another, they do not do much harm and can be regarded as an innocuous form of madness. It is only when they fight and persecute one another that things get really bad." But even in this dry formulation of the idea there is a rhetorical trick which, however, I find it impossible to eliminate because it is contained in Voltaire's conception itself. It is the unexpected contrast of religion and business, in which business is placed higher, practically and morally, than religion. The very device of coupling the two, as though they were forms of human endeavor on the same plane and to be judged from the same viewpoint, is not only an impertinence; it is a specific approach or, if one prefers, an experimental set-up, in which religion is ipso facto deprived of what constitutes its essence and its value. It is presented in a position in which it appears ridiculous from the start. This is a technique which sophists and propagandists of all times have employed with success, and Voltaire is a master of it. It is for precisely this reason that here, where he wants to demonstrate the blessings of productive work, he chooses neither a farm nor a business office nor a factory but the stock exchange, where people of all faiths and backgrounds congregate.

The way he invites us to enter the stock exchange is almost solemn. He calls it a place deserving of greater respect than many a court, and its frequenters deputies of all nations foregathered in the interests of humanity. Then he turns to a more detailed description of its frequenters and observes them first in their activity at the exchange, then in their private life; in both cases he emphasizes their differing in religion. As long as they are at the exchange, the difference has no importance. It does not interfere with business. This gives him the opportunity to introduce his play on the word *infidèle*. But as soon as they leave the exchange—that peaceful and free assembly, in contrast to the assemblies of battling clerics—the disparateness of their religious views comes to the fore. What was just now a harmonious whole—a symbol as it were of the ideal cooperation of all human society—now falls asunder into numerous unrelated and indeed incompatible parts. The remainder of the passage is given over to a lively description of a number of these. Leaving the exchange, the merchants disperse. Some go to a synagogue, others go to have a drink. The syntactic parallel presents the two as equally worthy ways of passing the time. Then we get a characterization of three groups of pious frequenters of the exchange: Anabaptists, Jews, and Quakers. In each case Voltaire emphasizes a purely external detail which differs from and is in no way related to the next but which in every instance is intrinsically absurd and comic. What comes out is not really the true nature of Jews or Quakers, not the grounds and the specific form of their convictions, but the external aspect of their religious ceremonial, which, especially to the uninitiated, looks strangely comic.

This again is an example of a favorite propaganda device which is often used far more crudely and maliciously than in this case. It might be called the searchlight device. It consists in overilluminating one small part of an extensive complex, while everything else which might explain, derive, and possibly counterbalance the thing emphasized is left in the dark; so that apparently the truth is stated, for what is said cannot be denied; and yet everything is falsified, for truth requires the whole truth and the proper interrelation of its elements. Especially in times of excited passions, the public is again and again taken in by such tricks, and everybody knows more than enough examples from the very recent past. And yet in most cases the trick is not at all hard to see through; in tense periods, however, the people or the public lack the serious desire to do so. Whenever a specific form of life or a social group has run its course, or has only lost favor and support, every injustice which the propagandists perpetrate against it is half consciously felt to be what it actually is, yet people welcome it with sadistic delight. Gottfried Keller[2] describes this psychological situation very finely in one of the novellas in his Seldwyla cycle, the story of lost laughter, in which a campaign of defamation in Switzerland is discussed. It is true, the things he describes compare with what we have seen in our time as a slight turbidity in the clear water of a brook would compare with an ocean of filth and blood. Gottfried Keller discusses the matter with his calm clarity and lack of prejudice, without softening the least detail, without the slightest attempt to whitewash the injustice or to speak of it as a "higher" form of justice; and yet he seems to sense in such things an element that is natural and at times beneficial, because after all "more than once a change of government and the expansion of freedom have resulted from an unjust cause or untrue pretense." Keller was fortunate in that he could not imagine an important change of government which would not entail an expansion of freedom. We have been shown otherwise.

Voltaire concludes with an unexpected turn: *et tous sont contents.* With the swiftness of a prestidigitator he has, in three sharp phrases, parodied three creeds or sects, and the four concluding words are sprung at us just as swiftly, surprisingly, and merrily. They are extremely rich in content. Why is everybody satisfied? Because everybody is allowed to do business and grow wealthy in peace; and because everybody is no less peacefully allowed to cling to his religious madness, with the result that no one persecutes or is persecuted. Long live tolerance! It lets everybody have his business and his fun, whether the latter is taking a drink or persisting in some absurd form of worship.

The method of posing the problem so that the desired solution is

---

2. Keller, a Swiss-German novelist of the late nineteenth century, serves Auerbach as a contrast-comparison with Voltaire's focusing devices in the Philosophical Letter. The examples from the very recent past, to which Auerbach quietly alludes, were provided by the anti-Semitism of Hitler's Third Reich, which drove Auerbach himself into exile [*Editor*].

contained in the very way in which the problem is posed, and the searchlight technique, which overilluminates the ridiculous, the absurd, or the repulsive in one's opponent, were both in use long before Voltaire. But he has a particular way of handling them which is all his own. Especially his own is his tempo. His rapid, keen summary of the development, his quick shifting of scenes, his surprisingly sudden confronting of things which are not usually seen together—in all this he comes close to being unique and incomparable; and it is in this tempo that a good part of his wit lies. As one reads his marvelous rococo sketches, the point becomes strikingly clear. For example:

> Comme il était assez près de Lutèce,
> Au coin d'un bois qui borde Charenton,
> Il aperçut la fringante Marton
> Dont un ruban nouait la blonde tresse;
> Sa taille est leste, et son petit jupon
> Laisse entrevoir sa jambe blanche et fine.
> Robert avance; il lui trouve une mine
> Qui tenterait les saints du paradis;
> Un beau bouquet de roses et de lis
> Est au milieu de deux pommes d'albâtre
> Qu'on ne voit point sans en être idolâtre;
> Et de son teint la fleur et l'incarnat
> De son bouquet auraient terni l'éclat.
> Pour dire tout, cette jeune merveille
> A son giron portait une corbeille,
> Et s'en allait avec tous ses attraits
> Vendre au marché du beurre et des œufs frais.
> Sire Robert, ému de convoitise,
> Descend d'un saut, l'accole avec franchise:
> "J'ai vingt écus, dit-il, dans ma valise;
> C'est tout mon bien; prenez encor mon cœur:
> Tout est à vous.—C'est pour moi trop d'honneur,"
> Lui dit Marton. . . .

(Not far from Paris, at the corner of a wood which borders Charenton, he saw the dashing Marton, with her blond hair bound by a ribbon. Her waist is trim and her little skirt permits a glimpse of her slim white leg. Robert approaches: he finds a face which would tempt the saints in Paradise; a beautiful bouquet of roses and lilies lies between two alabaster apples which none can see without adoring; and the freshness and bloom of her complexion would have dulled the brightness of her bouquet. To speak plainly, the young miracle of beauty was carrying a basket in her arms and, with all her attractions, was on her way to market to sell butter and fresh eggs. Sir

Robert, shaken with unholy desire, dismounted at one jump
and frankly embraced her. Said he: "I have twenty crowns in
my valise; it is my entire fortune; take my heart to boot: the
whole is yours." "The honor is too great," Marton replied. . . .)

This passage is from a fairly late narrative in verse: *Ce qui plaît aux
dames*. It is composed with great care, as may be inferred from the
successive impressions the knight receives of Marton's beauty as he
admires it first from afar and then from nearer and nearer. A great part
of its charm lies in its tempo. If it were drawn out longer, it would lose
its freshness and become trite. And the tempo determines the wit of the
piece too. The declaration of love is so comical only because it states
the essential data with such astounding brevity. Here as everywhere else,
Voltaire's tempo is part of his philosophy. In this instance he uses it to
set in sharp relief the essential motives of human actions as he sees
them, to unmask them as it were and show their extreme materialism,
without ever permitting himself anything crude. This little love scene
contains nothing sublime or spiritual, all that comes out in it is physical
lust and the profit motive. The declaration of love begins with an unrhe-
torical statement of the business side of the transaction, and yet it is
charming, elegant, and far from pedestrian. Everybody knows—and
Robert and Marton are no exception—that the words, *prenez encor mon
cœur, tout est à vous*, are nothing but a flourish to express the desire
for instantaneous sexual gratification. And yet they have all the charm
and bloom which Voltaire and his time inherited from classicism (in
this case specifically from La Fontaine)[3] and which he presses into the
service of the materialistic Enlightenment. The content has changed
completely, but the pleasing clarity, *l'agréable et le fin*, of the classics
has remained. It is present in every word, in every phrase, in every
rhythmic movement. A specifically Voltairian feature is the swift tempo,
which never becomes unaesthetic despite the author's boldness, not to
say unscrupulousness, in moral matters and his technique of sophistic
surprise attacks. He is completely free from the half-erotic and hence
somewhat hazy sentimentality which we have tried to demonstrate in
our analysis of the text from *Manon Lescaut*. His unmaskings in the
spirit of the Enlightenment are never crude and clumsy; on the contrary
they are light, agile, and as it were appetizing. And above all, he is free
from the cloudy, contour-blurring, overemotional rhetoric, equally destructive of clear thinking and pure feeling, which came to the fore in
the authors of the Enlightenment during the second half of the century
and in the literature of the Revolution, which had a still more luxuriant
growth in the nineteenth century through the influence of romanticism,

---

3. La Fontaine, who lived in the seventeenth century, is best known for his *Fables*, light, quick, charming poems that don't take their moralities too seriously [*Editor*].

and which has continued to produce its loathsome flowers down to our day.

Closely related to rapidity of tempo, but more generally in use as a propaganda device, is the extreme simplification of all problems. In Voltaire's case the rapidity, one feels almost tempted to say the alertness, of the tempo is made to serve the purpose of simplification. This simplification is almost always achieved by reducing the problem to an antithesis which is then exhibited in a giddy, swift, high-spirited narrative in which black and white, theory and practice, etc., are set in clear and simple opposition. We can observe this point in our passage on the London stock exchange, where the contrast business versus religion (the one useful and advancing human cooperation, the other senseless and raising barriers between men) is displayed in a vivid sketch which vigorously simplifies the problem in terms of a partisan approach; with this, and no less simplified, the contrast tolerance versus intolerance appears. Even in the little love story, if not a problem, at least the subject of the occurrence is reduced to a simplified antithetical formula (pleasure versus business). Let us consider yet another example. The novel *Candide* contains a polemic attack upon the metaphysical optimism of Leibnitz's idea of the best of all possible worlds. In chapter 8 of *Candide*, Cunégonde—who was lost and has been found again—begins her relation of the adventures she has undergone since Candide's expulsion from her father's castle:

> J'étais dans mon lit et je dormais profondément, quand il plut au ciel d'envoyer les Bulgares dans notre beau château de Thunder-ten-tronckh; ils égorgèrent mon père et mon frère, et coupèrent ma mère par morceaux. Un grand Bulgare, haut de six pieds, voyant qu'à ce spectacle j'avais perdu connaissance, se mit à me violer; cela me fit revenir, je repris mes sens, je criai, je me débattis, je mordis, j'égratignai, je voulais arracher les yeux à ce grand Bulgare, ne sachant pas que tout ce qui arrivait dans le château de mon père était une chose d'usage: le brutal me donna un coup de couteau dans le flanc gauche dont je porte encore la marque.—Hélas, j'espère bien la voir, dit le naïf Candide.—Vous la verrez, dit Cunégonde; mais continuons.—Continuez, dit Candide.

> (I was in my bed, in a deep sleep, when it pleased Heaven to send the Bulgarians into our fair castle of Thunder-ten-tronckh; they cut my father's throat and my brother's, and chopped my mother to pieces. A huge Bulgarian, six feet tall, observing that I had fainted at the sight, began to rape me; that brought me to, I recovered consciousness, I screamed, I struggled, I bit, I scratched, I tried to tear out the big Bulgar-

ian's eyes, not knowing that everything that was happening in my father's castle was perfectly customary: the brute gave me a knife-thrust in my left side, of which I still bear the scar. "Alas! I hope that I shall see it," said the simple Candide. "You shall see it," said Cunégonde; "but let us go on." "Go on," said Candide.)

These dreadful incidents appear comic because they come hammering down with almost slapstick speed and because they are represented as willed by God and everywhere prevalent—which is in comic contrast to their dreadfulness and to the aims of their victims. On top of all this comes the erotic quip at the end. Antithetical simplification of the problem and its reduction to anecdotal dimensions, together with dizzying speed of tempo, prevail throughout the novel. Misfortune follows upon misfortune, and again and again they are interpreted as necessary, proceeding from sound causes, reasonable, and worthy of the best of all possible worlds—which is obviously absurd. In this way calm reflection is drowned in laughter, and the amused reader either never observes, or observes only with difficulty, that Voltaire in no way does justice to Leibnitz's argument and in general to the idea of a metaphysical harmony of the universe, especially since so entertaining a piece as Voltaire's novel finds many more readers than the difficult essays of his philosophical opponents, which cannot be understood without serious study. Indeed, even the observation that the supposed reality of experience which Voltaire builds up does not correspond to experience at all, that it has been artfully adjusted to his polemic purpose, must have escaped most contemporary readers, or if not, they would hardly have made much of it. The rhythm of the adventures which befall Candide and his companions is to be nowhere observed in the reality of experience. Such a relentless, unrelated torrent of mishaps pouring down from a clear sky on the heads of perfectly innocent and unprepared people whom it involves by mere chance, simply does not exist. It is much more like the mishaps of a comic figure in a farce or a clown in a circus. Even apart from this excessive concentration of mishaps and the fact that in all too many cases they bear no inner relation whatever to their victims, Voltaire falsifies reality by an extreme simplification of the causes of events. The causes of human destinies which appear in his realistic propaganda pieces for the Enlightenment are either natural phenomena or accidents or—insofar as human behavior is admitted as a cause—the promptings of instinct, maliciousness, and especially stupidity. He never pursues historical conditions as determinants of human destinies, convictions, and institutions. This applies both to the history of individuals and to that of states, religions, and human society in general. Just as in our first example (the London exchange) Anabaptism, Judaism, and Quakerism are made to appear meaningless, stupid, and accidental, so in *Candide* the wars, troop-levies, religious persecutions, and the views of the nobility or the clergy are made to appear equally meaningless, stupid, and accidental. For Voltaire, it is a perfectly self-evident premise that no one in his senses can believe in an inner order of things or an inner justification for views. With equal assurance he assumes as a demonstrated premise that any individual in his personal history may encounter any destiny which is in accordance with the laws of nature, regardless of the possibility of a connection between destiny and character; and he sometimes amuses himself by putting together causal chains in which he explains only the factors which are phenomena of nature and purposely omits anything to do with morals or the history of the individuals concerned. By way of example we may turn to the fourth chapter of *Candide*, where Pangloss discusses the origin of his syphilis:

> . . . vous avez connu Paquette, cette jolie suivante de notre auguste baronne; j'ai goûté dans ses bras les délices du paradis, qui ont produit ces tourmens d'enfer dont vous me voyez dévoré; elle en était infectée, elle en est peut-être morte. Paquette tenait ce présent d'un cordelier très savant, qui avait remonté à la source; car il l'avait eue d'une vieille comtesse, qui l'avait reçue d'un capitaine de cavalerie, qui la devait à une marquise, qui la tenait d'un page, qui l'avait reçue d'un jésuite qui, étant novice, l'avait eue en droite ligne d'un des compagnons de Christophe Colomb. . . .

> (. . . you knew Paquette, our august Baroness's pretty attendant; in her arms I tasted the joys of Paradise which produced the infernal tortures which you see devouring me; she was infected with them; perhaps she has died of them. Paquette had received the gift from a most learned Franciscan, who himself had gone back to the source; for he had got it from an old countess, who had received it from a cavalry captain, who owed it to a marquise, who had it from a page, who had received it from a Jesuit, who, as a novice, had received it in the direct line from one of the companions of Christopher Columbus. . . .)

Such an account, which regards only natural causes, and on the moral plane merely lays a satirical emphasis on the mores of the clergy (including their homosexuality), at the same time merrily whisking out of sight and suppressing all details of the personal history of the individuals concerned, although it is these details which brought about the various love affairs—such an account insinuates a very specific conception of the concatenation of events, in which there is room neither for the individual's responsibility for acts he commits in obedience to his natural instincts nor for anything else in his particular nature or his particular inner and outer development which leads to particular acts. It is not often that Voltaire goes as far as he does in this instance and in *Candide* in general. Basically he is a moralist; and, especially in his historical writings, there are human portraits in which the individuality comes out clearly. But he is always inclined to simplify, and his simplification is always handled in such a way that the role of sole standard of judgment is assigned to sound, practical common sense (the type of enlightened reason which began to come to the fore during his time and under his influence) and that from among the conditions which determine the course of human lives none but the material and natural are given serious consideration. Everything historical and spiritual he despises and neglects. This has to do with the active and courageous spirit with which the protagonists of Enlightenment were filled. They set out to rid human society of everything that impeded the progress of reason. Such impediments were obviously to be seen in the religious, political, and economic actualities which had grown up historically, irrationally, in contradiction to common sense, and had finally become an inextricable maze. What seemed required was not to understand and justify them but to discredit them.

Voltaire arranges reality so that he can use it for his purposes. There is no denying the presence, in many of his works, of colorful, vivid, everyday reality. But it is incomplete, consciously simplified, and hence—despite the serious didactic purpose—nonchalant and superficial. As for the stylistic level, a lowering of man's position is implied in the attitude prevailing in the writings of the Enlightenment, even when they are not as impertinently witty as Voltaire's. The tragic exaltation of the classical hero loses ground from the beginning of the eighteenth century. Tragedy itself becomes more colorful and clever with Voltaire, but it loses weight. But in its stead the intermediate genres, such as the novel and the narrative in verse, begin to flourish, and between tragedy and comedy we now have the intermediate *comédie larmoyante* [sentimental comedy]. The taste of the age does not favor the sublime; it seeks out the graceful, elegant, clever, sentimental, rational, and useful, all of which is more properly intermediate. In its intermediate level the erotic and sentimental style of *Manon Lescaut* coincides with Voltaire's style in propaganda. In both instances the people introduced are no sublime heroes detached from the context of everyday life but individuals embedded in circumstances which are usually intermediate, on which they are dependent, and in which they are enmeshed materially and even spiritually. A certain seriousness in all this cannot be overlooked, not even in Voltaire, who after all takes his ideas perfectly seriously. And so we must conclude that, in contrast to classicism, a mixing of styles now occurs once again. But it does not go far or very deep either in its everyday realism or its seriousness. It continues the aesthetic tradition of classicism inasmuch as its realism remains always pleasant. Tragic and creatural penetration and historical involvement are avoided. The realistic elements, however colorful and amusing they may be, remain mere froth. With Voltaire the pleasantness and frothiness of the realism, which is present only to serve the ends of Enlightenment ideology, have developed into such an art that he is able to use even the "creatural" premonitions of his own decrepitude and death which come to him during his last years, as material for an amiably jocular introduction to a popular philosophical disquisition. In this connection I will cite an example which has already been analyzed by L. Spitzer (*Romanische Stil- und Literaturstudien*, Marburg, 1931, 2, 238ff.) It is a letter which the gaunt seventy-six-year old patriarch with the fleshless mask, whom everybody remembers, wrote to Mme Necker[4] when the sculptor Pigalle had come to Ferney to do a bust of him. It reads:

A Madame Necker.
Ferney, 19 juin 1770

Quand les gens de mon village ont vu Pigalle déployer quelques instruments de son art: Tiens, tiens, disaient-ils, on va le disséquer; cela sera drôle. C'est ainsi, madame, vous le savez, que tout spectacle amuse les hommes; on va également aux marionnettes, au feu de la Saint-Jean, à l'Opéra-Comique, à la grand'messe, à un enterrement. Ma statue fera sourire quelques philosophes, et renfrognera les sourcils éprouvés de quelque coquin d'hypocrite ou de quelque polisson de folliculaire: vanité des vanités!

Mais tout n'est pas vanité; ma tendre reconnaissance pour mes amis et surtout pour vous, madame, n'est pas vanité.

Mille tendres obéissances à M. Necker.

(When the people of my village saw Pigalle lay out some of the instruments of his art: "Why, look," said they, "he's going to be dissected; that will be curious." So it is, Madame, as you well know, that any spectacle amuses mankind; people go indifferently to a marionette-show, to a Midsummer Eve bonfire, to high mass, to a funeral. My statue will make a few philosophers smile, and knit the practiced brows of some villainous hypocrite or some depraved hack: vanity of vanities! But all is not vanity; my fond gratitude for my friends and above all for you, Madame, is not vanity. A thousand fond homages to Monsieur Necker.)

4. This is the married name of Suzanne Curchod, whose melancholy letter to Edward Gibbon was noted above, p. 114, n. 3 [*Editor*].

I refer the reader to Spitzer's excellent analysis, which pursues and interprets every shade of expression throughout the text, and shall limit myself to adding or summarizing what is essential for the problem of style here under discussion. The realistic anecdote which serves as point of departure is either invented or at least rearranged for the purpose. It is not at all likely that peasants about the year 1770 should have been more familiar with anatomical dissection than with the sculptor's craft. Who Pigalle was must have been widely discussed; and that portraits should be made of the famous châtelain who had lived among them for a decade must have seemed more natural to them than the idea of dissecting a person who had quite recently still been seen alive. That some half-educated wit among them could have made a remark of this sort is of course not entirely impossible, but I imagine most readers confronted with this question will find it much more probable that Voltaire himself was the wit. However that may be, whether he arranged the setting himself (as I suppose he did) or whether chance supplied him with it exactly as he describes it, in either case, it is an extraordinary, much too pat, theatrical piece of reality, admirably and exclusively suited to what he appends to it: the trite bit of worldly wisdom, charmingly and amiably presented, the fireworks display of examples in which the sacred and profane are mixed together with the characteristic impertinence of the Enlightenment, the irony in regard to his own fame, the polemic allusions to his enemies, the summing up of the whole in the basic theme from Solomon,[5] and finally the recourse to the word *vanité* to find the turn of expression which concludes the letter and which radiates all the charm of the still amiable and still lively old man, all the charm of the entire century in the formation of which he played so prominent a part. The whole thing is, as Spitzer puts it, a unique phenomenon, the *billet* of the Rococo Enlightenment. It is so much the more unique in that the texture of worldly wisdom and amiable wit is here linked to an anecdote which conjures up the creaturality of the old man's decrepit body, but a step from the grave. Yet even with such a subject Voltaire remains witty and pleasing. How many different elements this text contains: there is the artfully arranged realism; there is the perfection of charm in social relations, which combine great warmth of expression with a high degree of reserve; there is the superficiality of a creatural self-confrontation which is at the same time the exalted amiability which refuses to let one's own somber emotions become a burden to anyone else; there is the didactic ethos which characterized the great men of the Enlightenment and which made them able to use their last breath to formulate some new idea wittily and pleasingly.

---

5. The basic theme of the book of Ecclesiastes, supposed to be written by King Solomon, is "Vanity of vanities! All is vanity!" [*Editor*].

I. O. WADE

[Voltaire and *Candide*]†

The *Journal encyclopédique*[1] was far from favorable in its review of *Candide*. Indeed, it was so severe that Voltaire felt constrained to take its editors to task for what he deemed their ineptitude. Their article, however, certainly merits attention, since it contains the type of ambiguous evaluation characteristic of all criticism of *Candide* down to the present day:

> How to pass judgment on this novel? Those who have been amused by it will be furious at a serious criticism, those who have read it with a critical eye will consider our lenity a crime. The partisans of Leibniz, far from considering it a refutation of optimism, will consider it a joke from one end to the other, a joke which may be good for a laugh but proves nothing; the opponents of Leibniz will maintain that the refutation is complete, because Leibniz's system, being nothing but a fable, can only be attacked effectively by another fable. Those who seek in fiction only a portrayal of the manners and customs of the age will find its touches too licentious and too monotonous. In short, it is a freak of wit which, in order to please a wide public, needs a bit of decency and some more circumspection. We wish the author had spoken more respectfully concerning religion and the clergy, and that he had not made use of the miserable story of Paraguay, which as it appears here contributes nothing new or amusing. . . .

Thus the author of the article assumed that if the conte were intended to refute Leibniz, its success would be doubtful, and even if it were effective as a refutation, it could not be considered a work of art because of its indecencies and exaggerations. In general, the *Journal's* criticism gives the impression that *Candide* can neither be taken seriously nor dismissed lightly.

Voltaire found present in his period this same peculiar ambiguity noted by the *Journal encyclopédique* in its review. At the time he was writing the conte, he commented again and again that Paris "qui chante et qui danse" [which sings and dances] had abandoned its frivolous air for the serious air of the English. Instead of being "singes" [monkeys] performing "singeries," [monkey-business] which was perfectly normal

† From I. O. Wade, *Voltaire and Candide* (Princeton, 1959) 311–22. Copyright 1959; reprinted by permission of the Princeton University Press. Quotations from the French have been translated by the present editor.
1. March 15, 1759, p. 103.

and natural, Parisians had become "ours," [bears] debating and prattling about serious things. One gathers from his comment that he deplored the change, and in fact he does so in his *Correspondance*, but in Chapter XXII of the novel itself, he condemns Paris "qui chante et qui danse," Paris of the "singeries." His attitude toward this situation is not the important thing, however; the author's attitude never is, in a work of art. What is really significant is that the conte has absorbed the ambiguity of its time and of its author. *Candide* is the product of those "qui dansent et qui chantent," the "singes" and their "singeries," but also of the "ours" who take themselves seriously. And it is difficult to know which is the real, authentic *Candide*.

Grimm's review in the *Correspondance littéraire*, less favorable still, did precisely what the author of the *Journal encyclopédique* article deemed impossible. Renouncing any attempt to treat the work seriously, Grimm insisted that the only way to handle it was to take it lightly. After finding the second half superior to the first, after condemning the chapter on Paris, after denying the conte every serious literary and phil-osophical quality, he found only Voltaire's gaiety to praise:

> Gaiety is one of the rarest qualities to be found among wits. It is a long time since we read anything joyous in literature; M. de Voltaire has just delighted [but *égayer* has also the sense of "mock"] us with a little novel called *Candide, or optimism*, translated from the German of Dr. Ralph. There is no need to judge this performance by high standards; it would never stand up to serious criticism. There is in *Candide* neither arrangement nor plan nor wisdom nor any of those happy strokes which one sometimes finds in English novels of the same sort; instead, you will find in it plenty of things in bad taste, low touches, smut and filth deprived of that discreet veil which renders them supportable; but gaiety and facility never abandon M. de Voltaire, who banishes from his most frivolous as from his most carefully worked writings that air of pretension which spoils everything. The fine touches and gay sallies which he gives off at every moment make the reading of *Candide* a very amusing experience.

Thus *Candide* became for Grimm what Voltaire often called it: "une plaisanterie" [a jest].

Mme. de Staël, on the other hand, takes a position the very opposite of Grimm's. She admits willingly that the book abounds in laughter, but considers it in no way a "plaisanterie," for this laughter contains something inhumanly diabolical. She concedes that *Candide* basically was directed against Leibniz, but stresses that it was directed against the fundamental propositions which preoccupy mankind, especially those philosophical opinions which enhance the spirit of man. Nothing could be more serious:

> Voltaire had so clear a sense of the influence which metaphysical systems exert on the direction of our thinking, that he composed *Candide* to combat Leibniz. He took a curious attitude of hostility toward final causes, optimism, free will, and in short against all these philosophic opinions which tend to raise the dignity of man; and he created *Candide,* that work of diabolic gaiety. For it seems to have been written by a creature of a nature wholly different from our own, indifferent to our lot, rejoicing in our sufferings, and laughing like a demon or an ape at the misery of this human race with which he has nothing in common.

While Grimm stresses the conte's gaiety, and Mme de Staël its seriousness, Linguet in his *Examen des ouvrages de M. de Voltaire* (Bruxelles, 1788) notes its dual character, that is to say, the glee with which Voltaire destroys the philosophy of optimism by graphically describing the tragic miseries of humanity:

> Candide offers us the saddest of themes disguised under the merriest of jokes, the joking being of that philosophical variety which is peculiar to M. de Voltaire, and which, I repeat, seems like the equipment of an excellent comedian. He makes the *all's well* system, upheld by so many philosophers, look completely ridiculous, and cracks a thousand jests even as he holds before our eyes at every instant the miseries of society and portrays them with a very energetic pencil (p. 170).

Without being too dogmatic, we can confidently assert that these four opinions, though based on the same fundamental ambiguous assumptions, are widely divergent and represent the cardinal points of all *Candide* critics. There are those who, like the author of the *Journal encyclopédique,* feel that the work can be taken neither seriously nor lightly, those who maintain with Grimm that it must be treated only lightly, those who aver with Mme de Staël that it can be taken only seriously, and finally those who like Linguet, find that it must be taken seriously and lightly at the same time.

This double quality of gaiety and seriousness, so characteristic of Voltaire and of his time, is apparent at every turn throughout the conte, but it is not a simple matter to grasp the deep ambiguity of its personality. When the reader is ready to revolt in horror, a sudden reflection, a quick turn in events, an unexpected quip, or the mere insertion of a remark brings him back to normal. When he is inclined to levity, an incident, an observation, or an injustice brings him back to consider the deadly earnest attack which is being made on all aspects of life.

The difficulty in harmonizing these two attitudes in the reader's understanding has led to divers partial interpretations of *Candide*, practically all of them valid in their way but each woefully deficient in itself. If the book is to be taken lightly, how lightly? Can it be dismissed as the "crème fouettée de l'Europe," [whipped cream of Europe] or is it a "bonne plaisanterie," with a "fonds le plus triste" [an undertone of sadness]? Does Candide, like Figaro, rail at everything to keep himself from weeping? Is it, as Montaigne once said of Rabelais, "simplement plaisant" [naïvely comic] on the surface, but "triste" underneath? There is a similar progression in the opposite attitude. How far does Voltaire go in his satire? Does he, for instance, merely castigate the social conditions of his time, as Boileau or Horace had done before him, or does he satirize the fundamental conditions of life, like a Homer or a Racine, or does he push his revolt to the point of satirizing the Creator of life? These are difficult, almost irreverent, questions. The answers must always be yes, although every yes is contradicted by another yes, or a yes and no by another yes and no. Far from being a structure of "clear and distinct ideas," *Candide* is confusion confounded. But it is the confusion of a universe clearly and distinctly controlled. Whatever happens may be terribly and devastatingly irrational, but once it has been sifted through Voltaire's intelligence, it has been ordered by the keenest sort of criticism into a created form which does not differ from the form of life itself. *Candide* embraces everything that has occurred in the life of Voltaire as well as everything that had occurred in the eighteenth century. It is astounding in its comprehensiveness, and quite as remarkable in other aspects: the rhythmical arrangement of the above-mentioned phenomena, the careful selection and presentation, the exact apportionment, and the very orderly expression.

That is the reason why every judgment of *Candide* is bound to be partial, one-sided, contradictory, and vague, just like every judgment we make of life or of our individual lives. Since every man is a "Démocrite" and a "Héraclite," he must be "Jean-qui-pleure" and "Jean-qui-rit."[2] But every man must be these two characters at the same time: he is neither optimist nor pessimist, rebellious nor submissive, free nor enslaved, formed nor unformed, real nor unreal. He must make a reality of these necessary contradictions.

The four opinions expressed above, while representing the four cardinal positions in *Candide* criticism, in no way exhaust the range of partial interpretations given the work. I pass over Voltaire's own sly

2. Title of a poem by Voltaire, which concludes: "We're formed of clay divine, so much I know,/ And all, one day, will rise to heavenly glory./ But here on earth we see a different story./ Souls are machines, which fate bids stop or go./ Watch nature change her giddy mood;/ Although, like Heraclitus, he was sad,/ Let business suddenly be good,/ And man will, like Democritus, be glad" [*Editor*].

remark that it was written to convert Socinians, as well as the superficial, but amusing, epigram current at the time of its appearance:

> Candide is a little crook,
> Shameless and weak in the head;
> You can tell by his sly look,
> He's kid brother to *The Maid*.[3]

> His old dad would give a pack
> Just to be young again:
> His youth will come back,
> He's writing like a young man.

> Life isn't great, take a look,
> He proves it six different ways,
> You'll even see in this book
> Things really stink, like he says.

Of more importance is the qualification printed in the *Nouvelles ecclé-siastiques*:[4] "Bad novel, full of filth, perhaps the most impious and pernicious work ever to come from the pen of M. de Voltaire," or the opinion attributed to the Patriarch [i.e., Voltaire himself] by the un-known author of the *Confession de Voltaire*:[5] "It follows from the reading of *Candide* that the earth is a sewer of horror and abominations [with a quotation from Job 10:22 'A land of misery and shadows, where is no order but eternal horror dwells']; more than one chapter of it was com-posed during attacks of migraine. . . ." or the more drastic qualification of Jules Janin in *Le dernier volume des Œuvres de Voltaire*.[6]

> The book was much read in high society, where it was not understood. People saw nothing but romantic adventures where Voltaire with fiendish logic had intended to ridicule God.

After so many categorical statements, made with appropriately French nuance, it may seem idle to seek a clearer view of *Candide's* reality. It is quite possible to agree that the work is a "vaurien" [no good], or obscene, or perhaps the most impious ever written by Voltaire, or that its portrayal of the earth is abomination and horror incarnate. One might even go so far as to agree with Janin that "Voltaire avait voulu railler Dieu" [Voltaire intended to ridicule God]. But to understand that the work is at the same time a revolt and a submission, an attack and a defense, a joy and a suffering, a destruction and a creation requires more than ordinary insight, patience, and serenity. There is, indeed,

3. Voltaire's *La Pucelle*.
4. September 3, 1760, p. 158.

5. Geneva, 1762, p. 39.
6. Paris, 1861, p. 103.

the temptation to dismiss it as only one thing, as too simple, too superficial.

What is dangerous in *Candide* is not its simplicity, but its duplicity. *Candide* is always deceptively two. Its unremitting ambiguity leads inevitably to a puzzling clandestinity, and the reader, beset with difficulties in forming a well-considered opinion, settles for trite commonplaces. The work actually encourages him in this. Let us take as an example the oft-repeated remark that Voltaire attacked Leibniz. Though true, this statement adds nothing to the comprehension of *Candide's* reality.

It would be useful, nevertheless, to understand the relationship between *Candide* and Leibniz.[7] Undeniably, Voltaire satirized Leibnizian terminology in his conte but ample testimony has been adduced to show that he never rejected Leibnizianism: he rejected some things in it— the theory of monads, for example—but he readily accepted other ideas such as the principle of sufficient reason. We have already shown that he needed Leibniz's principles, just as they were needed by the eighteenth century at large. It is a particularly carefree criticism that envisages the development of ideas as a matter of acceptance or rejection. Voltaire was certainly more realistic in his attitude. What he satirized was the terminology; not the philosophy, but what in that philosophy was now contributing to making life sterile. Moreover, at the moment he was writing *Candide*, he stated explicitly that people had ceased paying attention to what Leibniz said. Soon after, when a new edition of Leibniz's works was published, he complimented the editor. The truth of the matter is that Voltaire, like his time, had to integrate Descartes, Pascal, Leibniz, Spinoza, Malebranche, Locke and Newton in order to create an Enlightenment philosophy. Leibniz was as important to that philosophy as any of the others, and fully as useful. It is probable that in 1750 he had played his role and in that sense had ceased to claim people's attention. But even this assessment is subject to caution.

This dilemma has led certain critics to insist that what Voltaire is attacking is not a philosopher, but a philosophy. Ever since the article of March 15, 1759, in the *Journal encyclopédique*, some critics have insisted that Voltaire definitely aimed his attack not against Leibniz or Pope, but against a system of philosophy to which Leibniz, Pope, and many others had contributed and which we now call optimism. Since he himself entitled his work *Candide, ou l'optimisme*, it would be extremely difficult to deny that he directed his satire at this way of looking at life. To conclude, however, with Linguet, that "il tourne complètement en ridicule le système du tout est bien" [he makes the *all's well* system look completely ridiculous"], or, with Lanson, that "le but est de démolir l'optimisme" ["his aim is to demolish optimism"], is misplacing the emphasis. It would not take a very skillful lawyer to prove

---

7. For this entire paragraph, it would be useful to refresh one's memory of "Summary: The Intellectual Backgrounds," above, pp. 79–84 [*Editor*].

that Voltaire's treatment of optimism is quite as optimistic as the treatment of the optimists themselves, that he says no more for or against it than Leibniz, Pope, King, and hundreds of others. Voltaire is assailing all feeling of complacency which nullifies and stultifies human effort in a universe requiring a maximum of human effort to realize itself—he is assailing, in a word, all restraints upon the creative spirit of man.

It must be admitted that his attitude toward optimism is difficult to trace because of the ambiguity of his position. He was congenitally opposed to any attitude which complacently asseverated that "tout est bien," mainly because such a belief limited human effort. But he was quite as opposed to any attitude which despairingly asserted that "tout est mal," chiefly because such a standpoint also limited human effort. But other considerations were important, too. Voltaire knew that "tout n'est pas bien" because there are numerous concrete cases of evil, and he knew also that "tout n'est pas mal" because there are many concrete cases of good. Throughout the conte, he draws a constant parallel between the wretchedness of others and his own happiness, and he continually wavers between the achievements of his time and its follies. He weighs facts as scrupulously as Montaigne weighed truth: the facts prove two things, two exasperatingly contradictory things. Cacambo's friendship and loyalty make him "un tres bon homme" [a very good man], while Vanderdendur's duplicity makes him "un homme très dur" [a very hard man], but both are realities, just as the "duretés" of the "homme noir" and the kindness of the "bon Jacques" are realities. There is thus in Candide a compensatory quality, common to all Voltaire's works and to the eighteenth century in general, that is, that good is counterbalanced by evil. This is no new attitude: it is evident throughout his works from the Epître à Uranie to Candide. Le Monde comme il va, Micromégas, Zadig hold steadily to this idea.

It is not the view, however, that is important, but the conclusion to be drawn from it. Should one conclude for optimism, or surrender to pessimism? Should one be content with weighing impassively this against that, refusing to take sides, enjoying fully his own happiness? This skeptical conclusion, characteristic of the Renaissance in general and of Montaigne in particular, did not find favor with Voltaire, although he, like most Frenchmen, was strongly attracted to it. The ambiguity of Candide's garden, and of its actual prototype at Les Délices and Ferney, was occasioned in fact by this skeptical conclusion. But Voltaire's skepticism, which is as positive as Montaigne's, is no proof against his cynicism. It was impossible to "jouir largement de son être" [enjoy freely his existence] in 1758 after the fiasco at Berlin, the Lisbon Earthquake, and the Seven Years War. It was possible, perhaps, to criticize, blame, satirize, laugh mockingly, always with indifference, in this completely mad world. Voltaire attempted to adopt this attitude also but found it quite unsatisfactory.

Candide is thus in its inner substance not *wholly* optimistic, or pessimistic, or skeptical, or cynical: it is *all* of these things at the same time. Since every created thing resembles its creator and the moment of its creation, it is precisely what Voltaire and his time were: optimistic, pessimistic, skeptical, and cynical, a veritable "moment de la crise" [moment of crisis]. Facts had produced ideas, it is true, but ideas had not yet produced ideals, and no one knew what *to do*.

There are, of course, several ways of meeting this situation. First, there is resignation: Christian or even philosophical resignation, both unacceptable to Voltaire. Having rejected Christianity, dogma and all, he could find no solace in an attitude leading to consequences that he could not accept, and having long since adopted libertine Epicureanism, he saw no sense in any form of stoicism, Christian or pagan.

Second, there is the way of attack, for if conditions are intolerable, they can be denounced. It is as easy to ridicule distasteful facts, offensive people, disagreeable incidents, and unfair judgments as to satirize an unacceptable view of the universe. Voltaire responded freely and fully to this temptation: the list of things and persons he assails is practically endless: kings, religious intolerance, the Inquisition; Fréron, Vanduren, Trublet; war, inequality, injustice; disease, earthquake, tidal waves; petty thievery, rape, social pride; Jesuits, Jansenists, slavery. In this mass and single attack there is a complete upheaval of the social order; in the political area we find deep criticism of monarchy, the policing of the state, the lack of freedom and equality before the law. In the realm of religion there are powerful accusations against persecution, intolerance, useless dogma, and hierarchical institution. In the moral order, dishonesty, shame, false pride, prostitution, rape, all the petty inhumanities of man against man are viciously assailed. In the natural order, disease, cataclysms, malformations are damned with an irreverence barely short of blasphemy. And yet, though *Candide* attacks, it does not ultimately destroy. The reason for this is very simple: life is full of miseries, but it also has its pleasures. It is perhaps true that few people would like to relive it, but also true that few voluntarily renounce it. Voltaire was certainly not one to abdicate.

Nevertheless, as the crisis developed, he was torn between cynical renunciation and the urge to create. He was completely aware that the forces restraining this urge were powerful enough to eliminate not only the desire but the person desiring. Experience had taught him the stupidities of man, the horrors of war, the power of kings, and the eccentricities of nature. Any one of these could easily suppress him and his urge to create. He was thus literally reduced to living by his wits, like J. F. Rameau and Figaro,[8] and living by his wits meant very literally

---

8. *Rameau's Nephew* is a character sketch by Diderot of a parasite; Figaro is the hero of Beaumarchais's play (and Rossini's opera) *The Barber of Seville*. Both characters are clever rogues [*Editor*].

indeed the application of wit to all this stupid phenomenon. The world had become a paradox and Voltaire responded with a revolt.

It is imperative to understand the nature of this revolt, since the whole eighteenth century and subsequent centuries have derived from it. Voltaire's response was born of both anger and despair. He was "fâché" [angry] with kings, "fâché" with earthquakes, "fâché" with God. Agamemnon, the great Earthshaker and Zeus had "let him down," just as they had seemed to abandon Achilles in a far distant moment. The two urns which stand at the feet of Zeus poured forth both good and evil upon the old Patriarch and he, in his frustration, became deeply unhappy, the more so since events transcended all understanding by the human mind:

> Poor feeble reason, blind, misled, bemused,
> If with God's insights it be not suffused,
> Will ne'er conceive what power out of hell
> Mingled so much of ill with what is well.

Voltaire's attitude toward Providence must be considered very carefully if we are to grasp the meaning of *Candide*. It was perhaps well to ask ourselves what role Rousseau's letter played in the composition of the conte. While it is extremely unlikely that the *Lettre sur la Providence* provoked *Candide*, as Rousseau would have us believe, it is nevertheless true that Rousseau's defense of Providence touched Voltaire in his sensitive spot. The conclusion of *Zadig*, it will be recalled, had definitely been a defense of Providence, along more rational, Popian lines than Rousseau's later defense. The problem is therefore posed as to Voltaire's subsequent attitude.

If, to be specific, Voltaire felt that Pope's arguments no longer "justified the ways of God to man," and Leibniz's were equally deficient, did he think that he had better ones, or that he could find better ones elsewhere? In other words, was his quarrel with the optimists whose arguments could not justify God's ways or with God whose way could not be rationally justified? And did he assail the philosophers with fiendish glee because he did not know how to attack Providence which was really responsible for evil? Why did he not heed Rousseau's letter as the Duke de Wurtemburg thought he should have done? Why was it rather an incitement to *Candide*, just as Rousseau thought? These are strange and almost irreverent questions, and totally unanswerable in any critical way, but necessary in divining Voltaire's state of mind. It is undoubtedly true that his act was not a critique but a revolt, a titanic revolt brought about by a breakdown in the power of critique. Having reached the place where understanding was irrational, Voltaire had no other resource than to attack overtly those who thought they understood, and who gave good rational reasons for their comprehension. Simply put, he could only attack the irrationality, the ambiguity of the universe by annihilating rationally all rationality. In that respect his wit is a spiritual, not a rational, instrument for assailing the ambiguity, the clandestinity of a universe which refuses to make itself known.

This state of things explains why one never knows in reading *Candide* whether to laugh with Voltaire or at him, whether to laugh with the philosophers or at them, whether indeed to laugh with or at Providence; whether, in fact, to laugh at all. In uncertainty and despair there is much ground for hesitation, uneasiness, bitterness, frustration. Taken seriously, the moment of *Candide* is a tragic affair. But should it be taken seriously? Mme d'Epinay in her characterization of Voltaire states that when he has become most serious he immediately starts making fun of himself and everybody else. This reaction seems to hold true for *Candide*. Certainly no one takes himself too seriously in *Candide*. When the moment of revolt becomes too intense, each person resorts to his wit to save the situation. Thus wit is not only a means of revolt, it is at the same time an instrument for the release of intolerable pressures and better still, it serves as a release for the inner forces of man; it is a force, too, a creative effort, an urge to be. Standing face to face with the power of annihilation, impotent to solve either the rationality or the irrationality of things, witness to an impossibly ludicrous cosmic tragedy, *Candide* proclaims loudly, not that

> The play is the tragedy Man
> And its hero, the Conqueror Worm[9]

but that the play is puny, insignificant, unregenerate man, and its hero an unconquerable, defiant, eternal wit.

J. G. WEIGHTMAN

The Quality of *Candide*†

It may seem late in the day to ask how good a book *Candide* really is. Has the world not been long agreed that it is a masterpiece? It started triumphantly by being banned in Paris and Geneva, and has gone on selling ever since. It has provided France and the world with two or three proverbial expressions. Schopenhauer praised it in the most emphatic terms;[1] Flaubert said that it contained the quintessence of Voltaire's writings;[2] H. N. Brailsford declared that it "ranks in its own way

9. From Edgar Allan Poe, "The Conqueror Worm" [Editor].
† From *Essays Presented to C. M. Girdlestone* Durham, 1960) 335–47. Reprinted by permission of J. G. Weightman. Quotations from the French have been translated by the present editor.

1. "I can see no other merit in Leibniz's *Theodicy* except that of having furnished the great Voltaire with the occasion of his immortal *Candide*." Quoted in *La Table Ronde*, Feb., 1958, p. 111.
2. *Correspondance*, ed. Conard, II, p. 348.

with *Don Quixote* and *Faust*".[3] So alive is it, indeed, that it was recently turned into an American musical and has thus shared with *Manon Lescaut* and *Les Liaisons dangereuses* the honour of being relaunched in the twentieth century as a work with a universal appeal for mass audiences.

But, on second thoughts, this may appear a doubtful honour and make us wonder on what level of success *Candide* has been operating. *Manon Lescaut* and *Les Liaisons dangereuses* are perhaps compromising connections, since their moral and aesthetic acceptability has often been questioned by literary critics. And it is true that Voltaire himself is still often referred to as if he were, generally speaking, rather disreputable; irreverent, outmoded, a mere maker of debating points. Faguet's 'un chaos d'idées claires' [a chaos of clear ideas] is a Voltairean jibe that has been used, effectively, against Voltaire. Mr. Martin Turnell, a contemporary English critic with a stern approach to French Literature, refers briefly to 'the flashy vulgarity of *Candide*'.[4] Even those people who have a genuine interest in Voltaire often imply that we should not look for depths or complexities in him. Carl Becker, after doubting whether Voltaire really understood the brilliance of his own witticisms, suggests that his scepticism did not amount to much, and that *Candide* is not a central text:

> The cynicism of Voltaire was not bred in the bone . . . It was all on the surface, signifying nothing but the play of a supple and irrepressible mind, or the sharp impatience of an exasperated idealist. In spite of *Candide* and all the rest of it, Voltaire was an optimist, though not a naïve one.[5]

The late Professor Saurat, introducing a selection of Voltaire's tales, differs from Becker in crediting Voltaire with deep feeling. However, he then goes on to deny him depth of intelligence:

> The jesting of *Candide* is the mournful levity of a belief expiring in the face of the facts, but which nonetheless persists. He would have preferred Leibniz to be right; but his intelligence, though so quick, was not deep enough to let him see that Leibniz was right.[6]

Professor Saurat does not explain in what way Leibniz is in the right. Already in 1913, in his critical edition of *Candide*, André Morize

3. *Candide and Other Tales*, Everyman's Library, 1937, p. xxiv.
4. *The Novel in France*, Hamish Hamilton, 1950, p. 189.
5. *The Heavenly City of the Eighteenth Century*

Philosophers, Yale University Press, 1957 edition, pp. 36, 37.
6. *Le Taureau blanc*, etc., The Hyperion Press, 1945, p. 5.

had emphasized that Voltaire did not appear to have a detailed knowledge of Leibniz's arguments:

> Candide or Optimism is by no means the product of a me-
> taphysician to whom Leibniz and the Theodicy were familiar.[7]

Richard Aldington, in his introduction to the Broadway Translation of 1927, gives a summary of the philosophical controversy from which Candide emerged, because—he says—the book 'is often represented as a merely amusing squib'. But his own conclusion seems strangely self-contradictory:

> Its popularity is due to its amusing adventures, its clear rapid
> style, its concentrated wit, its vitality and alertness, and to its
> triumphant disposal of facile optimism. Whether it really proves
> anything may admit of doubt . . .[8]

Dr. W. H. Barber, who gives a beautifully clear and meticulous account of the shifts in Voltaire's position with regard to optimism, makes a comment on Candide which might appear to reduce the book to personal satire on minor Neo-Leibnizians:

> Voltaire is not concerned to refute a doctrine by careful ar-
> gument; his object is to ridicule a band of enthusiasts whose
> ideas he thinks absurd; and the immediate and lasting popu-
> larity of Candide is some measure of his success.[9]

A similar statement is made by Hugo Friedrich in a special number of La Table Ronde devoted to Voltaire:

> At bottom it was not Leibniz whom Voltaire attacked, but the
> cheap optimism fashionable in Paris salons, as seasoned with
> obscure German lucubrations. We must not read Candide as
> a novel with a thesis . . . we must let ourselves be amused by
> watching a free spirit playing with very grave questions for lack
> of power to resolve them.[1]

All these judgements must seem rather slighting to anyone who has a high regard for Candide, because they suggest that the book is, in fact, more of a squib than anything else. Consequently, there may be a case

---

7. Librairie E. Droz, p. xiii.
8. Routledge, p. 16. My [Weightman's] italics.
9. Leibniz in France, O.U.P., 1955, p. 232.
1. La Table Ronde, February 1958, pp. 111–115.

for reopening the argument and trying to decide what exactly *Candide* achieves.

The first thing to establish, if possible, is that *Candide* is basically serious. Of course, Voltaire was never at any time fair-minded, and there seems every reason to believe that he did not bother to reread, or even read, Leibniz's *Théodicée* before writing his satire. As both Morize and Barber point out, he mixes up the two main forms of the theory of optimism: the belief that evil is an effect of the human angle of vision, and the belief that evil is a necessary part of creation. He makes no attempt to distinguish between the different degrees of sophistication represented by Leibniz, Pope and Wolff. Leibniz neither denied the existence of evil nor held the simple finalistic views which Voltaire attributes to Pangloss. Also, as Barber shows, Leibniz was an activist whose purpose was to encourage men to virtuous initiative within the all-embracing framework of God's will, and as such he was, in a sense, on Voltaire's side. If one wished to press the accusation of superficiality still further against Voltaire, one could recall that he himself began by being an optimist who declared in the *Traité de métaphysique* that moral evil was 'une chimère' ["a dream"] and the notion of evil a relative one:

> To be quite sure that a thing is evil one must see at the same time that something better is possible.[2]

The Angel Jesrad in *Zadig*, which comes before *Candide*, is on the whole Leibnizian in his statement that a world without evil would be another kind of world. So is the Quaker, Freind, in the very late conte, *L'Histoire de Jenni*. In other works of his later years—the *Homélies prononcées à Londres en 1765*, *Questions sur l'Encyclopédie*, *Il faut prendre un parti* and *Fragments historiques sur l'Inde*—Voltaire contradicts himself, saying in one place that God is obviously limited and repeating in another that evil exists only from the human point of view and must be unknown to God in His perfection.

Have we to conclude, then, that Voltaire had a shallow mind which casually adopted different sets of ideas at different times? Is *Candide* an irresponsible attack on beliefs that he was capable of putting forward as his own, when they happened to serve his purpose? Is he simply a jester who does not understand what the philosophers are about? I do not think so. The extraordinary resonance of *Candide* and the strange frenzy in which Voltaire seems to have lived during most of his life, and particularly during the latter half, point to a very different conclusion. Here was a man who, through his personal experience, his reading of history and his observation of contemporary events, gradually came to

2. *Traité de métaphysique*, ed. H.T. Patterson, Manchester U.P., 1937, p. 16.

be obsessed with the scandal of the presence of evil in the universe. At the same time, with his clear and vigorous brain he could only suppose that God was an immeasurably greater Voltaire who had organized the universe on rational lines and was not, ultimately, responsible for evil. How could God have willed evil since Voltaire, like any decent person, found it intolerable? Yet evil existed, and God must be good. But how could a good God . . . etc. He never escaped from the dilemma, but tried out different verbal solutions at different stages and was presumably never convinced by any of them. Through some psychological accident of which we shall no doubt always remain ignorant (perhaps he went through a phase like Shakespeare's tragic period), he produced *Candide* at a time when his awareness of evil was at its most violent and his vitality at its strongest. In this one book, the horror of evil and an instinctive zest for life are almost equally matched and it is the contrast between them, inside the paragraph and even inside the sentence, which produces the unique tragicomic vibration. The lesson of *Candide* is the permanent one that there is no verbal, that is intellectual, solution to the problem of evil, but that we go on living even so, and even when we think we have no faith.

If this interpretation is correct, two consequences follow. In the first place, Voltaire is not simply attacking Pope or Leibniz or the Neo-Leibnizians or J.-J. Rousseau; he is also attacking himself, because when he trusted to the philosophical use of language, he found himself arguing like them. He himself is Pangloss, just as he is Candide, Martin and Pococurante. The book is a transposition of his inner debate. And it is surely an underestimation of his wit to imply that his rapid jokes are not valid against the more elaborate explanations of evil. They are genuine caricatures. To the question: 'Why, if God is good (and we must suppose that He is), does evil exist?' there is no articulate answer which is not a juggling with words. Book VII of St. Augustine's *Confessions* is quite elaborate, but are its logical fallacies not obvious? Chapter VII of Book III of St. Thomas's *Summa Contra Gentiles* seems no less purely verbal. And when we open Leibniz to see how Voltaire misunderstood him, we find this sort of argument:

> For God sees from the beginning of time that there will be a certain Judas; and the notion or idea that God has of him contains this future free action. Only this question now remains, why this Judas, the traitor, who is only a possibility in the idea of God, exists in actuality. But to this question there can be no answer here below, except that in general one can say that since God found it proper that he should exist in spite of the sin He foresaw, it must be that this evil will be repaid with interest somewhere else in the universe, that God will

derive a greater good from it, and in short it will be found that
the sequence of events which includes the existence of this
sinner is the most perfect of all those which were possible. But
to explain in every instance the admirable economy of a particular choice, that cannot be done while we inhabit this tran-
sitory sphere; it suffices to know it without understanding it.[3]

The 'admirable economy' of a choice we know nothing about and only
suppose to have existed is an excellent example of Panglossian applauding
of the cosmos. Before Leibniz wrote the *Théodicée*, Bayle had said all
there was to be said about this kind of circular argument in dealing with
Lactantius, St. Basil and Maximus of Tyre,[4] and he was not adequately
refuted by Leibniz. In particular intellectual gifts, Bayle and Voltaire
may have been much inferior to Leibniz, but on this precise issue they
saw more clearly the futility of verbalizations. As Barber says:

> Leibniz . . . never really abandons *a priori* argument. He bases
> his knowledge of God's nature on *a priori* rational consider-
> ations . . . and once God's infinite goodness and wisdom have
> thus been established, all else also follows deductively. Thus
> he never really meets Bayle on his own ground. To all Bayle's
> paradoxes he has at bottom only one reply, though his subtlety
> of argument sometimes conceals the fact; the world as it is is
> God's creation, therefore no better world is possible.[5]

In the second place, *Candide* is not in the last resort a message of
hope, or at least not exactly in the way suggested by some critics who
take a favourable view of it. Morize, Barber and René Pomeau, the
author of *La Religion de Voltaire*, all seem to me to underestimate the
virulence of the work. Morize writes:

> The world is in shambles, blood flows, Jesuits and Molinists
> rage, innocents are slaughtered and dupes exploited; but there
> are in the world delicious asylums, where life remains possible,
> joyous, and sweet: let us cultivate our garden.[6]

This suggests an ability to shut out the spectacle of the world which
Voltaire never possessed, and does not correspond to the tone of dogged
persistence in the final chapters of *Candide*. According to Barber:

3. *Discours de Métaphysique*, 30, in *Leibnizens
Gesammelte Werke*, Hannover 1846. [Once again
the reader is referred to "Summary: The Intellectual Backgrounds," pp. 79–84, for explanation of
the major allusions in Weightman's argument—
[Editor.]

4. Voltaire's incisive analysis of verbal circularity
in Lactantius (above, pp. 85–86) illustrates sufficiently the character of Bayle's more wide-ranging
exposés [Editor].

5. *Leibniz in France*, p. 88.

6. Librairie E. Droz, p. xlvii.

The practical philosophy to which Candide finally attains is
the application to the limited field of personal activity of that
espérance [hope] which Voltaire had offered to humanity on
a transcendental level in the conclusion of the *Poème sur le
désastre de Lisbonne.*

In rejecting the doctrines of Pangloss and his like . . . he
is seeking . . . a safe foundation in an insecure world for that
profound belief in the value of activity which is characteristic
of European man and was particularly strong in him.[7]

But does he find any such foundation? There is no evidence in *Candide*,
and very little in his biography, that he had a profound belief in the
value of activity. He believed in man's need for activity and he himself
had a tremendous urge to be active, but these can be independent of
any conviction of value. Would it not be more plausible to suppose that
his feverish busyness was the only relief he could find for his acute
awareness of evil? Pomeau speaks of the "epicurean motive for action
which is the last word of the tale" and says that Voltaire "will make a
philosophy of activity . . . A lesson revolutionary in its banality." No
doubt, Voltaire borrowed the image of the garden from Epicurus,[8] but
he has no trace of Epicurean serenity or moderation. Actually, Pomeau
is uncertain about the ultimate significance of the work. In *La Religion
de Voltaire* (1956), he declares roundly:

Is the philosophy of *Candide* a philosophy of the "absurd"?
Certainly not. Candide is not, any more than Jacques or Figaro, a hero tragically abandoned in a wrong world. Whatever
surprises existence may hold for them, these wanderers are not
"outsiders" . . . Amid the worst disasters, Candide's universe
always furnishes a lifesaving plank.[9]

However, in his critical edition of 1959, after making some excellent
remarks about the poetic quality of *Candide*, he contradicts his earlier
statement:

Spontaneously, from the poetry of the unforeseen, there arises
a philosophy of the absurd.[1]

Only one critic appears to have stressed unequivocally the strength of
the dark side of Voltaire's temperament, which is so obvious in *Candide*

---

7. *Leibniz in France*, p. 233.
8. Epicurus, the classical philosopher who made
pleasure the supreme goal of life, had a famous
garden, where he lived an impressively moderate

and contemplative existence [*Editor*].
9. Librairie Nizet, 1956, p. 305.
1. Librairie Nizet, 1959, p. 70.

and in the correspondence. This is André Delattre, in his stimulating little book, *Voltaire l'impétueux*, where we read:

> It is only when, in *Candide*, he accepts certain perspectives of Pascal's, it is only when he ceases to strain against a dark and healthy pessimism, and ceases to hold open the empty sack of his optimism, that he finally creates, after his sixtieth year, his real masterpiece.[2]

This is a good pointer to the quality of the work. *Candide* is not just a clever, unfair satire on optimism which concludes with the bracing recommendation that we should do what we can to improve matters in our immediate vicinity. It is a work in which an unappeasable sense of the mystery and horror of life is accompanied, at every step, by an instinctive animal resilience. Negative and positive are juxtaposed (as they are, indeed, in some religious temperaments) with no unsatisfactory ratiocinative bridge between them. Voltaire has a faith, but it is not a political faith nor an easily defined religious one. It is the sort of faith that keeps the severed fractions of a worm still wriggling, or produces laughter at a funeral. In this sense, Voltaire's humanism is a very basic and simple characteristic, exceptional only in that it has at its service extraordinary intelligence and wit.

I say 'at its service' advisedly, because *Candide* is not, in the first place, an intellectual work. Its driving force is an intellectual bewilderment, which is felt as a strong emotion. Pomeau makes the interesting suggestion that the chronological irregularity in the composition of the *contes* is proof of their springing from a level well below Voltaire's everactive, normal consciousness:

> The intermittent quality of the invention in the tales makes clear that here a deeper self is finding outlet, which does not get expressed every day.[3]

He also adduces evidence to show that *Candide*, instead of being a rapid improvisation as has often been thought, was probably written at intervals over a period of a year. He concludes that it shows signs of deliberate artistry:

> A work of spontaneous fantasy, no doubt, but in the course of working on it, retouchings and additions appear, which make plain a very conscious impulse toward artistic form.[4]

2. Mercure de France, 1947, p. 69.   4. Edition critique, p. 46.
3. Edition critique, p. 7.

I think it is possible to accept the first suggestion, while remaining unconvinced by the second. The alterations and additions Pomeau mentions are comparatively slight, and although *Candide* may have been in the making for a year, it could still be a happy fluke in which the artistry is largely unconscious. Voltaire himself seems never to have realized that it was his masterpiece, and he probably devoted more deliberate attention to denying its authorship than he had to its composition. His still-born tragedies he composed with great care, passing them round amongst his friends for comment and improvement. His tales were rattled off much more spontaneously, and he does not appear to have understood how original and gifted he was in this *genre*. If he had, he would presumably have taken more pains with some of the others, which are all either imperfect or slight. It is impossible not to agree with Delattre on this score:

> As for the tales, apart from *Candide* which is in a class by itself, they are really thin, quite slender.[5]

There is no progression up to *Candide*, nor any sign of further development afterwards. Good *contes* and less good were written higgledy-piggledy. *Zadig*, which came twelve years before *Candide*, and *L'Ingénu*, written eight years after, are probably the next best, but the first is uncertain in design and ends feebly, while the second begins in one tone and finishes rather abruptly in another, without the transition having been properly justified. Neither is firmly centered on a major theme. Other *contes*, such as *Le Monde comme il va* and *Micromégas*, which keep to one theme, repeat the same effect rather monotonously. It is very curious that, in *Zadig*, *Le Monde comme il va*, *Memnon* and *Scarmentado*, Voltaire should appear to be fumbling towards *Candide* and then, having produced his masterpiece, that he should go on to imperfect works such as *L'homme aux quarante écus* and *L'Histoire de Jenni*, which we would be tempted, on artistic grounds, to place before *Candide*, if we did not know their date of composition. *Candide* is the only *conte* which has an overall pattern, a major theme worked out with a variety of incidental effects, a full complement of significant characters and an almost constant felicity of style.

Some slight discrepancies show that Voltaire did not finish the work with absolute care. Pomeau mentions the abrupt change, between Chapters I and II, from a springlike atmosphere to a shower of snow. Voltaire could, no doubt, have replied that fine spring days are quite often followed by snowstorms. More definite slips are the attribution of young wives to old men in Chapter III, the use by the inhabitants of El Dorado of gold and precious stones for the adornment of their houses, while

5. Op. cit., p. 96.

referring to these commodities as '*boue*' [mud] and '*cailloux*' [pebbles] and the implication in Chapter XX that Manicheism is a belief in the all-powerfulness of evil. But these flaws pass unnoticed in the general effectiveness of the work.

I think H. N. Brailsford is right in saying that *Candide* "ranks in its own way with *Don Quixote* and *Faust*," and the reason is that, like them, it is a parable of an aspect of the human plight. It is a pilgrim's progress, only this pilgrim can find no meaning in life nor establish any relationship with the transcendent. Candide has, of course, a clear literary ancestry; he is adapted from the hero of the picaresque novel of adventure, who could so easily represent the post-Renaissance displaced individual engaged on some more or less significant journey. More immediately, he is Voltaire himself, who was *déclassé* [a social outcast] like the picaresque hero, had been beaten and snubbed, 'tremblait comme un philosophe' ["trembled like a philosopher"] and had been frequently on the move. But he is also a symbol of the central part of the human soul which never loses its original innocence and, as Simone Weil says, always goes on expecting that good will be done to it rather than evil. And again, in spite of Pomeau's denial, he is *l'étranger* [the outsider], a fatherless bastard whose cosy sense of belonging to a coherent society and a comprehensible universe is a childhood illusion, soon to be shattered at the onset of puberty. Cunégonde is at first Eve who tempts him, with the result that he is driven out of the early paradise by the irate master of his little world. Then Cunégonde becomes the symbol of a lost happiness which will be recovered in the future, when the world falls again into some pattern reminiscent of the patriarchal social cell which preceded adulthood. But gradually it becomes clear that the world has no pattern, all human communities are in a state of perpetual flux and strife, and the best Candide can do is to reconstitute the battered Westphalian society of his childhood as a refugee colony on the borders of barbarism, with himself as its disillusioned head, in place of the self-confident Baron Thunder-Ten-Tronckh. Pangloss, the linguistic part of the brain, is still looking irrepressibly for explanations, but the numbed soul now knows that the quest is futile.

Just as the Candide/Cunégonde conjunction is far more significant than the parallel couples, Zadig/Astarte and Ingénu/St. Yves, so the structure of *Candide* is more complex and much better balanced than that of the other *contes*. It is not just one story, like the adventures of Zadig or the Ingénu; it is an interweaving of several different stories, which are linked and knotted and contrasted in an almost musical way. Dorothy M. McGhee, in her study, *Voltairian Narrative Devices*,[6] gives an interesting diagram showing that one method of analyzing *Candide*

6. Menasha, Wisconsin, George Banta Publishing Co., 1933, p. 55.

is to see it as a series of oscillations between Candide's "mental path of optimism" and the "level of reality" to which he is always being brought back by disaster. But there is much more to it than this. In addition to the up-and-down movement, there are complexities in the linear development. The stories of Candide, Cunégonde and La Vieille [the Old Woman] follow each other like three variations on the same theme, each slightly more preposterous than the previous one and with an increasing urbanity of tone as the events become more shocking. The pope's daughter, whose exquisite breeding has remained unaffected by the excision of a buttock, gives her account while the scene of action is shifting from Europe to America. In the New World, the same figure is repeated once more with a final flourish in the Jesuit's story, which leads into the El Dorado episode. This is an interlude of calm, coming in Chapter XVII, almost exactly in the middle of the book. Candide is now as far away as he ever will be from Europe and from the realities of ordinary life. Then, since the beatific vision can never be more than a fleeting experience, he begins on his long return journey, picking up the threads in the reverse order. The second half is, however, different from the first in two important respects. Candide is no longer an underdog; he has acquired money and he sees the world from a new angle. At the same time, he has lost his initial freshness; Martin has replaced the absent Pangloss and the accumulated experience of horror has added a permanent sob to the gaiety of the music. The hero has mastered life to some small extent, in that the terrible accidents no longer happen so often to him, but this is a hollow achievement since it leaves him freer to contemplate the sufferings of others. The second half of the book may seem weaker, artistically, precisely because Candide has become a spectator, but it is psychologically true in the sense that adulthood involves awareness of general evil.

Other aspects of the musical dance of the characters provide further refinements in the pattern. Each is killed once or more and bobs up again with heartening inconsequentiality. Voltaire expresses the strength of man's unconquerable soul by making Pangloss and the Baron, for instance, step out of the galley and begin at once behaving with characteristic foolishness, as if they had never been hanged, stabbed or beaten. He also balances the horror of evil by never leaving the hero in solitude for very long. Candide is always part of a group of two or more, and he is always assuming solidarity until it is proved illusory. A minority of human beings are, like himself, decent and well-meaning; the majority are selfish and stupid, but the implication is that all are involved in evil in more or less the same way. In this respect, Candide is both fiercely critical of human nature and curiously tolerant. The Grand Inquisitor, the brutal sailor and the *levanti patron* are carried along on the same inevitable melody as Maître Jacques or Martin. In this one work, es-

pecially, Voltaire strikes a note which is very much deeper than propaganda and which is perhaps in the last analysis, not very far removed
from inarticulate religious faith.

The parallel with music can be carried further. *Candide,* more clearly
than the other *contes,* is written in such a way that the reader has to
perform it mentally at a certain speed. As Pomeau says:

> That this style is not everyday prose, the loose style of the
> marketplace, is apparent in the first lines of the text.[7]

Voltaire is by no means the only eighteenth century author who can
write *allegro vivace* [quick and lively]. Lesage, in parts of *Gil Blas,* is
almost his equal.[8] Voltaire has Lesage's main qualities: an overall
rhythm, a euphemistically noble vocabulary and an ability always to
imply more than is actually said. But he also has features not to be
found in Lesage or the other gay stylists of the century. He uses repetition
and recapitulation very effectively in Candide to produce a constant
impression (which at first sight would seem difficult to achieve in a
typically eighteenth century style) of the welter of chance events. It is
astonishing that so short a book should create such a vision of the teeming
multifariousness of incomprehensible Necessity. His elliptical expressions are more frequent and more startling than those to be found in
the prose of his contemporaries, and so he jerks the reader again and
again into awareness of a metaphysical perspective behind his apparently
innocent recital of events. Each important character has his or her *motif*
which sounds at appropriate intervals; less obvious, but no less telling,
than Candide's simplicity or Pangloss's silliness are Cunégonde's accom-
modating sensuality and Cacambo's practical good sense. And the mixture of rapidity, irony, allusion, ellipsis, merciless satire of human nature
and affectionate understanding of the human plight produces an unmistakable, singing, heartrending lilt, of which only Voltaire is capable
in prose and that only Mozart, perhaps, could have transferred to the
stage. Admittedly, there are passages in *Candide* that might have been
written by Lesage; for instance, parts of the Old Woman's account, in
Chapter XI, of her sufferings at the hands of the pirates:

> It's a very remarkable thing, the energy these gentlemen put
> into stripping people. But what surprised me even more was
> that they stuck their fingers in a place where we women usually
> admit only a syringe. This ceremony seemed a bit odd to me,
> as foreign usages always do when one hasn't traveled.

7. Edition critique, p. 55.
8. See the excellent *'récit de Lucinde'* (Livre V,

Ch. I), which may have helped to suggest the stories of Cunégonde and La Vieille.

But in the more characteristic passages, Voltaire infuses feeling into this bright, eighteenth century melody, without falling into the sogginess of *sensibilité*, the usual weakness of eighteenth century writers when they try to be serious. Chapter I, in its deceptive simplicity, is no doubt the most perfect example of his style and one of the highest achievements in all French writing. However, practically every chapter contains what can only be described as unique, ironical prose poetry.[9] I quote, at random, the description of the auto-da-fe in Chapter VI:

> . . . Candide's mitre and *san-benito* were decorated with inverted flames and with devils who had neither tails nor claws; but Pangloss's devils had both tails and claws, and his flames stood upright. Wearing these costumes, they marched in a procession, and listened to a very touching sermon, followed by a beautiful concert of plainsong. Candide was flogged in cadence to the music; the Biscayan and the two men who had avoided bacon were burned, and Pangloss was hanged, though hanging is not customary. On the same day there was another earthquake, causing frightful damage
>
> Candide, stunned, stupefied, despairing, bleeding, trembling, said to himself:—If this is the best of all possible worlds, what are the others like? The flogging is not so bad, I was flogged by the Bulgars. But oh my dear Pangloss, greatest of philosophers, was it necessary for me to watch you being hanged, for no reason that I can see? Oh my dear Anabaptist, best of men, was it necessary that you should be drowned in the port? Oh Miss Cunégonde, pearl of young ladies, was it necessary that you should have your belly slit open?
>
> He was being led away, barely able to stand, lectured, lashed, absolved, and blessed, when an old woman approached and said,—My son, be of good cheer and follow me.
>
> Candide was of very bad cheer, but he followed the old woman. . . .

It is one of the mysteries of literary composition that the *Poème sur le Désastre de Lisbonne* should be so flat and unpoetical, whereas Voltaire's treatment of the same theme in prose is at once rich, funny and deeply moving. Perhaps the explanation is to be sought in the fact that

---

9. An exhaustive and useful analysis of Voltaire's irony has been made by Ruth C. Flowers in *Voltaire's Stylistic Transformation of Rabelaisian Satirical Devices*. The Catholic University of America Press, Washington, D.C., 1951. Dr. Flowers distinguishes (pp. 63 et seq.) eight varieties of 'Satirical Detail Elements' and nine varieties of 'Compound Satirical Devices' and concludes: 'Unquestionably, Voltaire is the greatest master of satire by "small art", a witty almost epigrammatic satire, a satire whose ironical impact depends entirely and exclusively on little things, strategically placed'.

It is ironical, however, that Dr. Flowers should not notice the emotion which governs the strategic placing of these little things. She says (p. 90) that Voltaire's heart is 'coolly detached, superficially moved'.

there is a philosophical ambiguity running through Candide, in addition to the contrast between vitality and awareness of evil. The *Poème* is a direct, but feeble, reproach to God, which ends with a still feebler hope that life will be better in the world to come than it is here. Voltaire was not, temperamentally, a God-defier. He invokes God convincingly only when it is a question of enlisting Him on the side of virtue, as in *Le Traité de la tolérance*. He was incapable of saying outright, with Baudelaire:

> For truly, Lord, this is the highest gage
> That we can offer of our dignity,
> This ardent sigh, which rolls from age to age,
> Dying on the shore of your eternity.

He can only criticize God freely when he does so, by implication, through human nature. It may be that the almost pathological violence of his onslaughts on the Church is to be accounted for, to some extent, by the transference of an unexpressed exasperation with the unknowable Creator onto a part of creation which is particularly irritating precisely through its claim to understand something about the Creator. At any rate, it is remarkable that, in *Candide*, the distinction between evil which is an act of God (and therefore from the human point of view gratuitous) and evil which is an effect of human wickedness or stupidity, is not clearly maintained. It is made, in Chapter XX, when Candide and Martin are watching the shipwreck, but in the form of a joke against Candide. God's indifference to humanity is again stressed in Chapter XXX when the dervish slams his door in Pangloss's face, and this time the joke—admittedly a rather sour one—is on Pangloss. It seems almost as if Voltaire were unwilling to come out into the open and accuse God, so much so that, from one point of view, the El Dorado episode can be seen as a logical flaw. That happy country, where the inhabitants never quarrel and worship God without a church, does not provide a fair contrast with the ordinary world; how would the people of El Dorado retain their serenity if their capital were shattered by an earthquake? The only way to justify the El Dorado chapters is to suppose that they are really a conscious or unconscious criticism of God. They occur as a sunny interlude between two series of disasters to show how happy and pious we might have been, had God not given us our ungovernable natures and put us into a world containing inexplicable evil. And the book as a whole, although so critical of mankind, tends to show human nature as a blind and passionate force driving helplessly on against a background of mystery. In other words, Voltaire, like Diderot, had not made up his mind about free-will, because the determinism/free-will dilemma is just another formulation of the God/no-God issue. The question is left open in Chapter XXI:

—Do you believe, said Martin, that hawks have always eaten pigeons when they could get them?

—Of course, said Candide.

—Well, said Martin, if hawks have always had the same character, why do you suppose that men have changed?

—Oh, said Candide, there's a great deal of difference, because freedom of the will . . .

As they were disputing in this manner, they reached Bordeaux.

Yet the whole weight of Voltaire's emotion is obviously against accepting the parallel between men and animals. *Candide* throbs from end to end with a paradoxical quality which might be described as a despairing hope or a relentless charity, and which comes from seeing the worst steadily, without either capitulating to it or sentimentalizing its impact. Although, as Delattre says, no great writer wrote more often below his best than Voltaire did, in this short tale he managed to hold fundamental opposites in suspense and so produced, from the heart of a century that wished to deny evil, an allegorical prose poem about evil which is still perfectly apt, exactly two hundred years later.

ERNST CASSIRER

[Voltaire's Escape from Pascal]†

["Pascal tormented Voltaire, as Montaigne had tormented Pascal." The epigram is by Raymond Naves (*Voltaire l'homme et l'oeuvre*: Paris, 1942, p. 129); and at first glance the saying bristles with problems. Pascal was born in 1623, thirty-one years after the death of Montaigne in 1592; Voltaire was born in 1694, thirty-two years after the death of Pascal in 1662. What art did these Frenchmen have to torment one another from beyond the grave?

To a remarkable degree, they were preoccupied with a single problem, that is, the relation between faith and reason, which is in effect the question of original sin. This had been the crucial controversy between Erasmus and Luther; it would be the theme of conflicts between Calvinists and Arminians on the Protestant side, between Jansenists and Jesuits within the Catholic party. Its importance is obvious. For if man's reason, no less than his will, is fatally corrupted from birth, his only hope of understanding himself or the world lies in supernatural faith. In opposition to this crucial point, all the Enlightenment philosophers united; and Voltaire, perhaps in part because the brother whom he hated was a Jansenist, powerfully impregnated

† From Ernst Cassirer, *The Philosophy of the Enlightenment*, tr. Fritz Koeller et al. Copyright 1951 Princeton University Press. © 1979 renewed by Princeton University Press. Excerpt, pp. 141–48 reprinted with permission of Princeton University Press.

with the doctrine of original sin, focused his criticism of the doctrine on its foremost Jansenist exponent, Blaise Pascal. Professor Cassirer selects out of the dispute's several European manifestations those of France, as they shaped Voltaire's efforts to settle the tenacious, deep-seated doubts raised by Pascal.]

*   *   *

First let us trace the problem as it appears in the intellectual history of France where it achieves its most fruitful formulation. With a perfection possible only to the French analytical mind, all the various aspects of the problem are elucidated and their logical consequences developed. The diverse possible approaches are set over against each other in a clear-cut antithesis, and the dialectical solution seems to spring spontaneously from this antithesis. The problem of original sin is again raised in French philosophy of the seventeenth century by one of its most profound thinkers. With almost unrivaled vigor and with the greatest clarity of presentation the problem appears in Pascal's *Thoughts* (*Pensées*). Its content seemed scarcely to have changed since Augustine, for through the mediation of Jansen's[1] great work on Augustine the formulation of the idea of original sin invariably recurs to this source. But the form and method of Pascal's reasoning distinguish him from Augustine and mark him as a thinker of modern times. Method in the age of Pascal is dominated by Descartes' logical ideal of the clear and distinct idea, and the Cartesian doctrine is applied even to the mysteries of faith. The result of this combination of Augustinian content with Cartesian method is a paradoxical mixture of ideas because the doctrine Pascal seeks to establish stands in sharp contrast to the procedure by which he reaches his conclusions. The thesis he defends is the absolute powerlessness of reason which is incapable of any kind of certainty by its own efforts, and which can arrive at the truth only by means of an unconditional surrender to faith. But the very necessity of this surrender is not demanded and preached; he sets out to prove it. He does not address the believers but the unbelievers, and he meets the latter on their own ground. He speaks their own language and offers to fight them with their own weapons. Pascal is an unrivaled master of the instrument of modern analytical logic which he had brought to a high degree of perfection in his mathematical works; he now wields this instrument in the service of a fundamental religious question. He approaches his problem, then, with the same methodological means which he had employed in his work on conic sections in the field of geometry, and which he had applied to a problem of physics in his essay on empty space. Here too the important thing is exact observation of phenomena and the power of hypothetical thinking. We possess no other means, and need no other means, to bring about a decision. Just as the physicist, in answering the

---

1. Cornelis Jansen (d. 1638) established the severe strain of Roman Catholicism that became known, after him, as Jansenism. Its roots were planted deeply in the teachings of Saint Augustine, on whom see "Summary: The Intellectual Backgrounds," above, p. 81 [*Editor*].

question of the character of a certain natural force, has no other resource than to survey the phenomena involved and to consult them in systematic array, so too the fundamental mystery of human nature must be solved. Here, similarly, we must require of every hypothesis that it do justice to the phenomena, and that it describe them completely. The postulate of the "rescue of the phenomena" is no less valid for theology than for astronomy. And it is on this point that Pascal challenges his opponents—the doubters and the unbelievers. If they reject the religious solution of the problem and refuse to accept the doctrine of the fall of man and of man's dual nature, then it is their responsibility to give another more probable explanation. It becomes their task to introduce simplicity in place of duality and harmony in place of discord. But this alleged unity and harmony will immediately clash with all the facts of human experience. For wherever we encounter man, we find him not as a complete and harmonious being but as a being divided against himself and burdened with the most profound contradictions. These contradictions are the stigma of human nature. As soon as he attempts to understand his position in the cosmos, man finds himself caught between the infinite and nothingness; in the presence of both, he is incapable of belonging to either one of them alone. Elevated above all other beings, he is also degraded below all; man is sublime and abject, great and wretched, strong and powerless, all in one. His consciousness always places before him a goal he can never reach, and his existence is torn between his incessant striving beyond himself and his constant relapses beneath himself. We cannot escape this conflict which we find in every single phenomenon of human nature, and there is no other way to explain it than to transfer it from the phenomena to their intelligible origin, from the facts to their principle. The irreducible dualism of human nature is resolved only in the mystery of the fall. Through this mystery that which had been cloaked in impenetrable darkness becomes at once manifest. Though this hypothesis is in itself an absolute mystery, it is, on the other hand, the only key to our deepest being. Human nature becomes comprehensible only by virtue of the incomprehensible mystery which underlies it. Thus all the standards of logical and rational knowledge are reversed. In this knowledge the unknown is explained by reducing it to a known quantity, but Pascal bases immediately given and existing phenomena on the absolutely unknown. This overthrow of all rational means and measures teaches us that we are dealing not with an accidental but with a necessary, not with a subjective but with an objective, limit of knowledge. It is not merely the weakness of our insight that prevents us from arriving at an adequate knowledge of the object, it is the object itself which defies rationality and is absolutely contradictory. Every rational measure as such is an immanent measure, for the form of rational knowledge consists in drawing conclusions from the real nature of a thing regarding properties which necessarily belong to it. But here we are dealing with a nature which contradicts itself; here it is immanence which turns into transcendence and negates itself as soon as we attempt to understand it completely. "Who will disentangle this turmoil? Nature confounds Pyrrhonists [sceptics] and reason confounds dogmatists. What will become of you then, O man, who try by your natural reason to discover what is your true condition? . . . Know then, proud creature, what a paradox you are to yourself. Be humble, impotent reason; be quiet, imbecile nature: *know that man surpasses man infinitely* and learn from your Master of our true condition, of which you are ignorant. Hearken unto God!"[2]

The most difficult and profound problem of eighteenth century philosophy is posed in these words of Pascal. In him this philosophy found an opponent of equal strength, who had to be reckoned with if it were to take a single step forward. If the spell of transcendence could not be broken at this point, and if man was and remained "self-transcendent," then any natural explanation of the world and of existence was checked at the start. It is, therefore, understandable that French philosophy of the Enlightenment recurs to Pascal's *Thoughts* again and again as if it were impelled from within, and that it repeatedly tests its critical strength on this work. Criticism of Pascal continues through all periods of Voltaire's career as a writer. This criticism begins in his first philosophical work, *Letters on the English*, and half a century later he comes back to this product of his youth in order to supplement it and support it with new arguments.[3] He accepted Pascal's challenge; he said he wanted to defend humanity against this "sublime misanthrope." But if one inspects his various arguments, it would seem as if he were trying to avoid an open fight. For Voltaire carefully avoids pursuing Pascal to the real core of his religious thinking and to the ultimate depths of his problem. He tries to keep Pascal on the surface of human existence; he wants to show that this surface is self-sufficient and self-explanatory. Voltaire treats Pascal's deep seriousness in his typical urbane manner; he answers the terse precision of Pascal's reasoning with intellectual agility, and the mystical depth of his feeling with the superficiality of the worldling. Common sense is invoked against the subtleties of metaphysics and made judge of these subtleties. What Pascal had called the contradictions of human nature become for Voltaire merely a proof of its wealth and abundance, of its variety and versatility. Human nature, to be sure, is not simple in the sense that it has a definite being and must follow a prescribed course; for it is forever venturing upon new possibilities. But according to Voltaire not the weakness but the strength of human nature lies in this almost unlimited versatility. However diverse the activity of man may appear, however difficult it may be to hold fast to any one

2. Pascal, *Pensées*, art. VIII (ed. Ernest Havet, fifth edition, Paris, 1897, vol. 1, p. 114).
3. Cf. Voltaire, *Remarques sur les Pensées de M.*

Pascal, Oeuvres, ed. Lequien, Paris, 1921, vol. XXXI, pp. 281 ff.

accomplishment and not be driven on from one goal to another and from one task to another, the true intensity and highest power of which human nature is capable is demonstrated by this very many-sidedness. In the display and unhampered development of all the various forces at work within him, man is what he can and should be: "Those apparent contrarieties, which you call *contradictions*, are the necessary ingredients which enter into the composite of man, who is, like the rest of nature, what he ought to be."

But Voltaire's philosophy of "common sense" is not his last word on this question. Little as he concedes to Pascal's arguments, one feels nevertheless that he is constantly disturbed by them. In fact we have now reached a point at which mere negation did not suffice, at which a clear positive decision was expected of the philosophy of the Enlightenment. If it rejected the mystery of original sin, it had to shift the cause and origin of evil to another quarter; it had to recognize and prove the necessity of the source of evil in the eyes of reason. There seemed, therefore, no escape at this point from metaphysics as such; for doubts regarding dogma compel us all the more inexorably toward the riddle of theodicy. This riddle exists too for Voltaire since he looks upon the existence of God as a strictly demonstrable truth. The proposition: "I exist; therefore a necessary and eternal being exists," has lost none of its force for Voltaire.[4] But if the Gordian knot of the problem of theodicy remains uncut as ever, how can we escape Pascal's conclusion that the coils of this knot lead us back to the "abyss" of faith?[5] Optimism, the philosophical solution of Leibniz and Shaftesbury, was consistently rejected by Voltaire; he looked upon optimism not as a philosophical doctrine but as something on a par with mythical phantasies and romances.[6] Those who maintain that all is well with the world are mere charlatans; we must admit that evil exists and not add to the horrors of life the absurd bigotry of denying them.[7] But if Voltaire here takes his stand against theology and metaphysics in favor of a theoretical skepticism, he is yielding indirectly to the reasoning of Pascal whom he intended to refute. For at least with respect to his achievement he now stands at exactly the same point where Pascal had stood. Pascal had come to the conclusion, which he never tired of stressing, that philosophy as such, that reason left to its own resources and deprived of the support of revelation, must necessarily end in skepticism: "Pyrrhonism is the truth."[8] Since on the problem of the origin of evil Voltaire had

4. Cf. *Additions aux remarques sur les Pensées de Pascal* (1743) in *op. cit.*, vol. XXXI, p. 334; "I exist, therefore something exists throughout eternity, is an evident proposition."

5. *Pensées*, art. VIII, *op.cit.*, p. 115: "The node of our condition has its folds and coils in that abyss, in such a way that man is more inconceivable without this mystery than this mystery is inconceivable to man."

6. Cf. especially, *Il faut prendre un parti ou le principe d'action* (1772), sect. XVII: "Des romans inventés pour deviner l'origine du mal." *Oeuvres*, vol. XXXI, p. 177.

7. *Ibid.*, sect. XVI, *Oeuvres*, XXXI, 174 ff.

8. Cf. *Pensées*, ed. Havet, XXIV, 1; XXV, 34, vol. 11, pp. 87, 156.

deprived himself of all the weapons against skepticism, he finds himself henceforth driven hither and yon in the skeptical whirlpool. He embraces all solutions and he rejects them all. Schopenhauer[9] often referred to Voltaire's *Candide* and he tried to use it as his most powerful weapon against optimism. But in a systematic sense Voltaire was no more a pessimist than an optimist. His position on the problem of evil is never the upshot of a sound doctrine; it is, and this is all it pretends to be, merely the expression of the transient mood in which he contemplates the world and man. This mood is capable of all nuances, and Voltaire likes to indulge in the play of nuances. In his youth Voltaire knows no pessimistic moments. He advocates a purely hedonistic philosophy whose justification consists in the maximum enjoyment of all the pleasures of life. To pursue any other wisdom seems to him as difficult as it is useless: "True wisdom lies in knowing how to flee sadness in the arms of pleasure."[1] Voltaire means only to be the apologist of his time in these words, the apologist of luxury, of taste, and of sensuous enjoyment undeterred by any prejudice.[2] Later on, however, as a result of the earthquake of Lisbon, Voltaire expressly retracts his glorification of pleasure. The axiom: "All is well," is now absolutely rejected as a doctrine.[3] It is foolish self-deception to close our eyes to the evils which everywhere confront us; all we can do is turn our eyes to the future hoping it will bring the solution of the riddle which is now insoluble: "*Some day all will be well*, is our hope; *all is well today*, is illusion." Again Voltaire accepts a compromise both in the theoretical and in the ethical respect. Moral evil too is undeniable but its justification consists in the fact that it is inevitable to human nature as it is. For were it not for our weaknesses, life would be condemned to stagnation, since the strongest impulses of life arise from our appetites and passions, that is, ethically considered, from our shortcomings. Voltaire gave his most pregnant expression of this outlook on the world and life in his philosophical tale *The World as It Is, Vision of Babouc* (*Le Monde comme il va, Vision de Babouc*, 1746). Babouc receives an order from the angel Ithuriel to go to the capital of his country and observe the manners and customs there, and his judgment is to decide whether the city will be destroyed or spared. He acquaints himself with all the weaknesses and faults of the city and with its grave moral shortcomings, but also with the full splendor of its culture and refined society. And on this basis he

---

9. German philosopher of the nineteenth century, famous for his implacable pessimism [*Editor*].

1. "La véritable sagesse
   Est de savoir fuir la tristesse,
   Dans les bras de la volupté."

2. Cf. the poem "Le Mondain" (1736) and "Défense du Mondain ou l'Apologie du Luxe," *Oeuvres*, vol. XIV, pp. 112 ff., 122 ff.—The following treatment of Voltaire and Rousseau has al-ready been published in part in a somewhat different form. Cf. the author's essay: "Das Problem Jean-Jacques Rousseau." *Archiv fuer Geschichte der Philosophie*, ed. Arthur Stein, vol. XLI (1932), pp. 210 ff.

3. "Poème sur le désastre de Lisbonne ou examen de cet axiome: Tout est bien" (1756), *Oeuvres*, vol. XII, pp. 179 ff.

passes judgment. He has a small statue made by the best goldsmith in the city; it is composed of all metals, the most precious and the most inferior. He brings this to Ithuriel and asks him: "Would you destroy this pretty statue because it is not composed entirely of gold or diamonds?" Ithuriel understands: "He resolves not to think of correcting Persepolis and to *permit it to go on as it is*; for, says he, if all is not well, all is tolerable." In *Candide* too, in which Voltaire pours out all his scorn for optimism, he does not deviate from this basic attitude. We cannot avoid evil and we cannot eradicate it. We should let the physical and moral world take their course and so adjust ourselves that we can keep up a constant struggle against the world; for from this struggle arises that happiness of which man alone is capable.

ROBERT M. ADAMS

Getting the Point†

—Is it true that they are always laughing in Paris? asked Candide.
—Yes, said the abbé, but with a kind of rage too; when people complain of things, they do so amid explosions of laughter. . . .

Chapter 22

The abbé, who must have been well acquainted with M. de Voltaire to describe his temper so precisely and concisely, isn't really entitled to the wit and insight that *Candide* bestows on him. His character in the story is that of a shabby trickster and a sleazy go-between; he introduces Candide into the company of some card-sharks and sets him up with a "marquise" who is little better than a prostitute with a few pretensions. For his part, the abbé is interested in nothing but getting a part of the money that's so easily extracted from Candide. His explanation of the Parisian temper doesn't serve any of his immediate purposes; it isn't especially in character. But there's a lot of loose wit as well as some accumulated malice flying around the story, and some of it drops on him. Voltaire was a Parisian by birth and by unchangeable affection; but since the summer of 1750 he had been in effectual exile (not by formal decree but by the pointed, implacable hostility of the king and the Catholic hierarchy); he would not see Paris again till 1778, when he returned for a few months, already a dying man. Thus Paris, which sings and dances but is also capable of atrocious cruelties and gross stupidities, is an object of mixed hatred and longing. He places his feelings about the city, and his understanding of those feelings in himself, in the mouth of an ambiguous, murky rascal. A brilliant insight about the book as a whole drops casually from the source in the story where

† First published in this Norton Critical Edition.

one would least expect it. The moment illustrates a frequent quality of transparency in Voltaire's narrative surface. At any moment it is liable to be penetrated from behind by the lean finger and glittering satiric eye of M. de Voltaire in person. What we call the "point" of a passage is never more clear than when the pen of M. de Voltaire stabs directly through the narrative page to make it.

But there are some other episodes in the book where the point isn't so clear—where the story-teller withholds his presence or conceals his concerns behind the texture of the story, which doesn't itself point in an unequivocal direction. These may be worth discussing, but only in an interrogative mode, to see if they could profit by some further pointing up, or if their apparent pointlessness isn't in fact the point. Where there is so much in the *conte* that is brilliantly clear, passages that still harbor shadows of mystery invite special attention.

For instance, those two girls whom Candide and Cacambo spy while camped on the border of the Biglug territory (ch. 16). There can be very little doubt about the function of the Biglugs themselves. In their harum-scarum flight from Spanish pursuit, our heroes are bound to have adventures good and bad; and in the South American rain forests, most of them will probably be bad. The Biglugs, in proposing to cook the two travelers for dinner, are a thoroughly bad scene. They are bad too, in a way that interests Voltaire, who has Cacambo deliver an eloquent speech (out of the *Dictionnaire philosophique portatif* article "Anthropophages") to the point that eating your enemy isn't as bad as killing him in the first place. So the Biglugs provide a peril for Candide to overcome and a way for Voltaire to needle a pious prejudice. They also protect the fabled land of Eldorado, which would be overrun in an instant by European adventurers if there weren't some grisly characters to keep them out. The two girls serve a story function in discovering the travelers and complaining of them to the Biglugs. But why have they taken monkeys as lovers? Why, when Candide sees them, are they running away from their lovers in such evident distress that Candide shoots the monkeys? Voltaire may be satirizing the behavior of women, who (it was traditional to say) like to be chased but not caught. But why have they taken monkey-lovers in the first place? Cacambo, who took a thoroughly philosophic view of cannibalism, seems to assume an equally accepting attitude toward intercourse between the species. Are we to understand that here again Candide is being liberated from narrow prejudice? But of course in the world of *Candide* (elastic though it may be in many respects) intercourse with the animals isn't normal at all. Perhaps it is only in the state of nature that such connections are common. Voltaire himself seems to have some misgivings about representing (though not about implying) intercourse; his monkeys leap about the girls and snap at their buttocks, but that could be play as well as foreplay. If the naturalness in nature of any sort of sexual connection is the point here, Voltaire may be glancing back at human narrowmindedness and overrestriction earlier in the story. The girls playing joyously with monkeys could be understood to contrast with those deadly regulations about genealogical quarterings, that cruel judgment passed on the Biscayan for marrying his child's godmother in Chapters 1 and 3.

On the other hand, if the conclusion of Voltaire's argument against bigotry and snobbery is a ringing endorsement of bestiality, it's not clear that he's helped his cause very much. To look back one more stage of speculation, we might recognize as a contributing influence the fact that sometime in the 1740s he had taken as mistress his niece, the newly widowed Mme. Denis. This, though improper and duly hushed up at the time, was not so scandalous in the eighteenth century as might be thought. For a relatively small sum of money, Voltaire could have got the bounds of consanguinity overlooked. But then he would have had to marry Mme. Denis, and he would have had to obtain all sorts of permissions from the church, at the cost of his demonic pride. So he accepted in daily practice the illegitimacy of the connection; but perhaps in the imaginative freedom of South American jungles he imagined that things could have been natural and right. Reinforcing the parallel are physiological facts. Mme. Denis in her person was as remarkably plump as Voltaire was preternaturally lean. His enemies did often refer to him as an ape, and that was the sort of insult that stung. When we put all these considerations together, we don't have a single formula to explain the episode's artistic point, but we may have some points of departure from which to approach, one at a time, its tendency, its positioning, and a couple of its emphases.

Less speculative is the incident of dinner at Venice with six ex-kings (ch. 26). Here it's less the nature of the episode that's in question than its literary quality. The ex-monarchs are seated *incognito* at a tavern in Venice; one by one they are revealed to be royalty; one by one they explain perfunctorily what country they used to rule and how they lost their thrones. The sixth king being totally destitute, the other five take up a subscription for him, but are outshone by Candide, who, though only a commoner, gives a hundred times more than any of them. The episode, though clearly imaginary in its shape, clearly reflects the historic fact that a good deal of redundant, unattached royalty was floating around Europe in the mid-eighteenth-century. Not very far or well concealed behind the story-surface is the fact that Voltaire was one of the richest men of his day, who had money on loan to at least three crowned heads and could easily have outdone most ex-kings in a generosity contest. This personal financial situation does something to account for the text as we have it, but doesn't help us over a strong sense of flatness. Indeed, the six kings demonstrate persuasively the mutability of human political arrangements (and that will be the theme of Pangloss's concluding tirade), but after the first two chapters of *Candide*, who needs that demonstration? The episode may carry a monitory overtone: if all these kings have lost their thrones, the surviving ones had better watch out. Imaginatively, the warning issued from one republic, Venice; historically, it issued from another, Geneva. It is a muted warning, as Voltaire often muted his satiric savagery when it came close to the rich and powerful, but it builds toward the other muted warning, in chapter 30—muted because ostensibly it applies only to events in Turkey, but just as general in implicit application as the round-table in chapter 26.

Another order of considerations regarding the episode of the six kings is narrative in nature. After Eldorado Candide is exempt from violent physical abuse, and his stay in Venice is not otherwise very animated. Paquette turns up with Fra Giroflée just for a moment to keep her in the story; the visit to Lord Pococurante is an exercise in boredom and vacancy. Voltaire may have wanted to give his readers a touch of exotic color in the course of his hero's visit to one of the world's cultural centers. And the carnival season, just at its height, brings with it the tradition of masquing, which may have pleased him with its resemblance to the momentary disguise of monarchy. Yet at the same time the fall of princes is described as a routine, commonplace procedure, and comparing it with the procession of cadis, pashas, and effendis arriving at Constantinople and departing shortly thereafter as severed heads (ch. 30), one can't help feeling that the monotony of the process is part of Voltaire's point. And, glancing backward, the defile of kings—stiff, formulaic, almost identical—can be thought to resemble processions in the old morality plays, on tapestries, or on decorative friezes, where steady repetition of a single formula provides a ground bass for other melodies.

That the kingdom of Eldorado in South America resembles closely More's kingdom of Utopia, also in South America, is pretty apparent, and most apparent in the matter of precious metals and rare jewels. Both societies are closed enclaves, carefully isolated from the world and having no use for the world's common medium of exchange. Treasure being inexhaustibly plentiful in Eldorado, and the inhabitants of a philosophic temper, gold is mud and precious stones mere pebbles, just as in Utopia. But Voltaire has little use for the ascetic disciplines and rigid controls of More's society; rather, he attributes the prosperity and libertarian lifestyle of the Eldoradans to the absence of priests, monks, and persecution. There is no daily labor in Eldorado, and there is nothing to pray for (as the king tells Candide), since nature and the God of nature provide, automatically and gratuitously, whatever people want. The food in Eldorado is lavish beyond the dream of any jungle-dweller in South America, and the dusky maidens of the community are much in evidence—it's a Voltairean twist to have them members of the royal guard. So, apart from the aching absence of Miss Cunégonde, there is only one obvious difficulty with this ideal land, and that is boredom. But Voltaire wants to save that rich and untapped topic for the visit to Lord Pococurante in Venice, where boredom can be shown to erode all the luxuries of civilization—music, food, literature, art, drama, and sex—all at once. (And, incidentally, wasn't Voltaire the first to raise ennui from a mere local irritation to the major human affliction that it becomes in nineteenth-century poets like Baudelaire and Leopardi?) In fact, Voltaire in writing the Eldorado unit of *Candide* must have foreseen the great yawning execration of boredom that would comprise so much of chapter 30—as a result of which he has left the departure of the two travelers from the earthly paradise perceptibly undermotivated.

In the economy of the book, separating Candide from his Eldorado money substitutes in the later chapters for the kickings, beatings, and physical mishaps so prominent in the first part. This is an improvement, to be sure; but, Voltaire points out, possession of money brings with it anxiety over losing it and also problems about how to use it. Candide and Cacambo never do anything with their riches that gives them the slightest pleasure; and the money they give to Paquette, or use to ransom Pangloss and the baron, earns the donor no gratitude and (so far as we can tell) gives the recipients only momentary pleasure. At the end of the book, when he's lost most of his money, Candide is actually in a position to get some pleasure from his tiny remainder; the parallel with Miss Cunégonde is close, if not exact.

Cruelty mingled with explosions of laughter is most apparent in the atrocious violence inflicted on various characters—brutalities from which they immediately recover, then presenting themselves as good as new. A mere fraction of the brutal beating visited on Candide by the Bulgars would leave him crippled for life—if he had a real life. No matter; in a few pages he is ready to go to war, survive beggary, shipwreck, and earthquake in order to be savagely beaten again in the auto-da-fé. Pangloss cheerfully survives burning, hanging, and vivisection; yet of all the damage inflicted on him only the venereal infection picked up from Paquette leaves any permanent traces, and it reappears only for a moment in the course of an affectionate recognition-scene with the little trollop who bestowed the disease on him. This is part of Voltaire's tangible economy for the book, a way of keeping himself present in the story yet out of it. In the same way, Cunégonde becomes strikingly ugly (after having been, the last we saw her, ravishingly beautiful) just in time to serve Voltaire's dramatic purposes by staggering Candide. Paquette and Fra Giroflée never suffer the effects of the fearful disease with which she devastates Pangloss, for no better reason than that Voltaire does not want it so.

Our hero is, of course, indestructible. Like one of those toy soldiers with a lead weight in his round foot, he pops upright no matter how many times he is knocked down. Moreover, he changes not a hair nor the shadow of a feature in the course of the narrative. From the jungles of Brazil to the boulevards of Paris, the canals of Venice, and the mosques of Constantinople, whether opulent or beggarly, he remains the same modest, trim little figure, unmarked and untouched. The little family he gathers round him at the farm outside Constantinople are all derelicts of one sort or another. But among the battered specimens, so reminiscent as a group of Voltaire's miscellaneous family circle at Ferney, only Candide remains pristine, as white as when he came from his Maker's hand.

Two contrasting figures, the dervish and the "good old man," usher Candide into the moment of repose and balance that marks the book's conclusion. They look like antithetical personae, representing dogmatic religion and practical wisdom; and so, to some extent, they are. The dervish first tells Pangloss to shut up and then slams his door in the face of the irrepressible babbler. The good old man chats with Candide and his friends, then opens his door and invites them in for refreshments and conversation. It's clear enough who is the fresh voice in the book as well as the more humane neighbor, and Candide seems by now (at last) to have enough practical sense to avoid the dervish and imitate the good old man. This seems like a strong, if slightly flat, note on which to end. Sitting under one's vine or one's figtree is an activity with biblical precedent going back to 2 Kings 4. And the image of sitting crosslegged and at rest under an orange grove while imbibing cool sherbets and contemplating the traffic of the world has an undeniably restful finality. But for Voltaire, the dervish's sour, sardonic "Hold your tongue" ("Te taire") may have seemed particularly appropriate to these endlessly verbose unbelievers. Constantinople was no paradise of free speech, and Voltaire knew it. Among the *Questions sur l'encyclopédie* (1770) a little note under "Raison" tells the brief, bitter story of a man who was always right—"qui avait toujours raison." He went to the intendant general of France and laid out for him the principles of a sensible economy, along the lines of those in "L'homme aux quarante écus"; when he got out of French jail, he went to Rome and instructed the pope on the behavior proper to Saint Peter's successor; when he got out of the papal dungeon, he went to Venice and made some sardonic jests about pretending to marry the sea every year. His lecture earned him a stay in the gloomy *stinche*, or prison-cells—after which he went to Constantinople to provide the Turks with some plain truths about the Mohametan religion. That finished his career of being right in the wrong place; the Turks promptly impaled him on a pointed stake.

So while the old man has found in hard, steady work a cure for the three big evils of need, vice, and boredom, the dervish has supplied an indispensable preliminary. "Keep your mouth shut"—it was advice that Voltaire had good reason to present as the cornerstone of his practical wisdom because he had himself paid so often and so poignantly for disregarding it. And it enters into the symphonic balance of that quiet, stupid ending that Flaubert admired so extravagantly.

It's not just a joke to say that *Candide* has more points than a barrel cactus, and that picking around in them can yield you a lot more than lacerated fingers.

THE CLIMATE OF CONTROVERSY

Extended critiques of *Candide* do not start appearing till more than a century and a half after its publication; but Voltaire was a figure so central to French intellectual life and so deeply imbedded in it—he was such a fighter, and took memorable positions on so wide a range of topics—that his name, and that of his most famous story, crop up again and again in the great controversies of the nineteenth and twentieth centuries. For a Frenchman, one's opinion of Voltaire is like one's opinion of the Church or the Revolution or Napoleon—it is a key to one's whole historical and ethical outlook. Wherever a crucial issue of French civilization makes its appearance, there will also be found an epigram of Voltaire's, lucid, cocksure, infuriating, and unforgettable. Even when Voltaire is not himself the subject and center of a conversational storm, he is often brought in to illustrate an argument, deplore a tendency, or formulate an attitude. His vast and miscellaneous production lends itself to occasional use. People can discuss Voltaire without declining at once into literary shop-talk, can make use of his phrases for practical purposes without the uneasy sense of desecrating a literary masterpiece. Voltaire is wonderfully accessible to the popular mind.

Put to so many different purposes, seen from so many different points of view, he fractures remarkably. The cast of features that one man describes as the bestial rictus of a malicious satyr will seem to another the compassionate visage of a Saint of Humanity. But he becomes deeper and more complicated, too. In the course of this continuing controversial discussion of Voltaire, many of the most acute and penetrating observations upon his mind and character get made—as by-blows, many times, in the course of a larger controversy. Even when they are not explicitly controversial, little passing comments about Voltaire run like a murmuring undercurrent through French intellectual life of the nineteenth and twentieth centuries. In a phrase of a letter-writer or an observation of a journal-keeper, one will find commentary on Voltaire serving to define some purpose of the writer's, some aspect of contemporary literary endeavor. Properly speaking, this sort of incidental discussion is not literary criticism; but it may serve to represent a current of literary opinion within which Voltaire has never ceased vitally to exist, and which has defined a whole series of still agitated questions about his nature and influence. All translations of the selections that follow have been made by the present editor.

1. VOLTAIRE'S FAITH

VOLTAIRE: Letter on the Subject of *Candide*

[We begin with a letter by Voltaire himself on the subject of *Candide*. It pretends to be a response to a notice of *Candide* that had appeared in the *Journal encyclopédique* of March 15, 1759 (Professor Wade's essay reproduces that notice, see above, p. 144). But though this letter of Voltaire's is dated April 1, 1759, it appeared only on July 15, 1762. The date of April 1 suggests that it is an April Fool's joke, a *poisson d'avril*; and in fact it is a piece of obvious hocus-pocus. But, as usual, Voltaire was doing something quite serious behind his foolery. A controversy had broken out in 1762 regarding the political role of the Jesuits; Voltaire's letter was designed to stir up hostility against them by bringing once again to public attention the fact that Jesuits had not always been docile servants of secular governments. In addition, its claim that *Candide* was written to convert the Socinians raises a real question about Voltaire's own creed.]

Gentlemen,

You say, in the March issue of your journal,[1] that some sort of little novel called *Optimism* or *Candide* is attributed to a man known as Monsieur de V . . . I do not know what Monsieur V . . . you mean; but I can tell you that this book was written by my brother, Monsieur Demad, presently a Captain in the Brunswick regiment; and in the matter of the pretended kingdom of the Jesuits in Paraguay, which you call a wretched fable, I tell you in the face of all Europe that nothing is more certain. I served on one of the Spanish vessels sent to Buenos Aires in 1756 to restore reason to the nearby settlement of Saint Sacrament; I spent three months at Assumption; the Jesuits have to my knowledge twenty-nine provinces, which they call "Reductions," and they are absolute masters there, by virtue of eight crowns a head for each father of a family, which they pay to the Governor of Buenos Aires—and yet they only pay for a third of their districts. They will not allow any Spaniard to remain more than three days in their Reductions. They have never wanted their subjects to learn Spanish. They alone teach the Paraguayans the use of firearms; they alone lead them in the field. The Jesuit Thomas Verle, a native of Bavaria, was killed in the attack on the village of Saint Sacrament while mounting to the attack at the head of his Paraguayans in 1737—and not at all in 1735 as the Jesuit Charlevoix has reported; this author is as insipid as he is ignorant.

---

1. N.B. This letter was lost in the post for a long time; as soon as it reached us, we began trying—unsuccessfuly—to discover the existence of Monsieur Demad, Captain of the Brunswick Regiment [Note by the *Journal*].

Everyone knows how they waged war on Don Antequera, and defied the orders of the Council in Madrid.

They are so powerful that in 1743 they obtained from Philip the Fifth a confirmation of their authority which no one has been able to shake. I know very well, gentlemen, that they have no such title as King, and therefore you may say it is a wretched fable to talk of the Kingdom of Paraguay. But even though the Dey of Algiers is not a King, he is none the less master of that country. I should not advise my brother the Captain to travel to Paraguay without being sure that he is stronger than the local authorities.

For the rest, gentlemen, I have the honor to inform you that my brother the Captain, who is the best-loved man in his regiment, is an excellent Christian; he amused himself by composing the novel *Candide* in his winter quarters, having chiefly in mind to convert the Socinians. These heretics are not satisfied with openly denying the Trinity and the doctrine of eternal punishment; they say that God necessarily made our world the best of all possible ones, and that everything is well. This idea is manifestly contrary to the doctrine of original sin. These innovators forget that the serpent, who was the subtlest beast of the field, tempted the woman created from Adam's rib; that Adam ate the forbidden fruit; that God cursed the land He had formerly blessed: *Cursed is the ground for thy sake: in the sweat of thy face shalt thou eat bread.* Can they be ignorant that all the church fathers without a single exception found the Christian religion on this curse pronounced by God himself, the effects of which we feel every day? The Socinians pretend to exalt providence, and they do not see that we are guilty, tormented beings, who must confess our faults and accept our punishment. Let these heretics take care not to show themselves near my brother the Captain; he'll let them know if everything is well.

I am, gentlemen, your very humble, very obedient servant,

Demad

At Zastrou, April first, 1759

P.S. My brother the Captain is the intimate friend of Mr. Ralph, well-known Professor in the Academy of Frankfort-on-Oder, who was of great help to him in writing this profound work of philosophy, and my brother was so modest as actually to call it a mere translation from an original by Mr. Ralph. Such modesty is rare among authors.

[Voltaire's little joke that *Candide* was written to refute the "Socinians" is a proper bit of ironic duplicity. As the Socinians (Polish followers of Faustus and Laelius Socinus, sixteenth-century theologians) were convinced optimists, *Candide* could appropriately claim to refute that part of their creed. But they were much better known for their denial of original sin—that, not optimism, was what made them heretical—and Voltaire could not very well refute that belief, because, as an active and prominent deist, he shared it.[2] Or did he? A curious figure in *Candide* is that officer of the Inquisition who peeps into the last half-page of chapter 5, utters two sentences which hang up Pangloss like a split fish, and then disappears forever. His argument is that the "all's well" philosophy, by denying original sin and the fall of man, removes all grounds for belief in supernatural reward or punishment; and by making God wholly and directly responsible for the present wretched state of the world, it destroys the possibility of human freedom.

Now these were arguments with which Voltaire was thoroughly familiar. They had been used against him, several years before *Candide*, by an orthodox critic named Bouillier, who had caught up some overoptimistic statements to which Voltaire committed himself in the *Remarques sur Pascal* (Article XVIII).[3] The heart of them is the reaffirmation of the doctrines of fall and redemption. Voltaire evidently saw the strength of the position as Bouillier used it against him, for he transferred the arguments to his own armory, using them again and again—in the Preface to the *Poème sur Lisbonne*, for example, and in a letter to Pastor Elie Bertrand dated February 28, 1756. It is odd enough to see Voltaire, in his own person, vindicating the supernatural dogmas of the Christian faith against unbelieving optimists; but even odder to see him, in his fiction, assigning to an officer of the hated Inquisition an argument which he had made seriously in his own person. Perhaps Voltaire, like many later unbelievers, especially those with Jesuit training, continued to respect the logic of the church in which he no longer believed. Or perhaps, like many good controversialists, what he believed in at heart was neither one cause nor the other, but sharp weapons skilfully wielded. It is the economy of the poursuivant's style—the snip-snip of his logical scissors on the sleazy texture of Pangloss's verbosity—that represents his triumph in Voltaire's eyes. In any event, one could argue that the officer of the Inquisition is, metaphysically speaking, a hero of the book; the point would be that, like the tough-minded dervish of the last chapter, he has his philosophical legs under him.]

PETER GAY: [What Did Voltaire Mean by *l'Infâme*?]†

[Throughout the latter part of his life, Voltaire fought most of his many battles under a slogan, a battle-cry, that he made his own: *Ecrasez l'infâme*. What did he mean by it? *Ecrasez* is perfectly clear; it means "wipe out." But what are the boundaries of the "infâme" that we are to wipe out? The

2. From an orthodox point of view, Voltaire pluming himself on having refuted the "Socinians" is like a policeman posing as an enemy of crime because he has given a speeding ticket to robbers on their way home from looting a bank. "Socinians" were especially useful to Voltaire as a stalking-horse because there weren't very many of them, they were far away (the sect had its roots in Poland), and nobody was quite sure what they believed, since one of their chief tenets was that nobody was bound to believe anything against his conscience.

3. Voltaire's "Anti-Pascal" was first published in 1733 and variously modified thereafter; Bouillier's sharp attack on his excessive optimism appeared as an *Apologie de la Métaphysique* (Amsterdam, 1753); the argument that optimism is unchristian appears on p. 83. See Lanson's edition of the *Remarques sur Pascal*, 2. 209.
† From *Voltaire's Politics: The Poet as Realist*, Second Edition, by Peter Gay, pp. 239–40. Copyright © 1988 by Yale University Press. Reprinted by permission.

word means "infamy," but that's not very specific; probably Voltaire did not mean to be completely specific. But the way he uses the word makes clear some of the things he means by it. Peter Gay lays out clearly and concisely four alternative meanings for the word, depending on how much ground one understands it to cover. The problem may be solved either by finding one meaning better than the others or by defining circumstances under which any one of the four may seem to predominate over, without erasing, its rivals.]

* * * After two centuries of debate there remain four distinct interpretations: fanaticism, Catholicism, Christianity, and religion. The writers who restrict *l'infâme* to fanaticism point out that Voltaire never openly left the faith into which he was born and that he occasionally practiced it, that other educated Catholics objected to fanatical and superstitious displays as violations rather than manifestations of true Roman Catholicism, that he treated his Jesuit teachers with respect and affection, and that his violent diatribes against Christianity may be dismissed as the hyperbole of propaganda. Those who enlarge the term to mean Catholicism call attention to his membership in a Masonic order which was Christian but anti-Catholic, his statements that Protestantism is greatly preferable to Catholicism, his friendships with Genevan pastors whose philosophical Protestantism resembled his own religious convictions, his obvious admiration for the freedom and toleration of Protestant countries, his contention that deism had grown naturally from the Protestant Reformation. Those who interpret *écrasez l'infâme* as an attack on supernatural religions in general and Christianity in particular cite the vehemence of Voltaire's assault on doctrines shared by Catholics and Protestants, his conviction that all forms of Christianity are the source of fatal infection, his disappointment in the Genevan clergy, and the famous line in his *Henriade*:

> Je ne décide point entre Genève et Rome,
> [I make no decision between Geneva and Rome]

which they take as a rejection of both. Finally, those who expand *écrasez l'infâme* into a war against all religion stress his Aesopianism, his need to mask his dangerous opinions, his skepticism which they think is ill-disguised behind a polite deism.

ANDRÉ DELATTRE†

Let's try for a hypothesis which will explain adequately this religious or anti-religious (no matter which) obsession. The origin of the deepest emotion in his life can only be of an emotive order; it was for no purely

† From *Voltaire l'impétueux* by Andre Delattre, pp. 67–69. Copyright 1957 by Mercure de France. Reprinted by permission.

intellectual reasons that he persecuted *l'infâme* with ever-growing enthusiasm for more than sixty years.

Voltaire, son of a bourgeois Jansenist, was situated from his birth in the opposition, and he would become a leader of it. Jansenists in France, like Puritans in England, were both a religious movement and the central political force of the rising bourgeoisie; both currents, being essentially united, made up between them a dynamism, perhaps the most powerful of the age. But between the Jansenist father with his austerities and the frivolous son, there was a clash, or could one perhaps say a traumatic breach with determining effects? We recall that Voltaire's mother died when he was seven years old. Then, the second son of M. Arouet was in further conflict with his older brother Armand, a fanatical Jansenist who finally became a convulsionary.[1] This older brother was tough and made his sibling suffer * * * Later, Voltaire disputed with his brother over the affections of their sister's children * * * In the matter of religion, Voltaire himself flatly opposed his attitude to that of Armand Arouet * * *

So far we deal with matters of unquestioned fact. The hypothesis begins here: this hostility against father and older brother, could it have caused in Voltaire's sensibility a wound sufficient to determine his entire life? Is it possible that Voltaire was anti-lyric, anti-mystic ("the mystics," he said, "are the alchemists of religion"—*Works*, ed. Moland, XV, 73)—anti-dionysian in a word, as a reaction against Armand, that dionysian miracle-maker? * * * Let us embroider freely: through the mask of Pascal whom he attacks, he is striking at his Jansenist brother. His profound repulsion in his youth for this pious, hard, dry brother turned him toward the rational, the clearly defined things of this earth, the anti-supernatural; and it knotted up within him a whole creative, vital, poetic self to which, nonetheless, he struggled to give expression—vainly. Voltaire clings desperately [to the material] in order to keep himself from plunging into that mysticism toward which his powerful primitive impulses keep dragging him.

2. VOLTAIRE'S GREATNESS

Whether Voltaire was really a great man and, if so, what his greatness consisted in, were questions in which shifting political passions and shifting literary tastes played a major role. His voluminous production seemed to include no single outstanding book, no unquestioned masterpiece. Though they continued to hold the stage well into the nineteenth century, Voltaire's tragedies came under increasingly heavy fire as being pompous and dull.

---

1. M. Arouet was pleased with neither of his boys, and used to say he had two madmen (*fous*) for sons, one in verse and one in prose.

His poetry fell by the wayside even earlier, and his histories (with the possible exception of *Le Siècle de Louis XIV*) lost stature with the passage of time. At the same time his little short stories, farces, and entertainments—which were certainly not pompous but sometimes uncomfortably irreverent—came to the fore. Thus conservatives who despised Voltaire's principles but remained susceptible to his rhetoric were often found to rank him higher in the literary pantheon than those who admired his ideas but deplored his neo-classic taste.

JOSEPH DE MAISTRE†

* * * His much-vaunted wit is far from unblameable; the laugh it raises is never legitimate; it is a grimace. Have you never noticed that God's anathema was written on his face? After so many years, it's time to look and see. Go, look at his face, in the Hermitage;[1] I never see it without rejoicing that it was not recorded for us by an artist of Greece, who would have spread over it the veil of ideal beauty. Here everything is natural. There is as much truth in this head as in a death-mask. Look at this low brow, to which shame will never bring a blush, these two cold craters where one still seems to see the last bubblings of luxury and hate. This mouth—I speak evil, perhaps, but it is not my fault—this horrible rictus, running from one ear to the other, these lips pinched tight by cruel malice, like a coiled spring ready to let fly some blasphemy or sarcasm. Don't talk to me of that man, I can't support the very idea of him. Ah! what harm he has done us! Like that insect, the bane of gardens, which seeks out and gnaws the roots of the most precious plants, Voltaire, with his needle-pointed style, stabs continually at the two roots of society, women and young people; he fills them full of his venoms, which he transmits thus from one generation to the next. It is in vain that his stupid admirers, trying to cover up his inexpressible crimes, deafen us by repeating the sonorous tirades in which he has spoken worthily of the most venerable topics. These selfblinded folk don't see that, in this way, they complete our condemnation of this guilty writer. If Fénelon, with the same pen which depicted the joys of Elysium,[2] had written the book of *The Prince*, he would be a thousand times more vile, more guilty, than Machiavelli. The great crime of Voltaire is the abuse of his talent, the deliberate prostitution of a genius created to celebrate God and virtue. He could not plead, as so many others have

† From *Les Soirées de Saint-Pétersbourg*. "Quatrième Entretien." *Loquitur* le conte. The date is 1831.

1. De Maistre's imaginary conversations are supposed to take place in St. Petersburg (modern Leningrad), where the great picture gallery called the Hermitage is located. Voltaire, needless to say, had been dead for more than thirty years when the dialogues were actually published. His portrait in the Hermitage is of doubtful authenticity.

2. In the course of his didactic romance about Telemachus, son of Odysseus, Fénelon has his hero visit the Elysian fields. The speaker is upset that someone who can write "virtuous" books may also write "bad" ones.

done, youth, carelessness, the force of passion, or, in short, the melancholy weakness of our nature. Nothing absolves him; his corruption is of a sort which belongs to him alone; it is rooted in the deepest fibres of his heart, and fortified with all the energy of his understanding. Always akin to sacrilege, it defies God while destroying man. With unexampled fury, this insolent blasphemer rises to the height of declaring himself the personal enemy of the Savior of mankind; he dares, from the depths of his nothingness, to give Him a ridiculous name, and that marvellous law which the Man-God brought to earth he refers to as *"l'infâme."* Abandoned by God, who punishes by withdrawing, he knows no rein or check. Other cynics astonished the virtuous. Voltaire amazed the vicious. He plunges into filth, rolls in it, saturates himself; he yields his imagination to the enthusiasm of hell, which lends all its forces to drag him to the absolute limits of evil. He invents monsters, prodigies which cause one to blench. Paris crowned him, Sodom would have banished him. Shameless profaner of the universal tongue and its greatest names, the last of men after those who admire him! How can I tell you what I experience at the thought of him? When I see what he could have done and what he actually did, his inimitable talents inspire in me nothing more than a kind of sacred rage for which there is no name. Torn between admiration and horror, sometimes I think of raising a statue for him—by the hand of the common hangman.

VICTOR HUGO†

* * * I have pronounced the word "smile." Let me pause over it. In Voltaire an equilibrium always re-establishes itself ultimately. Whatever his first rage, it passes, and the aroused Voltaire yields to the pacified Voltaire. Then, in that deepset eye, the smile appears.

This smile is wisdom. This smile, I repeat, is Voltaire. This smile broadens sometimes to a laugh, but then a philosophic melancholy tempers it. Against the mighty it is mocking; in behalf of the weak, it is tender. It disturbs the oppressor and comforts the oppressed. Against the mighty, raillery; for the little people, sympathy. Ah! let us be touched by that smile. He experienced the clarities of dawn. He illuminated the true, the just, the good, and what there is of honesty in the useful. He lit up the interior of superstitions; these ugly sights are good for us to see, and he showed them. Being luminous, he was prolific. The new society, the desire for equality and justice and that first stage of brotherhood which is called toleration, mutual good will, the due propor-

† From "Le Centenaire de Voltaire" (30 mai, 1878), in *Œuvres Complètes de V.H.* ("Actes et Paroles," 1940) 3: 298–306. Though Victor Hugo tended to make a public ceremonial performance out of every minor occasion, the centenary of Voltaire's death called for an authentic celebration. The faithful reporter has duly recorded crowd reactions.

tioning of men and rights, the recognition of reason as a supreme law, the eradication of prejudices and preconceptions, the serenity of the soul, the spirit of indulgence and pardon, harmony, peace—that is what came forth from the great smile.

The day, soon to dawn no doubt, when the identity of justice and mercy will be recognized, the day when the amnesty will be declared, I tell you now, among the stars on high, Voltaire will be smiling. (*Triple salvos of applause. Cries of Long live the amnesty!*)

Gentlemen, there exists between two servants of humanity who appeared eighteen hundred years apart, a mysterious connection.

To combat the pharisees, unmask the hypocrites, humble the tyrants, usurpers, bigots, liars, and persecuters, to demolish the temple in order to rebuild it—that is, to replace the false with the true—to attack the ferocious magistrates and the bloody-minded priests, to take a whip and drive the moneychangers from the temple, to reclaim the heritage of orphans, to protect the weak, the suffering, and the humiliated, to struggle in behalf of the persecuted and the oppressed: that is the war of Jesus Christ. And who is the man who fought that war? It is Voltaire. (*Bravos.*)

The work of the evangelist is fulfilled in the work of the philosopher; what the spirit of inspiration began, the spirit of toleration continues. Let us say it in a spirit of deepest respect, Jesus wept, Voltaire smiled; and it is from this divine tear and this human smile that the glory of modern civilization is compounded. (*Prolonged applause.*)

EDMOND AND JULES GONCOURT†

[Magny's was a restaurant in the Latin Quarter, i.e., the student district, of Paris, where for a time in the mid-nineteenth century, literary figures used to gather for dinner and conversation. Most intellectual discussions in France, wherever they begin, come back to the Revolution and one's attitude toward that colossal event. The session described by the Goncourts begins with Voltaire's literary merits and ends with the proposal to erect his statue on the Place Louis XV, known nowadays as the Place de la Concorde, but notable earlier in its history as the spot where Louis XVI went to the guillotine. Putting a statue of Voltaire on that spot would be like putting a statue of John Wilkes Booth in front of the Lincoln Memorial.]

28 March. Dinner at Magny's. The new member of the circle is Renan. The conversation turns naturally to religion. Sainte-Beuve says that paganism was originally a fine thing, but then it became a rotten mess, a pox * * * And Christianity was the mercury that cured the pox, but the dose was too strong, and now humanity must be cured of the remedy
* * *

† From *Journal of the Goncourts*, March 28, 1863.

And the battle is over Voltaire. Both of us, in discussing this writer, set aside his political and social influence, we challenge his literary value, we dare to repeat the sentence of the Abbé Trublet defining Voltaire's genius as "the perfection of mediocrity," we grant him only the value of a popularizer, a publicist, nothing more, a man possessed of wit if you will, but of wit no loftier than that of all the witty old women of his day. His plays can't be discussed. His history is lies, the same old pompous and stupid conventions repeated by the most conventional and antiquated historians. His science, his hypotheses, are objects of ridicule by contemporary men of learning. Finally, the only work by which he deserves to live, his famous *Candide*, is LaFontaine in prose, spoon-fed Rabelais. What are these eighty volumes of his worth, alongside *Rameau's Nephew*, alongside *This is not a Story* [both by Diderot]—this novel and this story which contain in germ all the novels and stories of the nineteenth century?

The whole company falls upon us, and Sainte-Beuve ends by saying that France will be free only when Voltaire has his statue on the Place Louis XV.

3. VOLTAIRE'S COHERENCE

If Voltaire, without writing an unqualifiedly great book, managed nonetheless to give the very general impression of being a great author, we should not be startled to find that without having a coherent philosophy he gave the general impression of being a systematic thinker. But this reputation faded too, and the brothers Goncourt, in their assault on the Patriarch, could toss aside his intellectual achievements with a contemptuous phrase. Yet precisely out of the ruins of his reputation as a systematic philosopher sprang the seeds of other valuations.

EMILE FAGUET†

These are petty reasons for a great reputation. There are better ones. It is much rarer than people think for a great man of letters to be the perfect expression of his native land, to represent brilliantly the spirit of his country. Neither Corneille nor Bossuet nor Pascal nor Racine nor Rousseau nor Chateaubriand nor Lamartine gives me the idea—even an enlarged, improved, and purified idea—of a Frenchman as I see and know him. What they represent, each of them, is an aspect of the French character, a single one of the intellectual qualities of the French race, picked out of many and carried to a point of excellence. This is why—

† From "Voltaire" in *Dix-Huitième Siècle* (Paris, 1895) 286–87.

as much because of their narrow range as because of their superiority within it—they scarcely represent us at all. But Voltaire is like us. The average spirit of France is in him. A man more witty than intelligent, and much more intelligent than artistic, is a Frenchman. A man of great practical good sense, swift in repartee, quick and brilliant with the pen, and who contradicts himself abominably as soon as he ventures on the great issues, is a Frenchman. A man impatient of minor restraints and docile under the heaviest ones is a Frenchman. A man who thinks himself an innovator and who is conservative to the bottom of his soul, who in literature and art is strictly attached to tradition as long as he has the right to be disrespectful toward it, is a Frenchman. Voltaire is light, impulsive, a fighter; he is a Frenchman. He is sincere, by intention anyway, and among all his faults he does not have those of pedantry or charlatanism; he is a Frenchman. He is almost incapable of metaphysics or poetry; he is a Frenchman. He is gracious and charming, in verse or prose, and eloquent on occasion; he is a Frenchman. He is radically incapable of understanding the idea of liberty, and knows only how to be a malicious slave or a gleeful tyrant; he is a Frenchman. At heart he loves despotism, and expects all progress from the State, from an enlightened savior; he is a Frenchman. He is not very brave; and this is not French at all, but the French have recognized so many of their other qualities in him that this one aberration they have forgiven.

DANIEL MORNET†

Voltaire outlines, with a marvellously sure hand, the architecture of an epic poem which will conform with all the rules of the most harmonious construction—and the most boring. He is just as good, or just as puerile, an architect in his tragedies. But there is no longer a question of order, or even of equilibrium, in most of his stories. What he proposes to study there is precisely the quirks of fate, the disordered complexity of existence. He will pursue this disorder, which is both picturesque and necessary, in *Zadig*, in *Candide*, and *l'Ingénu*. Accident still serves as a link in these works. But Voltaire will reach the stage of giving up linkage of every sort. In order to publish the confused body of reflections stirred up within him by the confusion of human affairs, he will have to forego writing a treatise, a discourse, or even an essay. He will jumble all his ideas into those *Questions on the Encyclopedia* which eventually become the *Philosophical Dictionary*; logical order is thus reduced to alphabetical order. Faguet said of Voltaire that he was "a chaos of clear ideas." It was a reproach. I should almost be tempted to think it a grounds for praise. The same chaos is found in a good number of his contemporaries.

† From Daniel Mornet, *Histoire de la Clarté Française* (Paris, 1929) 110. Reprinted by permission of Editions Payot, Paris.

It is the consequence of a prodigious influx of new ideas; it results above all from a renunciation of the classic spirit, which, for fear of losing its way, was reduced to turning forever in a narrow and monotonous circle.

RAYMOND NAVES†

Fréron first set in motion against Voltaire a critical procedure which has enjoyed some success among his adversaries down to the present day: it consists of carefully selecting phrases, detaching them from their context, and putting them in contradiction with one another. The task presents no difficulties when one is dealing with a body of work that, as we've seen, depends closely on particular circumstances. Even serious critics have sometimes repeated this charge of inconsistency, persuaded of its validity by a sort of tradition and relying on a superficial reading of the texts. Chateaubriand said "Voltaire was always taking stands both for and against." Nisard thought he could distinguish the chaff from the grain by attributing to the philosopher a laudable structure of thought but malignant, almost demoniacal, intentions. Faguet popularized the "chaos of clear ideas," skillfully presenting Voltaire's politics and his morality as bodies of "discontinuous" thought.

This impression, which gains credibility if one simply adds up isolated patches without any control from history, disappears as soon as one reestablishes the man behind the work. In the first place, Voltaire's thought displays a psychological unity. One finds everywhere the same impatient, ransacking spirit, hostile to posturing and mystery, taking hold of every subject with the same passion for clarity; and already that sort of appetite, that disposition that gives primacy to the the free mind, and encourages it.

But, as we've already noted, there's also a critical unity in this thought: hostility to absolutes and certainties, condemnation of all excesses and fanaticisms, in the name of humanity to be sure, but also in the names of logic and science, in the name of nature too, since it doesn't befit a creature who is limited, ignorant, and mortal to impose his judgments on others by bestowing on them an unquestionable privilege. In every area of thought, Voltaire pursues this educational goal with impressive persistency. The *Questions on the Encyclopedia*, forty-five years after the *Letters from England*, resound with the same blows showered on the same adversaries. And for that matter, those who complain of contradictions rarely fail to bring against Voltaire another charge, not very congruent with the first, "that no writer ever repeated himself so much." Repetitions are at least evidence of continuity.

Yet evolution on certain points of detail did take place, didn't it? Real

† From *Voltaire l'homme et l'oeuvre* (1942; Paris, 1955) 149–65. Reprinted by permission of Hachette, Paris.

changes (not reducible to a mere difference of lighting) are in fact very few. In the literal sense, Voltaire moved slowly toward a wider and more relaxed taste, more receptive to fantasy and spectacular innovations; but this results from an increase in his powers—the change was already being contemplated in his first works. Philosophically, there is a drift toward determinism, particularly noticeable in the redoubling of his attacks on providence, which had earlier been treated with an indulgent smile. But this deepening of pessimism is nothing but the consequence of repeated disillusions, a fleeting reflection from life, rather than transformation of the thought which as early as 1730, in the *Remarks on Pascal*, conceived of an equilibrium to which, after every variation of humor, the mind would return. The only important change concerns his work in history; here the writer has formally spoken of a reconsideration after having earlier lost sight of the fact that his subject should be the study of civilizations, not that of a few great men; but here again it's more a question of development than of rejection, and in any case the lucidity of the evolution can only accentuate a spiritual unity underlying the historian's effort toward greater human richness.

[Voltaire, Naves argues in an omitted passage, was a consistent, if always developing, humanist; but the concept of humanism, by itself, extends in so many different directions that the sense in which it applies particularly to Voltaire requires a definition as cogent as it is concise.]

Humanism may be a pious inventory of the treasures bequeathed us by the past; in this sense, Voltaire is very little of a humanist. He sets little store by all the "old stuff"; like Pococurante, he doesn't hesitate to say that he's often bored by Homer and that Virgil is very often frigid. Not that he despises the old works as such, but they were good for their period, and each new period has its own needs. He is a resolute modernist, ready to sacrifice cheerfully the old monuments in the name of health and urban growth. And it's from the same point of view that he passes judgment on primitive traditions and beliefs; no man ever had as few scruples as he about profaning the past and discarding such antiquity as had no other claim than its antiquity. Examining things for himself and without preconceptions, that principle he upholds without any exceptions.

Humanism can also be a meditation on the experiences of our species. Here, Voltaire finds a position, and rejects no document from the past that throws light on our history. Not that he tries, like Montaigne, to back up everything he says with allusions and citations from an immense collection. But he is a historian by temperament; his epic, his tragedies, his philosophic articles are all bathed in the waters of history; all his life he was researching, annotating, and commenting on documents—and with a determination that one wouldn't expect of a poet or of a polemical writer. His wisdom is at bottom historical; the same men whom as a militant modernist he disdained, he studied as a moralist, and made use of their examples to paint his vast panorama of "the customs and spiritual life" of nations. But his meditations on history always culminate in the present; the works of the past were essentially pioneering works, enriching us less by their success than by their experimental nature.

This leads us to a last form of humanism, which is the flowering of a human heritage and the love of humanity as an organism both fragile and perfectible. This sort of humanism Voltaire cultivates passionately, and this is what creates the profound unity of his constructive thought. From one end of his work to the other, there is only one basic concern, man; just one basic reality, man. This man he has scolded and bullied in every possible way, but his irritations are those of love, as of a father trying by rebukes and sarcasms to direct a fractious child. He never ceased, after everything, to have confidence; from so many satirical pages there emerges, not a sullen melancholy, but an energetic spirit of activity and perseverance. Quite unlike La Rochefoucauld, very different even from La Bruyère, who quickly tires, Voltaire in his criticisms excites us; even as he destroys, he builds up.

What then did he build truly, and what remains today of his work? He built above all a morality destined to replace the one whose rubble he shuffled underfoot. The old morality had in his eyes two fatal flaws. It was attached to dogmas, and rational discussion of those dogmas threatened to discredit the morality by contagion; and it exalted values highly suspect in themselves, such as authority based on tradition, and obligatory conformity. Voltaire tried, then, to separate morality from dogma in order not to shackle the necessities of practical life by linking them to shifting and uncertain beliefs. And he tried also to make morality less automatic, at least for the minority capable of rising to the superior morality, which is considered and free consent.

4. VOLTAIRE'S HUMANITY

Whether Voltaire laughed with the human race or at it, whether he pitied men or sneered at them, whether his famous smile was a benediction or a grimace, these were questions that centered rather closely on *Candide*.

MADAME DE STAËL†

[*After a passage explaining why serious German philosophy has trouble gaining a hearing in a flippant and worldly society*]
    The philosophy of sensations is one of the principal causes of this

† From *De L'Allemagne* 3.4, "Du Persiflage." The book was written in 1810 but published only in 1813.

frivolity. Since people have taken to considering the soul passive, a great number of philosophic works have fallen into contempt. The day when it was announced that there were no more mysteries in the world, that all ideas reached us through our eyes and ears, and that nothing was real which was not palpable, every individual who enjoyed the full use of his senses supposed himself a philosopher. One continually hears it said of people who have enough sense to make money when they are poor and to spend it when they are rich, that they have the only reasonable philosophy, and that only dreamers spend their time thinking of other matters. And in fact the senses can teach us nothing much more than this; if one can know nothing but what they teach, we must dismiss as madness everything which is not grounded on material evidence.

But if one should admit that the soul acts of its own accord; that it can sink into itself, and find truth there; and that this truth can be grasped only with the aid of a profound meditation, since it is not within the sphere of terrestrial experiences, then the entire direction of our thoughts would be changed. Men would no longer reject disdainfully exalted thoughts because they require careful consideration; what they would find insupportable is the superficial and the commonplace, for the void in the long run is singularly heavy.

Voltaire had so clear a sense of the influence which metaphysical systems exert on the direction of our thinking, that he composed *Candide* to combat Leibniz. He took a curious attitude of hostility toward final causes, optimism, free will, and in short against all those philosophic opinions which tend to raise the dignity of man; and he created *Candide*, that work of diabolic gaiety. For it seems to have been written by a creature of a nature wholly different from our own, indifferent to our lot, rejoicing in our sufferings, and laughing like a demon or an ape at the miseries of this human race with which he has nothing in common. The greatest poet of the age, the author of *Alzire, Tancrède, Mérope, Zaïre,* and *Brutus,* repudiated in this novel all the great moral truths which he had so worthily celebrated.

When Voltaire, as a tragic author, felt and thought in the character of another, he was admirable; but when he remained in his own character, he was a trifler and a cynic. The same mobility which allowed him to take on the lineaments of those characters he wished to depict, was only too effective in inspiring a language which, at certain moments, was appropriate to the character of Voltaire himself.

Candide sets in action this mocking philosophy, so indulgent in appearance, so ferocious in reality: it presents human nature under the most deplorable aspect, and offers us, as our only consolation, the sardonic laugh which exempts us from pity toward others by inviting us to renounce it for ourselves.

GUSTAVE LANSON†

[Voltaire was such a fighter by nature that his sympathy for the good guys very often took the form of savage attacks on the bad guys. This may make his humanity difficult to detect. But, whatever his personal motives, we can hardly be in doubt that just about every cause for which he fought, and which sooner or later triumphed, resulted in a widening of human freedom, an enriching of human potential. He was one of the great liberators of the modern mind.]

And if we just consider a bit, if we pause to visualize the France of Louis XV with all its many abuses and shortcomings: the capricious despotism of its government; the self-centered, extravagant court; the powerful clergy and judiciary, both more concerned with their special privileges than with the general welfare; the financial disorder and oppressive fiscal system; the poverty of the parish priest; the chaotic condition of the laws; the confused conflict between various authorities and their jurisdictions; the intolerance that condemned Protestants to concubinage or hypocrisy and dismissed their pastors to the galleys; the multitude of rules and privileges that were nothing but so many sources of vexation and misery for the common people—if we compare to those conditions the reforms Voltaire advocated, and if into this Catholic, monarchical France of the old regime we introduce tolerance, freedom of the press, a graduated tax-scale, a uniform code of laws, reforms in criminal procedure, a subordinate, salaried clergy, a program of public assistance, liberal and peaceful principles of government, and honest, conscientious administration, public servants truly concerned with the public interest—then, and only then, can we realize the extent of the transformation that Voltaire's critiques aimed at bringing about. Only then do we realize how wrong-headed it is to regard Voltaire's work as negative and timid. His criticism labored to produce a new and different France, a France extricated from an old feudal and monarchical chaos that was Roman and ecclesiastical, anarchic and tyrannical. It was a new France that was becoming, under the Very Christian Bourbon king, something like the France that emerged during the peaceful moments of the [Napoleonic] Consulate or the Second Empire [of Louis Napoleon]. More precisely, the Voltairian reform in its main outlines—except for the two-chamber system—was the design for the bourgeois government of Louis Philippe (1830–48). It is the France that would have come into being had Turgot been able to stay in power for twenty years and been permitted to do what he

† From *Voltaire* (Paris, 1906) 189–90. Copyright © Hachette, 1906. Reprinted by permission of Hachette, Paris.

wanted.[1] Broadly speaking, Voltaire was the journalist and propagandist for the work of which Turgot was the statesman.

5. VOLTAIRE'S STYLE

It has been said that one of the great misfortunes is to be born with a witty mind but outside of France. There's a sort of truth to the saying, but discriminations must still be made. The French find Molière irresistibly witty, but, like certain delicate vintages, he doesn't travel at all well; something essential seems to evaporate when he's translated into English. Not so with Voltaire; like the ruler of Eldorado, and no less astonishingly, his witty sayings, even when translated, still seem witty. The reason can hardly be the profundity of his thought; rather, it is the concentrated brilliance of his style—the quicksilver effects of which still challenge analysis or even description.

HIPPOLYTE TAINE[†]

"I've done more in my time," he says somewhere, "than Luther and Calvin"; and in that statement he's wrong. But the truth is that he has something of their spirit. Like them, he wants to change the predominant religion, he behaves like the founder of a sect, he recruits, proselytizes, bands his allies together; he writes letters of exhortation, of indoctrination, and direction; he sends out passwords and gives "to his brothers" special insignia; his passion resembles that of an apostle or a prophet. Such a spirit is not capable of reserve; by nature, he's a militant and an enthusiast; he rebukes, he insults, he improvises, he writes under the spur of his first impression, he makes use of every word in the language, even the most crude. He thinks in explosions, his emotions are convulsions, his images fly up like sparks; he gives himself up to his thought body and soul, surrenders himself to the reader and so takes possession of him. Impossible to resist him, the contagion is too strong. Creature of air and flame, the most excitable that ever existed, composed of atoms more volatile and vibrant than those of other men, he has the most delicate of mental structures, the most unstable, and the most precise. You could compare him to one of those extremely delicate balances

1. Turgot managed to remain comptroller-general of France for a scant two years (1774–76). The changes he proposed—tax-reform, limitation of monopolies, freer trade, strict economy in government—might, if followed out, have modified the ferocity of those discontents that broke out in the Revolution. Lanson's impressive list of freedoms we "now" enjoy could be vastly expanded "now,"

almost a century after he wrote. Voltaire didn't fight for all the changes that make the world "modern," and wouldn't have liked many of them, but their roots can often be traced back to reforms he did propose.

† From *Origines de la France contemporaine* (1876; Paris, 1880) 1: 342–45.

that a breath of air disturbs, yet in comparison with which all other measuring apparatus is clumsy and inexact. In such a balance you can't place anything but very light weights, mere scruples; under those circumstances, it weighs every substance precisely. So it is with Voltaire, involuntarily, as a result of his makeup, when he is writing for himself as well as for the public. An entire philosophy, a theological treatise in ten volumes, an abstract science, a specialized library, an entire body of learning, experience or invention reduces itself in his hand to a phrase or a verse. From an enormous mass of rough and rugged ore he extracts for us the precious essence, a grain of gold or copper, a specimen of the the rest, and presents it to us in the handiest, most convenient form, in a comparison, a metaphor, an epigram that becomes a proverb. In this respect no writer, ancient or modern, even comes close to him; at simplifying and popularizing, he has no equal in the world. Without departing from the tone of ordinary conversation, and almost playfully, he puts into little portable phrases the greatest discoveries and most daring hypotheses of the human mind, the theories of Descartes, Malebranche, Leibniz, Locke, and Newton, the various religions of antiquity and of the modern world, all the known systems of physics, physiology, geology, morality, natural law, and politics—in a word, all the general conceptions that the human race had achieved in eighteen centuries.

His leaning in this direction is so strong that it carries him away; he diminishes important matters in order to make them accessible. You can't reduce everything to current conversational small-change in this way—religion, legend, the ancient popular poetry, the spontaneous creations of instinct, the demivisions of the primitive ages; these are not topics of witty or clever conversation. A snappy saying can't express such subjects; it has to be a parody. But what an attraction for Frenchmen, for people of the world: what reader could possibly resist a book where the sum of human knowledge is set forth in witty expressions?

For in fact it's a question of the sum of human knowledge, and I don't see what important ideas a man would be missing who took as his breviary the *Dialogues*, the *Dictionary*, and the *Novels*. Read them over five or six times, and only then will you appreciate everything that they contain. It's not just views on the world and on man that abound there, nor general ideas of almost every sort, but particular information and practical techniques; thousands of little exact facts swarm through his writings, precise and interrelated facts about astronomy, physics, geography, physiology, statistics, innumerable personal experiences of a man who has himself read the texts, handled the instruments, visited the countries, worked in the industries, consulted with the managers, and who, by the sharpness of his alert imagination, can see or summon up again, as with an inner eye, everything that he's discussing even as he describes it. It's a unique ability, all the more rare in a classic century, and the most valuable of all, since it consists of seeing things, not through the gray mist of general phrases, but in themselves, as they are in nature and history, with their colors and forms as we know them, with their individual shapes and outlines, with their circumstances and surroundings in time and space. We see a peasant in his cart, a quaker in his congregation, a German baron in his castle, Dutchmen, Englishmen, Spaniards, Italians, and Frenchmen all in their native habitats, a fine lady, a conniving woman, yokels, soldiers, sluts, and the rest of the human pell-mell, from every level of the social ladder, each caught up in a phrase and held in the momentary light of a fleeting beam.

And this is the most striking quality of the style, its prodigious rapidity, the dizzy, dazzling passage of things forever new—ideas, images, events, landscapes, stories, dialogues—in a series of miniature paintings, which fly past as if projected by a magic lantern, withdrawn almost as soon as they are put forward by the impatient magician, who in the wink of an eye, races around the globe, and who, now astride of history, now of fable, now truth, now fantasy, now present, now past, frames his work sometimes into a parade as grotesque as that of a fair, sometimes into a spectacle more magnificent than that of the Opera.

JOHN MORLEY†

[Early commentators on Voltaire were most interested in his religious views, his humanitarian principles, his neoclassical tragedies, and his encyclopedic histories. The light verse and the stories (*contes*) by which he survives today, they barely noticed. And they said little or nothing about his literary style, which they largely took for granted. Oliver Goldsmith, for example, was an enthusiastic admirer, but his tribute to Voltaire, in *The Citizen of the World*, has nothing to say of the wit, irony, and concision of Voltaire's story telling. Only after the earthquake of the French Revolution had subsided into aftershocks did the Victorian liberal establishment try to make room (mostly by softening and smoothing over the sharp angles) for the great French iconoclast. John Morley's *Voltaire* (1872) was one of the most successful of such domesticating enterprises. Though he was (for his day) a liberal man politically, Morley felt he had to soft-pedal many of Voltaire's libertine ideas, overlook some of his sexy jocosities, and tone down his bitter raillery against priestcraft and superstition to make him acceptable. In this process of Gladstonizing (so to speak) the great mocker, the concept of literature and the value assigned to literary style became of primary importance. Morley was not himself a complex or sensitive mind; his outstanding qualities as a politician and a man of letters were directness, simplicity, and transparent honesty. And those, by no coincidence, are just the qualities that he praises in Voltaire. How appropriate they were to Voltaire needn't be decided here;

---

† From *Voltaire* (1872; London, 1923) 118–26.

they did lead Morley to an eloquent and influential appreciation of Voltaire's prose eloquence and its social influence.]

* * *

What is it then that literature brings to us, that earns its title to high place, though far from a highest place, among the great humanizing arts? Is it not that this is the master organon [methodology] for giving men the two precious qualities of breadth of interest and balance of judgment; multiplicity of sympathies and steadiness of sight? Unhappily, literature has too often been identified with the smirks and affectations of mere elegant dispersiveness, with the hollow niceties of the virtuoso, a thing of madrigals. It is not in any sense of this sort that we can think of Voltaire as specially the born minister of literature. What we mean is that while he had not the loftier endowments of the highest poetic conception, subtle speculative penetration, or triumphant scientific power, he possessed a superb combination of wide and sincere curiosity, an intelligence of vigorous and exact receptivity, a native inclination to candour and justice, and a pre-eminent mastery over a wide range in the art of expression. Literature being concerned to impose form, to diffuse the light by which common men are able to see the great host of ideas and facts that do not shine in the brightness of their own atmosphere, it is clear what striking gifts Voltaire had in this way. He had a great deal of knowledge, and he was ever on the alert both to increase and broaden his stock, and, what was still better, to impart of it to everybody else. He did not think it beneath him to write on Hemistichs[1] for the Encyclopædia. 'Tis not a very brilliant task, he said, but perhaps the article will be useful to men of letters and amateurs; 'one should disdain nothing, and I will do the word Comma, if you choose.'[2] He was very catholic in taste, being able to love Racine without ignoring the lofty stature of Shakespeare. And he was free from the weakness which so often attends on catholicity, when it is not supported by true strength and independence of understanding; he did not shut his eyes to the shortcomings of the great. While loving Molière, he was aware of the incompleteness of his dramatic construction, as well as of the egregious farce to which that famous writer too often descends.[3] His respect for the sublimity and pathos of Corneille did not hinder him from noting both his violence and his frigid argumentation.[4] Does the reader remember that admirable saying of his to Vauvenargues; '*It is the part of a man like you to have preferences, but no exclusions*'[5]? To this fine principle Voltaire was usually thoroughly true, as every great mind, if only endowed with adequate culture, must necessarily be.

---

1. The hemistich is a half-verse or fragment, often set off from the rest of the verse by a caesura; Voltaire's article, unusually full and careful, will be found in volume 8 of the *Encyclopédie*.

2. *Correspondence*, ed. Besterman, #6894.

3. "Temple du Goût," *Oeuvres complètes de Voltaire*, ed. Lequien, 1825, *Poésies*, I, pp. 326–27.

4. Letter to Vauvenargues, 15 April, 1743, Besterman, #2567.

5. *Oeuvres de Vauvenargues* (Paris, 1821), II, 252.

Nul auteur avec lui n'a tort,
Quand il a trouvé l'art de plaire;
Il le critique sans colère,
Il l'applaudit avec transport.[6]

Thirdly, that circumfusion of bright light which is the highest aim of
speech, was easy to Voltaire, in whatever order of subject he happened
to treat. His style is like a translucent stream of purest mountain water,
moving with swift and animated flow under flashing sunbeams. 'Voltaire,' said an enemy, 'is the very first man in the world at writing down
what other people have thought.' What was meant for a spiteful censure,
was in fact a truly honourable distinction.

The secret is incommunicable. No spectrum analysis can decompose
for us that enchanting ray. It is rather, after all, the piercing metallic
light of electricity than a glowing beam of the sun. We can detect some
of the external qualities of this striking style. We seize its dazzling
simplicity, its almost primitive closeness to the letter, its sharpness and
precision, above all, its admirable brevity. We see that no writer ever
used so few words to produce such pregnant effects.[7] Those whom brevity
only makes thin and slight, may look with despair on pages where the
nimbleness of the sentence is in proportion to the firmness of the thought.
We find no bastard attempts to reproduce in words deep and complex
effects, which can only be adequately presented in colour or in the
combinations of musical sound. Nobody has ever known better the true
limitations of the material in which he worked, or the scope and possibilities of his art. Voltaire's alexandrines, his witty stories, his mock-
heroic, his exposition of Newton, his histories, his dialectic, all bear the
same mark, the same natural, precise, and condensed mode of expression, the same absolutely faultless knowledge of what is proper and
permitted in every given kind of written work. At first there seems something paradoxical in dwelling on the brevity of an author whose works
are to be counted by scores of volumes. But this is no real objection. A
writer may be insufferably prolix in the limits of a single volume, and
Voltaire was quite right in saying that there are four times too many
words in the one volume of D'Holbach's System of Nature.[8] He main-
tains too that Rabelais might advantageously be reduced to one-eighth,
and Bayle to a quarter, and there is hardly a book that is not curtailed
in the perfecting hands of the divine muses.[9] So conversely an author
may not waste a word in a hundred volumes. Style is independent of

---

6. From "Temple du gout," *Poésies*, ed. Lequien,
1825, I, 327. The verses could translate: "No author can be wholly bad/(He thinks), who's learned
to give delight;/His criticism doesn't snarl or bite,/
And praising others seems to make him glad."
7. Voltaire's wit tends to create a quiet, inward
smile; his sarcasms are not, as a rule, broad enough
to produce guffaws [*Editor*].
8. Holbach's *Systéme de la Nature* (1770) was recognized at once as prolix. [*Editor*].
9. "Temple du Goût," *Poésies*, ed. Lequien,
1825, I, 323.

quantity, and the world suffers so grievously from the mass of books that have been written, not because they are many, but because such vast proportion of their pages say nothing while they purport to say so much.

No study, however, of this outward ease and swift compendiousness of speech will teach us the secret that was beneath it in Voltaire, an eye and a hand that never erred in hitting the exact mark of appropriateness in every order of prose and verse. Perhaps no such vision for the befitting in expression has ever existed. He is the most trenchant writer in the world, yet there is not a sentence of strained emphasis or overwrought antithesis; he is the wittiest, yet there is not a line of bad buffoonery. And this intense sense of the appropriate was by nature and cultivation become so entirely a fixed condition of Voltaire's mind that it shows spontaneous and without an effort in his work. Nobody is more free from the ostentatious correctness of the literary precisian, and nobody preserves so much purity and so much dignity of language with so little formality of demeanour. It is interesting to notice the absence from his writings of that intensely elaborated kind of simplicity in which some of the best authors of a later time express the final outcome of many thoughts. The strain that society has undergone since Voltaire's day has taught men to qualify their propositions. It has forced them to follow truth slowly along paths steep and devious. New notes have been struck in human feeling, and all thought has now been touched by complexities that were then unseen. Hence, as all good writers aim at simplicity and directness, we have seen the growth of a new style, in which the rays of many side-lights are concentrated in some single phrase. That Voltaire does not use these focalising words and turns of composition only means that to him thought was less complex than it is to a more subjective generation. Though the literature which possesses Milton and Burke need not fear comparison with the graver masters of French speech, we have no one to place exactly by the side of Voltaire. But, then, no more has France. There are many pages of Swift which are more like one side of Voltaire than anything else that we have, and Voltaire probably drew the idea of his famous stories from the creator of Gulliver, just as Swift got the idea of the Tale of a Tub from Fontenelle's History of Mero and Enegu (that is, of Rome and Geneva). Swift has correctness, invention, irony, and a trick of being effectively literal and serious in absurd situations, just as Voltaire has; but then Swift is often truculent and often brutally gross, both in thought and in phrase. Voltaire is never either brutal or truculent. Even amid the licence of the Pucelle[1] and of his romances, he never forgets what is due to the French tongue. What always charmed him in Racine and Boileau, he tells us, was that they

1. The "Pucelle" (1755) is a mock-epic on Joan of Arc; it has to be defended, as Morley does, on the score of observing the decencies of the French language, because there are no other decencies of any sort that it does observe [Editor].

said what they intended to say, and that their thoughts have never cost anything to the harmony or the purity of the language.[2] Voltaire ranged over far wider ground than the two poets ever attempted to do, and trod in many slippery places, yet he is entitled to the same praise as that which he gave to them.

Unhappily, one of the many evil effects which have alloyed the revolution Voltaire did so much to set in motion, has been both in his country and ours that purity and harmony of language, in spite of the examples of the great masters who have lived since, have on the whole declined. In both countries familiarity and slang have actually asserted a place in literature on some pretense that they are real; an assumed vulgarity tries to pass for native homeliness, and, as though a giant were more impressive for having a humped back, some men of true genius seem only to make sure of fame by straining themselves into grotesques. In a word, the reaction against a spurious dignity of style has carried men too far because the reaction against the dignified elements in the old order went too far. Style, after all, as one has always to remember, can never be anything but the reflex of ideas and habits of mind, and when respect for one's own personal dignity as a ruling and unique element in character gave way to sentimental love of the human race, often real, and often a pretence, old self-respecting modes of expression went out of fashion.[3] And all this has been defended by a sort of argument that might just as appropriately have been used by Diogenes, vindicating the filthiness of his tub against a doctrine of clean linen.

To follow letters, it is important to observe, meant then, or at least after Voltaire's influence rose to its height, meant distinctly to enter the ranks of the Opposition. In our own time the profession of letters is placed with other polite avocations, and those who follow it for the most part accept the traditional social ideas of the time, just as clergymen, lawyers, and physicians accept them. The modern man of letters corresponds to the ancient sophist, whose office it was to confirm, adorn, and propagate the current prejudice. To be a man of letters in France in the middle of the eighteenth century was to be the official enemy of the current prejudices and their sophistical defenders in the church and the parliaments. Parents heard of a son's design to go to Paris and write books, or to mix with those who wrote books, with the same dismay with which a respectable Athenian heard of a son following Socrates. The hyper-hellenistic collegian need not accuse us of instituting a general parallel between Socrates and Voltaire. The only point on which we are insisting is that each was the leader of the assault against the sophists of his day, though their tactics and implements of war were sufficiently

2. *Correspondance*, ed. Besterman, #1935.

3. Writing in 1872, Morley is undoubtedly reacting here to the poetry of Swinburne, which combined political radicalism with sexual suggestiveness in a manner very distressing to the critic's middle-class, midlands, nonconformist values [*Editor*].

unlike. To the later assailant the conditions of the time made the pen the most effective instrument. The clergy had the pulpit and the confessional, and their enemies had the press.

6. SHORT TAKES

Not all good ideas appear before us wearing top hats and swell clothes. A sharp eye and a lively imagination can find a welcome acquaintance in a little ragamuffin idea that seems to have slipped in among the august pronouncements almost by accident.

ANATOLE FRANCE†

Comedy turns sad as soon as it becomes human. Does not *Don Quixote* sometimes make you grieve? I greatly admire those few books of a serene and smiling desolation, like the incomparable *Don Quixote* or like *Candide*, which are, when properly taken, manuals of indulgence and pity, bibles of benevolence.

GUSTAVE FLAUBERT††

As for novels, Voltaire wrote just one, which is a summary of all his works * * * His whole intelligence was an implement of war, a weapon. And what makes me cherish him is the disgust I feel for his followers, the Voltaireans, those people who laugh at great things. Did he laugh, himself? He ground his teeth.

GEORGE SAINTSBURY§

* * * Mademoiselle Cunégonde (nobody will ever know anything about style who does not feel what the continual repetition in Candide's mouth of the "Mademoiselle" does) * * *

ANDRÉ BELLESSORT‖

We may say that the French Revolution began on 10 February 1778, the day that Voltaire entered Paris.

† From *The Garden of Epicurus*, in *Oeuvres* IX (Paris, 1927) 9: 412. Reprinted by permission of Calmann-Lévy, Paris.
†† From a letter to Mme. Roger des Genettes (1859–60?).
§ From *A History of the French Novel* (London, 1917) 1: 382. Reprinted by permission of MacMillan Ltd., London.
‖ From *Essai sur Voltaire* (Paris, 1925) 365. Copyright © Librairie Académique Perrin. Reprinted by permission.

EMILE FAGUET†

He's one of those people of whom it's said that they frequently change their *idées fixes* * * * This great mind is a chaos of clear ideas.

FREDERICK THE GREAT††

Two years after Voltaire's death in 1778, Frederick the Great told d'Alembert that in his morning prayers he never failed to include the phrase, "Divin Voltaire, *Ora pro nobis*" (Saint Voltaire, intercede for us). At various times in his life Frederick had referred to Voltaire as an unscrupulous liar, a malicious monkey, and much worse. There were two attitudes to take toward the philosopher, both of them extreme, and Frederick took them both.

S. G. TALLENTYRE§

"I disapprove of what you say, but will defend to the death your right to say it."

PETER GAY‖

His empiricism made him hostile to political theorizing, but throughout his life he intervened in political controversies; he meddled whether he was asked to or not, and even, as sometimes happened, when he was earnestly begged to mind his own business. He always said demurely that he was only cultivating his garden, but privately he defined his garden as Europe.

STENDHAL#

[Julien Sorel, in prison and facing the guillotine, dreams of a more honorable priest, a purer religion, and a more kindly God than he has ever known on earth:] "The good priest would tell us about God.

---

† From *Dix-huitième siècle: études littéraires* (Paris, 1890) 206.

†† From Lytton Strachey, "Voltaire and Frederick the Great," *Literary Essays* (1915 York, 1949) 105.

§ This invention was attributed to Voltaire in a book by Tallentyre, pseud. of E. Beatrice Hall, *The Friends of Voltaire* (London, 1907). Voltaire himself never said it.

‖ From *Voltaire's Politics* (1959; New York, 1965) 17. Reprinted by permission of Yale University Press.

From *The Red and the Black*, chapter 44.

But what God? Not that in the Bible, a petty despot, cruel, and thirsting
for revenge . . . but the God of Voltaire, just, kind, infinite. . . ."

RICHARD WILBUR: [Pangloss's Song]†

[A musical operetta based on *Candide* was produced in New York in 1956.
Leonard Bernstein composed the music, and Richard Wilbur was one of
several collaborating lyricists. The song that Pangloss sings to Candide combines Voltaire's wit with Wilbur's graceful, unstrained prosody.]

I

Dear boy, you will not hear me speak
    With sorrow or with rancor
Of what has paled my rosy cheek
    And blasted it with canker;
'Twas Love, great Love, that did the deed
    Through Nature's gentle laws,
And how should ill effects proceed
    From so divine a cause?

Sweet honey comes from bees that sting,
    As you are well aware;
To one adept in reasoning,
Whatever pains disease may bring
Are but the tangy seasoning
    To Love's delicious fare.

II

Columbus and his men, they say,
    Conveyed the virus hither
Whereby my features rot away
    And vital powers wither;
Yet had they not traversed the seas
    And come infected back,
Why, think of all the luxuries
    That modern life would lack!

All bitter things conduce to sweet,
    As this example shows;
Without the little spirochet
We'd have no chocolate to eat,
Nor would tobacco's fragrance greet
    The European nose.

† "Pangloss's Song" from *Advice to a Prophet and Other Poems*, copyright © 1957 and renewed 1985 by Richard Wilbur, reprinted by permission of Harcourt Brace Jovanovich, Inc., and Faber and Faber Ltd.

III

Each nation guards its native land
    With cannon and with sentry,
Inspectors look for contraband
    At every port of entry,
Yet nothing can prevent the spread
    Of Love's divine disease:
It rounds the world from bed to bed
    As pretty as you please.

Men worship Venus everywhere,
    As plainly may be seen;
The decorations which I bear
Are nobler than the Croix de Guerre,
And gained in service of our fair
    And universal Queen.

THOMAS JEFFERSON†

The truth of Voltaire's observation offers itself perpetually, that every man here must be either the hammer or the anvil. It is a true picture of that country to which they say we shall pass hereafter, and where we are to see God and his angels in splendor, and crowds of the damned trampled under their feet.

JACQUES VAN DEN HEUVEL††

Hence the remarkable continuity of this production [the *contes*]. Only compare the outlines of *Babouc, Zadig, Memnon, Scarmentado*, and *Candide*—you will find, in spite of the apparent diversity of their subjects, nearly always the same constant elements. At the center, a hero young and pure—as if Voltaire had tried from time to time to create himself anew in one of his characters—intellectually scrupulous, all loyalty and good faith. In effect, there's nothing less "Voltairian" than the heroes of Voltaire's *contes*. They have, if one may venture the expression, a mystique, and carry their own paradise within them.

† From Bernard Mayo, *Jefferson Himself* (Boston, 1942) 112–13.

†† From *Voltaire dans ses Contes* (Paris, 1967) 331.

ANDRÉ DELATTRE†

It's astonishing that whenever he deliberately designs the architectural structure of a work, he always comes a cropper—invariably, throughout one of the longest literary careers in the history of the world—while he displays the greatest of talents whenever he writes frivolities.

HUGO FRIEDRICH††

The dervish at the end of *Candide* "claque la porte au nez de Pangloss." In reality it is Voltaire who slams the door. At last the friends, newly reunited and still in shock from their miseries, are going to enjoy on their little farm a modest measure of happiness. To tell the truth, their situation isn't much different from that of their great misfortunes.

7. VOLTAIRE'S APOTHEOSIS

We conclude with a selection from the magisterial remarks of Paul Valéry, in a discourse pronounced at the Sorbonne on December 10, 1944. To pronounce Voltaire a classic is no longer enough, he has become the creator of the classic standard, the measure of the measure.

PAUL VALÉRY§

Voltaire was twenty-one at the death of Louis XIV. He was eighty-four when he perished himself, a monarch of the European mind. He led the funeral cortège of an age, of which the real strangeness, the complete originality, escape us, so familiar are we from childhood with its language and imposing discipline. It is pompous and simplified, this age; it combines the arbitrary and the logical; all the rigors of thought with the ostentation of appearances; will expresses itself in all forms of art, pursuing the natural by artifice and capturing it sometimes by abstraction. The severe goes hand in hand with the theatrical. In the life of the monarch himself, a sincere devotion and an exact observance of religious duties exist side by side with a succession of passionate attachments, known to everyone, of which the illegitimate products are publicly avowed, and take their place in the highest ranks of the state.

Voltaire lowers this century into its tomb. But with what respect, in

† From *Voltaire l'impetueux* (Paris, 1957) 88. Reprinted by permission of Mercure de France, Paris.
†† From an essay in *La Table Ronde* (February, 1958) 114.

§ From *Voltaire, discours prononcé le 10 Décembre, 1944, en Sorbonne* (Paris, 1945) 5–16. Reprinted by permission of Éditions Juridiques Associées, Paris.

what a finely finished casket does he commend it to its glory! He gives it the name of the king. He was the first to state that Europe, under this reign, recognized in our nation, in the order of its directing ideas and its general style of intellectual accomplishment, as well as in its manners, a supremacy which could be brought into question neither by abuses nor by defeats nor by the final exhaustion of the kingdom's resources. And he had the quite new and felicitous idea of introducing within his history an account of the state of arts and letters at the period he was describing. It was he who drew up, without error or omission, so that posterity has never erased or inserted a single name, the list of those great writers whom we call our classics.

He is the unquestioned inventor of this famous and imperious notion—completely French—of the classic, he who was able in his maturity to embrace within a single perfectly lucid glance the entire corpus of a first rate literary achievement which was just hardening into an authoritarian system of perfection. It was directly inspired by the purest models of antiquity, as far as its structure and its economy of effects were concerned; but nourished, on the other hand, in the sacred simplicity of the Vulgate;[1] and penetrated, lastly, by a sense of logical rigor which the taste for geometry had, since the day of Descartes, communicated to more than one thoughtful citizen.

And yet Voltaire was to spend his entire life in ruining, in consuming with the fire that was his being, what remained of the grand century, of its traditions, its beliefs, its pomps—but not its works. Between the time of his youth and that which saw him disappear, the contrast is striking. Had he lived ten years more, this man who could have seen Louis XIV could have seen the end of the Terror—supposing he had not perished at its hands before Thermidor.

Thus he may make us think of that god Janus to whom the Romans attributed two opposed faces, and who was the god of beginnings and endings. The face of young Voltaire looks toward the sumptuously melancholy evening, in the dark purple shades of which the Sun King sank to rest, overwhelmed by his glory, and abandoning himself to the dark like a solemn sun never to reappear. But the other face of this Janus, old Voltaire, looks toward the East, where some unfamiliar dawning gilds enormous cloud banks. At the level of the horizon throb a multitude of rays * * *

No, he is no philosopher, this devil of a man, whose mobility, whose complexity, whose contradictions make up a character which only music, and the liveliest of music, could follow and follow to his end.

---

1. I.e., of the Latin Bible.

For Further Reading

A languaged or even semilanguaged reader who wants to enjoy the *Contes et Nouvelles* of Voltaire in their original French will find them, handily packaged, among the Classiques Garnier, edited by H. Bénac. Theodore Besterman's biography *Voltaire* (Oxford, 1969), in addition to seven hundred tightly packed pages of information about its subject, contains at the end a polyglot bibliographical note of frightening proportions. *Voltaire's Politics*, by Peter Gay, provides another forty pages of bibliographical directions. Two other extensive bibliographies in French are those of Raymond Naves, *Le Goût de Voltaire* (1938) and René Pomeau, *La Religion de Voltaire* (1956). Following out these directives should occupy an avid student of Voltaire full-time for some years to come. His spare time might well be filled reading in Besterman's enormous edition of the *Correspondance* (twenty-thousand-plus letters) and the numerous, varied contributions to the periodical *Studies on Voltaire and the 18th Century*. Both provide limitless perspectives for exploration and sampling.

Wider reading in Voltaire himself might well begin with the *Philosophic Dictionary* in any of its several forms. The articles are short and snappy, the points always clear and strong. On the other hand, the *Age of Louis XIV* and the *Essay on Customs* are too vast to be swallowed whole (though Voltaire prepared a *Précis* of the former); but they are the basis for Voltaire's reviving reputation as a historian, as well as treasures of lively and curious lore.

As one would expect, there is a lot less commentary on Voltaire in English than in French. But a student could well begin his explorations with the several English books (e.g., those of Auerbach and Cassirer, Wade, and Weightman) from which this critical edition could present only excerpts. In addition one might investigate the following:

Norman Torrey, *The Spirit of Voltaire* (New York, 1938)
Nancy Mitford, *Voltaire in Love* (New York, 1957)
W. H. Barber, *Voltaire: Candide* (London, 1960)
Ruth C. Flowers, *Voltaire's Stylistic Transformation of Rabelaisian Satirical Devices* (Washington, D.C., 1951)
Dorothy McGhee, *Voltairian Narrative Devices* (Menasha, Wisconsin, 1933)
Leo Spitzer, *A Method of Interpreting Literature* (Northampton, Massachusetts, 1948)

—plus the many articles, studies, and full-length books to be discovered in the volumes of *Studies on Voltaire and the 18th Century*.

NORTON CRITICAL EDITIONS